PRAISE FOR *GUILT BY MATRIMONY*

"An amazing story about a homicidal web of deceit fueled by mental illness. It is not a typical true-crime tale—it is in a class by itself. *Guilt by Matrimony* by Nancy Styler with Daleen Berry makes the case that the hunt for justice in a murder investigation can create as many victims as the crime itself."

—Diane Fanning, national bestselling crime writer

"*Guilt by Matrimony*, a tale of murder and intrigue among Aspen's chic social set, is as invigorating as a lungful of crisp mountain air. The story revolves around Nancy Pfister, a ski-resort socialite found bludgeoned to death in her home, and Nancy Styler, her friend who stands accused of murder. This tale of two Nancys is a true-crime yarn with all of the vital ingredients, from high-life scheming to whiplash-inducing red herrings to a classic twist ending."

—John Temple, author of *American Pain: How a Young Felon and His Ring of Doctors Unleashed America's Deadliest Drug Epidemic*

"*Guilt by Matrimony* is the gripping tale of a woman whose unconditional faith in her one true love led her to be wrongly accused of the murder of an Aspen socialite. Daleen Berry, the award-winning crime writer behind *Pretty Little Killers*, helps Nancy Styler tell her tragic, true story."

—Judy Melinek & T.J. Mitchell, authors of *Working Stiff: Two Years, 262 Bodies, and the Making of a Medical Examiner*

GUILT BY
MATRIMONY

GUILT BY MATRIMONY

A MEMOIR OF LOVE, MADNESS, AND THE MURDER OF NANCY PFISTER

NANCY STYLER

with *Daleen Berry*

BenBella Books, Inc.
Dallas, Texas

This book is a work of non-fiction, however, certain liberties have been taken with scenes and dialogue in an attempt to recreate what happened the night Nancy Pfister was murdered. So, this is the authors' version of what might have happened that fateful evening, based on extensive research. It is their attempt to comprehend the incomprehensible. Some names and locations have been changed to protect the privacy and anonymity of the people they interviewed.

BenBella Books, Inc.
10300 N. Central Expressway
Suite #530
Dallas, TX 75231
www.benbellabooks.com
Send feedback to feedback@benbellabooks.com

Printed in the United States of America
10 9 8 7 6 5 4 3 2 1

Library of Congress Cataloging-in-Publication Data is available upon request.
978-1-941631-95-9

Editing by Erin Kelley
Copyediting by Karen Levy
Proofreading by Amy Zarkos and
    Brittney Martinez
Front cover design by Faceout Studio,
    Emily Weigel
Full cover design by Sarah Dombrowsky
Text design and composition by
    Aaron Edmiston

Cover photography courtesy of Daleen
    Berry (front, Pfister chalet), Facebook
    (front, Nancy Pfister), and Trey Styler
    (back, Phister chalet view)
Nancy Styler author photo by Donna Lee
Daleen Berry author photo by Kate
    Davis Photography
Printed by Lake Book Manufacturing

Distributed by Perseus Distribution
perseusdistribution.com

To place orders through Perseus Distribution:
Tel: (800) 343-4499
Fax: (800) 351-5073
Email: orderentry@perseusbooks.com

Significant discounts for bulk sales are available.
Please contact Glenn Yeffeth at glenn@benbellabooks.com or (214) 750-3628.

To Trey

CONTENTS

FOREWORD

Outside, sharp clouds billowed overhead, punctuating the crisp Colorado sky like pieces of cotton candy painted on a blue background. But inside, the scene changed abruptly, going from a vibrant Van Gogh to a dark, chaotic Jackson Pollack portrait. There, police found a woman's body stuffed inside a bedroom closet, along with a mattress. She had been bound and gagged, before being brutally murdered.

Seventeen years later, police stormed a chalet on Buttermilk Mountain, after receiving word of another death. This time the fifty-seven-year-old victim wasn't a homeless woman whose bipolar illness cost her two marriages. But Nancy Merle Pfister's erratic ways had exacted a heavy toll: once her alcoholism overtook her life, and her demands became too much, many of Pfister's friends began avoiding her.

Like the first victim, she was vivacious and loved making people laugh. Also like the other victim, she, too, had a mental illness. And she was found stuffed inside a closet, after being bludgeoned to death. Pfister was an Aspen, Colorado, heiress whose mother was a hero, having flown in World War II. Her maternal grandfather was a founding partner at Random House, and her family name still holds sway over polite Aspen society. But ultimately, none of those things could save Pfister.

***

Jodi Lynn Carrigg was only thirty-six when she was murdered in 1996 inside a Denver motel. No one witnessed her killer come or go near the intersection of Broadway and 11th Avenue.

This was equally true for Pfister, 160 miles away at her 1833 West Buttermilk home.

Though almost two decades apart, the two crimes were nearly identical, with the victims' bodies eerily hidden away in the same place, in almost the same manner.

Carrigg's killer was never caught. However, Pfister's killer was— yet almost two years after her death, many people in Aspen still don't believe the official account of what happened. If those people are right, and the confession was false, then police have closed the books on a case that is far from being solved. On a murder that may have connections to Carrigg's, which remains unsolved.

CHAPTER ONE

THE CRIMINALS IN ROOM 122

A persistent pounding woke Nancy Styler from a deep sleep at 5:30 a.m. on February 27, 2014. Even though she didn't sleep with her hearing aids, the pounding on the door of her motel room was so loud that Nancy could easily hear it. By the time she threw on her robe and walked the few steps to the door, only the security chain, straining at the force pushing against it, kept the door from opening entirely.

Nancy peeked through the crack. In the darkness she could make out several armed men wearing body armor. She immediately thought something bad was happening at the motel where she and her husband were staying, and a SWAT team had come to save them.

"Just a second." Nancy tried to open the door, but the pressure from the other side kept it so taut she couldn't move it. "Let me close the door so I can remove the chain." For a split second, the chain was loose enough that Nancy could slip it from the confines of its metal bar. The men surged into the room, bringing a blast of cold Colorado air with them.

"Nancy and William Styler, we have a judge's order to take you in." In the commotion, Nancy couldn't tell who was speaking, but she could make out clothing that said "Colorado Bureau of Investigation" and "Pitkin County Sheriff's Department."

Someone showed Nancy a subpoena. Distraught, she turned to her husband. William "Trey" Styler was still in bed, but struggling to sit up. "Trey, am I dreaming? Is this a dream?"

"No, there's a dead body," a voice from the middle of the pack answered curtly.

Nancy gasped. "Who? What? We don't know anything about a dead body."

No one answered her.

"We're taking you into custody for questioning," another man added.

"Please be careful! He's out of his medicine," Nancy said, seeing the men urging her husband to get out of bed. "He might fall."

"We had to hold him up, he was so weak," Detective Brad Gibson would later tell investigative reporter Daleen Berry. Gibson had been with the Pitkin County Sheriff's Department for fourteen years and was the agency's investigative coordinator. He was excited, because this was his first "hot" murder case.

As Trey stood, armed men began snapping photos. Everyone in the room could see that his torso and legs were emaciated, because he was naked. They could also see how unsteady he was.

"Remove your robe, ma'am," one of the men said. "We need photos of you, too."

Nancy, sixty-two years old, came fully awake then, her disbelief turning to shock. She wanted to refuse, knowing she was wearing nothing underneath her robe, but she was afraid. So she complied, dropping her robe on the bed. Someone ordered her to turn around, first this way, then that. Then they began taking close-up shots of Nancy's hands and arms. Then a voice stopped him.

"Yeah, but you know we aren't supposed to. Heather can get them for us, since she's a woman," the voice said.

Basalt City Officer Heather Nelson had received a 3:37 a.m. text message asking for her assistance in serving the warrant. She met up with Undersheriff Ron Ryan, Director of Operations Alex Burchetta, Director of Investigations Brad Gibson, Deputies Levi Borst and Monique Merritt, and Basalt city officer Ernie Mack at the Basalt police department at 5:15 a.m. There, a Colorado Bureau of Investigation agent briefed the group about their mission before everyone headed to the Aspenalt Lodge.

Officer Nelson was outside putting crime tape on the Stylers' Jaguar and arranging for the vehicle to be towed when an officer inside the room radioed her to come inside. She did and as Nelson took the camera, Nancy noticed the female officer's hand shaking and watched her draw a long, deep breath as if to steel herself. Then Nelson began snapping nude photos of Nancy.

Nancy felt like a cornered animal. Somehow, as if through a thick mist, Nancy heard her sixty-five-year-old husband's soft voice coming from between the two queen beds.

"Can you please close the door, officers? It's February. It's freezing in here."

No one responded, even though he kept asking periodically.

"Why are we being treated like this? We haven't done anything wrong," Nancy said, but no one seemed to be listening to her, either. "Are we being arrested?"

"No," one of the men replied. "You're being brought in for questioning."

"I really need to use the bathroom," Nancy said, trying to cover her private areas with both arms. "May I use the bathroom?"

Nancy fell silent and waited. The men started taking swabs from under Nancy and Trey's nails, from inside their mouths. Nancy knew they were collecting DNA samples. *This is absolutely crazy!* Nancy remembers thinking to herself.

Finally, the pressure on her bladder building, Nancy spoke. "Please, I really need to use the bathroom." The men ignored her. "Will someone please let me use the bathroom before I have an accident?"

"Heather, take Mrs. Styler to the restroom and keep an eye on her."

The women maneuvered around the uniforms and into the bathroom, while Nancy tried to shield her body with her arms. It felt so good to relieve her bladder that Nancy didn't even care about Heather—who had kindly averted her eyes—standing guard. By then, Nancy was beyond humiliated.

When the women returned to the bedroom, the room was a whirl of activity. One officer was dumping out their suitcases, another, her purse. Two others were helping Trey don an orange prison outfit and his custom-designed orthopedic shoes. Someone handed Nancy an oversized orange top and matching pants. "PITKIN COUNTY JAIL" was emblazoned across the back of the shirt. Nancy felt her stomach turn as she donned the outfit. A pair of tennis shoes four sizes too large was dropped in her lap.

She repeated her earlier question. "Whose body is it?" Again, no one answered her.

Handcuffed and shackled, they led her outside and placed her in the front seat of a waiting Pitkin County Sheriff's Office SUV. She watched other officers lead her husband outside. As the vehicle started to pull away, Nancy strained her neck to see Trey. The Aspenalt Lodge grew smaller and smaller as Nancy watched them place him in another vehicle. When the SUV turned a corner, Nancy could no longer see her husband.

She had never felt so alone in all her life.

***

As the cruiser moved through town, Nancy struggled to get comfortable. If she tried to move her wrists to relieve the pressure against her lower back, the handcuffs cut into her skin.

A dozen different scenarios ran through Nancy's mind—all of them bad. They involved her landlady, Nancy Merle Pfister; her friend Kathy Carpenter; and, of course, alcohol. Alcohol was always the culprit, when it came to the two women's fights. Nancy was afraid that this time Pfister may have gotten so angry that she killed Kathy. Or, she thought, Pfister, finally destitute, had killed herself.

Behind the wheel, the deputy was mostly silent, but he still treated Nancy humanely, asking her if the temperature was comfortable.

Suddenly, the police radio came alive. A voice on the other end said Christina and Suzanne were on the phone, asking for help. Nancy recognized the names—they were Pfister's sisters. Something must have happened to Pfister.

***

When the Stylers met Pfister four months earlier, the socialite told them all about her prestigious family. She was the daughter of Elizabeth "Betty" Haas, a female aviator and the woman who helped organize and even flew on rescue missions with the Pitkin County Air Rescue Group, and Arthur "Art" Pfister, who made millions buying up acres and acres of cheap Aspen land during the 1940s. In 1959, he and his neighbor, Friedl Pfiefer, turned it into Buttermilk Mountain, playground to the rich, the famous, and anyone who hoped to become so. Eventually, Art sold his share to Aspen Skiing Company. Pfister hated seeing her family's land parceled out to people who wouldn't care for it, love it, like she did.

"You're a writer?" she asked Trey.

He nodded. "Well, I like to write."

"I want you to write a book about my life and my mother's," Pfister said, opening a cabinet door to expose a tall stack of journals. "You can use my diaries. I want to call it 'My Mother Parked Her Helicopter in the Driveway.'"

Pfister, a gregarious, gracious host who offered Nancy and Trey a glass of Champagne, bragged about her other connections to wealth and fame. There was her grandmother, Merle Haas. "She translated the beloved children's book *Babar the Elephant* from French into English," Pfister gushed. Her maternal grandfather, Robert Haas, "was one of the founding publishers at Random House."

Pfister also told Nancy and Trey that she and her sister Suzanne hadn't spoken to each other for more than a year, after arguing over their mother's estate. Nancy Styler, whose own bond with her only sister, Cindy, was almost as close as the one she had with her adult son, couldn't imagine such a thing. She felt sorry for the two women when Pfister told her they fought about everything, from their mother's inheritance to her fancy dishes, fur coats, jewelry, and artwork. The strife had grown so bad that the women had taken their battle to civil court.

When she learned Pfister had been a trust-fund child, Nancy marveled at the irony: so was Trey, though his family's wealth couldn't begin to touch that of the Pfisters. His dad worked as a CPA and later became wealthy after several lucrative oil deals. Trey's trust-fund nest egg came from savvy investments his mother made after Trey's father died. Nancy's family had never had money, but after marrying Trey, she quickly grew accustomed to life's luxuries.

When Pfister invited the Stylers to stay at her Buttermilk Mountain chalet for free during the next month, Nancy and Trey were overwhelmed by her hospitality. They weren't there much, since they were busy making trips back and forth from Denver. And when they were, they were running errands for Pfister, or Nancy was cleaning her house. During that time, they only heard the socialite talk to her other sister, Christina. Nancy sensed theirs wasn't a close relationship, but unlike Suzanne, at least they still talked.

***

As the police radio came alive again with a crackle, Nancy snapped to attention. "Suzanne Pfister is on the phone. She wants a protective order against the subjects."

"Is Nancy Pfister dead?" The words escaped Nancy's mouth before she could stop them, and her eyes grew wide as she suddenly remembered what Pfister had told them during their stay at the chalet months earlier. "If anything ever happens to me, tell the police to look at my sister Suzanne."

CHAPTER TWO
FIVE DAYS EARLIER

Nancy Merle Pfister was restless and jetlagged. She looked at her iPhone, the digital display showing 1 a.m. Monday, February 24. No wonder she couldn't sleep. If she were still in Australia, where she had spent the previous three months, the evening would just be beginning. More dinners, more drinks, more people to befriend, and more excitement. She always craved more excitement.

Not today, though. Today she was in bed, buried under blankets back home in Aspen, which was also buried beneath a deep blanket of snow. Pfister sighed. The entire reason she left was to escape the winter weather. It was all their fault anyway—her tenants, Trey and Nancy Styler. They had left her high and dry without any money in Australia, forcing her to return to collect the three months' rent, $12,000, due her. Well, that's what she told the world, on her Facebook page.

But it wasn't true.

In truth, Pfister didn't care about the Stylers. Their rent was paid in full through February 22, according to the December 31 email from Trey to Kathy Carpenter. Kathy was Pfister's closest friend and the woman who cared for Pfister's affairs when she was traveling around the world. In turn, Kathy emailed Pfister, saying that she had taken the rent money and an additional $650 Trey paid for utilities on January 3 and deposited it all into Pfister's safety deposit box at Alpine Bank, where Kathy worked full time as a teller. Still, Nancy had kicked her tenants out three months early; that meant they couldn't open their mountain spa, as the three of them had discussed back in October when they first met. Originally, Pfister said they could have her place until May 22, when she was supposed to return from Australia. But then, when things didn't exactly work out in Australia and Pfister had to leave the country to renew her expired visa anyway, she decided to return home early, due to the pending sale of Pfister family land. She blamed the Stylers, though, for her return. But so what? She knew "those assholes"—or at least the wife—thought they were above her anyway. She would show them!

Local residents knew Pfister often rented out what she called her "chalet" while she flew around the globe from one foreign locale to another. Like so many of her previous tenants, whom she had also kicked out early, Pfister simply didn't care. She had to have a place to stay, and she would do whatever it took to get them out.

Pfister's colorful history of being at odds with people was well documented. While she was liked by her close friends, Pfister had a penchant for making enemies. Even her relationship with her sisters, Christina and Suzanne, was strained, to say the least. In fact, complete strangers who reached out to police after her death said Pfister had told them that if any harm ever befell her, the investigation should start at Suzanne's front door.

***

Getting the Stylers to leave her 1833 West Buttermilk residence hadn't even been that difficult. It had been like a game, really. She just got two of her good friends, Sheriff Joe DiSalvo and Bob Braudis, the former sheriff, involved, along with several other Aspenites she knew. And like Pfister told one of them, her friend Mimi Scott, in a February 18, 2014, email, "I just wanted to put a little fire under their ass!!!!"

No, Pfister wasn't worried about the Stylers. She didn't have time to worry about them. She was worried about money, though. Pfister always worried about money, even though she had even more money now than she did before she left the States: $664,837.20 more, from her deceased mother's estate. Instead, she was corralling the troops, wooing everyone to her side—for the real battle. It was just a week away, scheduled for Friday, February 28. That's when that trustee Andy

Hecht her father had put in charge of all the Pfister family property and funds was going to sell what was left of her daddy's land.

Hecht was a prominent local real estate attorney and investor in his own right. He was a long-time friend of Arthur Pfister and handled most of the Pfister family's legal affairs. Nancy Pfister did not trust him; whether paranoid, justified, or both, Pfister thought he mishandled the deathbed sale of a prime parcel of Pfister lakefront property. So the last thing she wanted was Hecht to know she was even thinking about the sale—or that she planned to make sure that neither he nor Pfister's sister Suzanne ripped her off in the process.

Of course, she was equally embarrassed about her dealings with her Aussie playmate, Richard. Their romp had ended badly in Australia, and Pfister didn't want word to get out about that, either. If it hadn't been for Suzanne bullying her, Pfister realized she might have caught on to Richard sooner—instead of not long after she arrived in Australia. Her younger sister, Christina, was right! She had called him "smarmy." Christina had tried to tell Pfister that Richard kept calling her repeatedly, trying to get information about Pfister's trust fund and the return she got on her investment, but she hadn't listened.

Christina asked Richard why he was interested, but all he would say was that he wanted to protect Pfister. At the time, Pfister truly believed him. But Christina, who said Richard "gave me the real hee-bie-jeebies," tried to warn her. Pfister kicked herself when she realized that she should have listened to her little sister.

Pfister's thoughts weren't very coherent and they bounced back and forth between the pending land deals, Richard, Christina, Suzanne, Hecht, and the Stylers. Just the thought of the couple—how arrogant and self-righteous they were—angered Pfister, who grabbed her iPhone. Using the voice-to-text feature (which often resulted in texts with errors throughout), Pfister dictated a quick message to Mimi at 1:32 a.m.

"Mimi did you win I haven't really checked my emails today but I'm call me it's Monday nowlagging [sic] in the middle of the morning so give seven my love and the kids too!!!! Can't wait to give you a big hug!!"

On a roll now, two minutes later, Pfister texted another friend, Sigrid Lee.

"Hey Sigrid give me a call when you get a chance will you yeah that looks like fun okay well I wish you would come and visit me if you can I can't move I'm too tired but I'd like to show you what a fucking wreck they've done to my house you won't believe it anyhow if you know of anybody that wants make some money I need to put the house back together okay I love you! Call when you get a chance."

Pfister had no way of knowing that was the last text message she would ever send.

***

Pfister picked up some papers from her nightstand and fingered the registration and insurance documents for the Stylers' car. The Stylers had switched vehicles with Kathy for the day: she got their small Jaguar in return for her roomier Subaru station wagon, better suited for moving their belongings out of Pfister's house at 1833 West Buttermilk. Pfister found the papers in the glove box of the Jag after Kathy picked her up from the airport Saturday afternoon, before Kathy and Trey exchanged cars again on Sunday. Pfister remembered the personal message she had Kathy deliver to Trey: she accused the Stylers of trashing her home and demanded that they pay her $14,000 in damages. She also refused to return their $150,000 in spa equipment—items they hadn't had time to remove from 1833 West Buttermilk, but which they needed to earn a livelihood—and threatened to obtain a restraining order if they tried to take it. She imagined what the equipment might fetch if she sold it on Craigslist. What a shame that would be for them, Pfister then thought. The legal documents—she wasn't quite sure what she was going to do with them, other than play a game of cat and mouse with the Stylers.

At that moment, Kathy was sleeping off the night before on the couch with Gabe, Pfister's black Labradoodle puppy. The two women had gone through two bottles of Champagne the night before to celebrate Pfister's return. Never mind that Kathy was back on the wagon and going to AA meetings; Pfister could always convince Kathy to drink with her.

Pfister knew Kathy might be hung over when she went to work the next day, but otherwise she would be fine. After all, how many brain cells were necessary to count cash for the customers who came to her teller window at Alpine Bank in downtown Aspen?

Pfister planned to show her face around town Monday afternoon, let the old gang know she was back. She was just dozing off when she was jolted awake: she had no way to get from her home in Snowmass to downtown Aspen. The snow was so deep that her little Toyota Prius had become embedded in a big chunk of ice and couldn't be moved.

Then she remembered: she had called her friend Patrick Carney sometime Sunday morning, telling him she was back from Australia and asking for a ride to town Monday. Patrick had told her he would come by after he went skiing, but she hadn't heard back from him, so she was a little miffed. Pfister got up and went downstairs, looking first in the fridge and then among the foodstuffs for something to eat.

Over on the couch, Kathy and Gabe were curled up. Kathy opened her eyes long enough to see Pfister come through the room, before she slipped back to sleep.

After a snack, Pfister went back to her room, closed the bedroom door like she always did, pushed her earplugs back into each ear, and slid her eye mask down over her eyes to block out the light. Finally, after a bit more tossing and turning, sleep overtook her travel-weary body.

***

While Pfister was resting and nursing her injured shoulder, Patrick Carney was doing the same. He was a patient in Aspen Valley Hospital after tumbling down one of the ski slopes Sunday afternoon and shattering his collarbone. The doctors put in fourteen pins and two metal plates and kept Patrick overnight. Swelling could be bad, and they didn't want that. Neither did Patrick, who was sleeping soundly, thanks to some very strong painkillers.

Patrick emerged from under the fog of painkillers his surgeon prescribed Monday morning. He found several text messages and voicemails on his cell phone. Pfister's message was among them. Patrick's entire arm was bandaged up and felt like lead as he returned her call. He got no answer, so he left a message, telling her he had been in the hospital overnight, after breaking his collarbone. Patrick said he'd give Pfister a ride after his doctor discharged him. Later, he tried Pfister's cell one more time, but when he got no answer, he popped another painkiller and fell back to sleep.

By Monday night, not having heard back from Pfister, Patrick tried once more to reach her. She didn't answer.

Patrick, having only been in the area for about eighteen months, was a relative newcomer to Aspen. He became Pfister's regular Thursday night dinner escort at L'Hostaria, where he nonetheless knew he would be expected to foot the bill. She never paid—not once—for any of their weekly dinners together.

"Nancy never stuck her hand in her pocket if her life depended on it," he would later tell police.

Patrick really liked Pfister even though, as he also told police, she was "drunk from the time she got up until she went to bed." As an Aspen outsider, Patrick had found it difficult to make friends when he first moved there, but Pfister befriended him immediately, so he was grateful for her companionship. He said it was platonic, that they were just good friends, nothing more. Pfister told him she had herpes and he, in turn, said that was a definite deal-breaker in his book, when it came to them being sexual partners. But witnesses later told defense investigators that Patrick had a tendency to become jealous if other men interacted with Pfister when he was with her.

As it turns out, Patrick Carney wasn't the only male friend who tried to contact Pfister in the days leading up to or after her return. So did local Aspen resident and Pfister's long-time buddy Billy Clayton, who says he was like Pfister's brother.

Pfister's friend Eric Todd, who lived in Taos, New Mexico, called Pfister twice—once on February 19, when he says, "Aloha my ass," and asked her to call him. His voice sounds seductive when he tells Pfister it's been a long winter in Taos, and he thought she was coming back.

Todd called again on February 21, the night before Pfister arrived back in Aspen. In that call, Todd's voice sounds slurred as though he's been drinking when he says he thinks he'll have to leave his beautiful world in Taos so he can come to Aspen to see her. He doesn't sound happy about it. Todd seemed angry at Pfister for neglecting him, and repeatedly tried to reach her.

Another gentleman was trying to reach Pfister, too, but no one knows who he was. The Sunday, February 23 call came from overseas. In his message, the foreigner with an accent calls her "honey."

From February 19 to 23, the men left Pfister messages saying "I love you," leading some Aspenites to believe one of the men had a jealous streak. Perhaps even enough to kill her.

Yet the police didn't even consider them suspects.

CHAPTER THREE
TREY TO THE RESCUE

W hile Pfister fell into a fitful sleep, Nancy Styler was also asleep inside her motel room at the Aspenalt Lodge. She and her husband, Trey, had spent all day Saturday trying to move everything they owned from Pfister's house before her scheduled return—but one problem after another cost them more time and money than they had left to their name. The stress and frustration wore Nancy Styler to a frazzle.

At one point she seemed to perk up when chatting with Kathy about the ride back from the airport. The two women had grown close during Pfister's absence, and Nancy had spent hours trying to build up Kathy's self-esteem. "How did it go last night? Did she give you any trouble?" Nancy had been worried about the reception Kathy might get if Pfister wasn't happy with the way the house looked.

"No, if she had given me any trouble I would have walked out," Kathy said.

"What about the house?" Nancy asked. "Was she happy with her bed?"

"No, she said it was too hot," Kathy replied.

They chatted for a few more minutes, then said goodbye.

Throughout the day, though, Trey grew more and more worried, especially when Nancy told him they "should take that drive now." It was a reference to the final famous suicide scene in the movie *Thelma and Louise*, where the two women drive off a cliff, but otherwise, except for sending a few text messages, Nancy slept most of the day.

As she and Trey were watching the Olympics on TV, Nancy texted their son, Daniel, at 7:20 p.m.: "Slept all day today. I really needed it. We are at the motel just watching Olympics. All is well. Is everything good there? Love you."

"Love you both, enjoy your curling," Daniel replied at 7:20 p.m.

He sent a second text right after that, also at 7:20 p.m. "Slept 'til 11 myself. I'm writing [a paper] . . . Finally [for the first time since you got it for me] had to get a SodaStream CO2 refill. Thing's efficient!"

Ten minutes later, at 7:30 p.m., Nancy texted Kathy: "How are things going? I slept all day. I am emotionally exhausted. How is your shoulder? How is the baby [Gabe] doing? Do you have him? I will talk to u tomorrow xo."

Before the Olympics were over, she was still so exhausted from the stress of the last few days that she couldn't stop yawning. "Goodnight, Trey," Nancy said, leaning over to give him a kiss as he played on his laptop.

"Goodnight, darlin'. I hope you feel rested tomorrow."

"So do I." She always removed her hearing aids when she slept, so she couldn't even hear his fingers, still clacking away at the keyboard. Nor did she hear Kathy's text much later that night, when it came through at 11:28 p.m. on her phone.

"I'm okay . . . met with Sarah today it was very therapeutic. The baby is fine. He hung out with me today. Glad you got some rest. Talk to you tomorrow. Xo."

***

When Trey woke up Monday morning, Nancy was still sleeping. He was surprised that she didn't wake up, and then he thought back to how much she had slept the day before and realized she must be overwrought with worry about their finances. He hated seeing her like that and he knew sleep was the best thing for her. He had never seen her so discouraged, so ready to give up. They had been through a lot together, and she was always right there, ready with an encouraging word or a positive pep talk. She was his cheerleader, but in the last week or two, she had lost her normal ability to bounce back from negative influences.

Trey was very worried. Even when his neurological illness, which everyone first believed to be a milder variation of Lou Gehrig's disease, or ALS, forced him to step down as chief of staff of the anesthesiology department at St. Joseph's Hospital in Denver, she cheered him on. And when he spent months and then years litigating a former employer over a piece of software he created that he believed they stole from him, Nancy's was the little voice in his ear that told him they would succeed. Even when his attorney in the case, John Powell, missed deadline after deadline, and failed to file the proper motions, eventually losing the case for Trey, Nancy was right there, cheerfully backing him up.

It wasn't until Nancy refused to write any more checks to Powell that the couple found themselves at odds. They had never argued about anything before, but Nancy had had enough. Yes, she went along at first, writing out checks to Powell for $10,000, then $14,000, and finally, the last one: $24,000. She was adamant: "No more, Trey!"

Of course, only later did Nancy learn about the credit card Powell had talked Trey into using. Trey had charged $30,000 on that card, giving every penny to Powell. When Nancy did the math, she calculated that over several months and then years Powell had bilked them for $670,000 in supposed legal fees—money he had done nothing to earn. That was when Trey saw Nancy's faith in him waver. Still, as loyal a wife as ever, Nancy told him it didn't matter. "We still have our home. And Danny, and each other," she said.

But their son Daniel, then away at college, had lost all faith in his father. Daniel had seen him throw the family's money away—including the trust fund Trey's mother had left him—fighting one lawsuit after another. Even so, Daniel was still close to his mother, and he hated seeing what his father's illness was doing to her.

By then, the cumulative effects of two lawsuits—one to gain control of the software he created, the other to force Powell to repay the money he stole from Trey and his family—along with the debilitating disease, had affected Trey's mind. Even the weekly visits to see his psychiatrist didn't help. They soon lost all their money and had to sell their refinanced $2.2 million Greenwood Village home at a loss, to prevent foreclosure. Trey never saw the darkness overtaking him. All he knew was his career, his health, his life's savings, his happiness, even his hobby helping Nancy tend her garden, everything had been stolen from him. What he didn't know was that his mind was going, too.

Having been reared by a father whose first priority was providing well for family, Trey knew what was expected of him. It was his responsibility, because that's what Trey's father had instilled in him: "We men always take care of our families, son. That's our job." He knew no other way to live—taking care of Nancy was his life's purpose. If he couldn't do that, he was a failure.

It was 2013, their money was all but gone and, in the midst of this dark depression, Trey began planning suicide. According to his warped sense of logic, Trey's death would provide Nancy with enough insurance money to survive—and allow him to die feeling like he was still able to take care of his family. Of his beloved wife. He became convinced the only way to do that was to kill himself. Unlike many modern insurance policies, his $1 million policy would still pay if his death were a suicide, so he had nothing to lose. He told Nancy of his plan—but she wouldn't hear of it.

"Trey Styler, I would rather live in a tiny cabin with you than anywhere else without you! Stop that crazy talk. We can make it," she said in her customary upbeat tone. "We still have a little money. We can use it to start over somewhere, maybe open up a little business that will bring in enough to get us through this rough patch. I'll go to work and support us, since you've worked so hard all these years."

For the last several years, that's exactly what she had done: she planned it all out fastidiously, as she did everything. She limited the amount of expensive clothes and shoes she bought, all to show him she was ready to support the family. She signed them both up for training in how to use a laser for cosmetic procedures; she took aesthetician classes, purchased the necessary equipment, and developed a business plan. He was going to be the medical director of "Mountain Oasis Spa" and she would perform most of the actual services.

Throughout, Nancy was still the effervescent cheerleader Trey needed, helping him regain his emotional perspective and pulling him back from the dark hole he was falling into.

***

Until now, he thought. Until Pfister. It was almost a fluke, how the sleepy town's most outrageous socialite became the Stylers' landlady: Pfister hailed from one of Aspen's founding families. When the Stylers answered her newspaper ad, Pfister called it "karma." Trey and Nancy were kind and generous, and they liked Pfister from their first meeting in October 2013. When she told them she wanted to invest in their world-class spa, they believed her intentions were genuine. After falling on hard times, they thought Pfister's offer to rent them her chalet while she was away in Australia was a miracle—and would provide them a much-needed chance to get back on their feet.

So the Stylers, not yet completely broke, went out of their way to please Pfister, continuing their lifetime habit of generosity. They gave her their frequent-flyer miles without thinking twice when Pfister asked them to purchase her first-class tickets to Houston, Texas, because she didn't like to fly coach. They bought her $1,000 worth of her favorite pink Champagne and never balked when she didn't pay them back. And when Pfister's boarding plans for Gabe fell through, just before she went overseas, they kept and cared for the puppy, even though they desperately needed to focus on getting their business off the ground.

In the meantime, during the month they lived with Pfister— rent-free in return for helping her around her house—the Stylers discovered Pfister was an alcoholic who lived to party. They watched as she talked one person after another into buying her expensive lunches and Champagne, and stuck them with the check. They saw Pfister get into loud screaming matches with Gabe's dog trainer, a personal organizer she hired, and a Hollywood producer. Pfister also expected Nancy Styler to drop everything for her at an instant—like Kathy later said Pfister had expected of her. However, Pfister found in Nancy Styler someone who wasn't used to such treatment, and who wasn't afraid to speak up for herself.

While enjoying her Australian getaway, Pfister began making wild demands for money far beyond what the couple owed her. Nancy and Trey became distraught when the landlady threatened to sue if they didn't give in to her extortion.

Pfister not only sabotaged their plans to open the spa—she also asked her friend Sheriff Joe DiSalvo to evict them. By then Trey wasn't the only one who was depressed and suicidal. So was his wife, his Nancy.

***

That crazy woman had driven them both to the edge with her changing terms, her outrageous lies, and her repeated threats. His Nancy was worn out from the stress and drama Pfister wrought upon them. Trey wasn't worried initially; he was angry, yes, angry that Pfister didn't seem to care that she was driving them to financial ruin, but he wasn't worried—because he knew Nancy would be right there to bolster him up, to bolster *them* up. She was their only buoy in a raging sea of crazy.

Except that during the last two weeks, she hadn't. Trey watched as his wife slowly grew more worried, the lines around her eyes more strained, but when she began repeating his own words back to him— "We should take that drive," the one Trey had repeatedly suggested— he grew terrified. He had to get them out of the mess Pfister created. After all, Nancy had wanted to move out of Pfister's home a week before Pfister flew to Australia. He was the one who convinced her to stay—a decision he now regretted with all his being.

"I hate that woman. I've never been so disrespected in my entire life," Nancy said in tears.

***

After hearing his wife voice the same suicidal sentence that Trey himself had begun repeating two years earlier, Trey wanted to let Nancy sleep. Just two days after they packed up and moved out of Pfister's house, he knew she needed it. He also knew his wife: if her phone was anywhere within reach, she would be making or taking calls. That's just who she was; she couldn't help herself; she was always available to her friends when they needed her. He picked up Nancy's iPhone 5, pocketed it, and took it with him on his errands.

Trey had been without some of his medications going on four days, so his thinking was a little muddled, which is why he didn't give a single thought to the business phone she had packed away in a suitcase. That was Nancy's iPhone 3, but they rarely used it.

As Trey quietly slipped out the door of the motel, he looked back and thought how peaceful Nancy looked in her sleep. Like always, Trey wanted to fix things for his beautiful wife. He wanted nothing more than to return the gift she'd given him during the last few tremulous years of his life. He would save her—somehow.

CHAPTER FOUR

MANY PEOPLE WITH A MOTIVE

A s Kathy Carpenter let herself out of Pfister's home very early on that Monday morning, she was careful not to bump her injured shoulder—still painful from injuring it Thursday after work while helping the Stylers move Pfister's furniture back into place. She closed the door behind her after posting a note on the main entryway, the front door of the basement: "Do not disturb, Nancy's sleeping," just like Pfister had asked her to the night before.

Then she drove to her apartment, a quaint place just five blocks from Alpine Bank where she worked. She quickly showered and cleaned up, before heading to her teller's position. It was the only company she'd worked for in the last fifteen years and she loved her job. Even though her alcoholism had caused her demotion from loan officer to teller, Kathy wouldn't trade it for anything. She loved her coworkers and the small home Alpine Bank provided her. Besides, she was on the wagon—determined not to drink again. Ever.

Kathy frowned, thinking of the Champagne she and Pfister had shared Saturday night, after she picked up her friend from the Aspen airport. Pfister had been so insistent—and the expensive pink Champagne Pfister loved to drink was so good—that Kathy finally gave in.

She had broken her promise to herself and Sarah, her AA sponsor, the one where she wasn't going to let Pfister manipulate her anymore. She told Sarah she was going to steer completely clear of Pfister and avoid any encounter that might involve alcohol. Yet she hadn't. The past few months had been so full of stress that Kathy had allowed herself to slip back into Pfister's grasp even before she got off the plane—a grasp that went back more than ten years, and involved an intimacy Kathy herself didn't even understand.

Her relationship with Pfister began when the well-known socialite went into the bank to open an account.

"You're fat!" Pfister told her.

Kathy promptly responded with, "And you're a bitch."

By the end of the day, the two women were drinking together. Before long, Kathy was acting as Pfister's personal banker, being her designated driver when needed, and in general watching over Pfister's place whenever Pfister flew to some foreign locale, which happened quite often. And once, when the place had no renters, Kathy and her son, Michael, even lived there for a time.

Everything was fine—until Carpenter joined Pfister for a drink. First it was one, then before she knew it, she would be drunk, even blacking out on occasion. The two women were alike in that way, and the drinking jags led to some pretty ugly scenes, like the time Pfister tried to force Kathy to drive them home in her Toyota Prius. Kathy refused, knowing she was drunk and shouldn't drive. Pfister called the police, insisting she was afraid of her intoxicated friend. But the ploy didn't go as planned because Pfister, so drunk she slurred her words, was arrested for DUI.

Pfister blamed Kathy for that, for the associated fines, court costs, and traffic classes she had to attend, insisting Kathy repay her the $2,500 she lost. Kathy tried to reason with her friend but it did no good, so in the end she stopped arguing and agreed to repay Pfister's money.

Standing behind the counter that morning at work, Kathy couldn't believe she was letting it happen all over again. She silently swore at Pfister, knowing she should never have let the woman talk her into spending the night after she drove her home from the airport. Every time she was around Pfister, she ended up drinking. Not when she was an alcoholic and had been working her AA steps so well! Hadn't Nancy Styler warned her about that very thing, before Pfister flew home? And in turn, Kathy had assured Nancy, her new friend, that Pfister wouldn't cause her to fall off the wagon again.

But she had. And now she had to start her sobriety all over again.

No good could come of any contact with Pfister. Kathy knew that. So she made herself another promise then and there: she wasn't going anywhere near Pfister or her home again. Even though they co-parented Gabe, the puppy Kathy had helped Pfister pick out, she was determined: Pfister could drop the puppy off at her home when it was Kathy's turn to keep him or when Pfister was leaving town, just like you'd exchange custody of children in a divorce—or else Pfister could make other arrangements for the animal. Kathy was not going down that road again. Not this time. She had too much to lose, and her self-respect topped the list. Kathy told herself she would do whatever it took to ensure she and Pfister were never together again!

* * *

Monday mornings were usually the busiest for Aspen attorney Andrew Hecht. One of the town's most prominent attorneys, he dabbled in real estate, making most of his money from handling family estates and trust funds, like the one Art Pfister left him in charge of all those years ago. He had quite a few things to do to prepare for the week, including the upcoming sale of two prime Pfister pieces of real estate. Hecht would never be so glad to conclude the sales, and he hoped it would lead to some peace between Suzanne Pfister Kelso and her younger sister, Nancy Merle Pfister.

* * *

A few miles away in Snowmass, Suzanne was also thinking about the upcoming sale. Suzanne, the eldest Pfister daughter, was not the giddy type—yet that day she was absolutely giddy, anticipating how much more money she would get for her property once the right-of-way was allowed to go through.

She and Pfister had become estranged over the two Tiehack lots their parents bequeathed them, among other things, because Pfister had repeatedly refused to grant Suzanne the right-of-way. But come Friday, that would all change. Nothing her little sister could do to try to stop the sale, to prevent the right-of-way, would work—because Hecht told her so.

Yes, on that Monday, February 24, Suzanne was quite happy about her upcoming plans.

CHAPTER FIVE

GET A CIVIL STANDBY

While Kathy was working her normal shift at Alpine Bank that Monday, Trey was wondering how to convince Pfister to let them get their spa and sewing equipment from her home. Nancy knew their landlord expected money for supposed damages to her home and for her to pay someone to rearrange it the way she wanted, but nothing more—because Trey skimmed over the details. He left out the part about another possible legal battle and her threats to keep their equipment. He was afraid Nancy would be too overwhelmed if she knew how events transpired during his Sunday afternoon meeting with Kathy.

By the time Trey returned from renting two storage units in Basalt, Nancy had already dressed and eaten. She asked Trey where he was, and he told her he checked out area storage companies, which turned out to be "a real hassle," but he finally found two units. They discussed getting their moving van—which they had to leave behind at Pfister's on Saturday because they hadn't yet secured a storage unit. Trey parked it up the hill from Pfister's driveway in a wide-open spot. That was their first priority Monday; then they would go straight to Pfister's about their equipment. They decided to ring up Pfister before driving up there, but Trey said his calls to her cell phone went unanswered, so he left her several voice mails. Nancy assumed she was simply unwilling to answer, but they were also worried because they didn't know their legal rights—and they certainly didn't want any further trouble. They were in a quandary, until Nancy had an idea.

27

"I'll talk to an attorney and see what to do," Nancy told Trey. She didn't know any local attorneys, so she called Merlin Broughton, a friend of Pfister's, as well as her handyman, to ask for the name of one; he suggested John LeSalle. But LeSalle couldn't help: "I'm sorry, I can't do anything. I've done work for the family before. Good luck with that one," he said.

LeSalle recommended another attorney, who referred Nancy to a third person—Basalt attorney Alan Adger. Finally, they found someone who had not worked with the Pfister family and was willing to give them legal advice. After hearing their concerns, Adger told Nancy she and Trey had legal standing to return to the house and get their belongings, and Pfister had no right to try to prevent that.

"I want protection from her lies. Is there any way to do that?" Nancy asked.

Yes, Adger said, advising her to request a civil standby before they went to Pfister's home. Nancy asked what that was and Adger explained: when someone anticipates problems arising in a tense situation like this one, they can call the local police and ask for an officer to "stand by"—that is, the Stylers should notify police that they anticipate problems and ask them to be on alert, in case they needed help once they reached 1833 West Buttermilk.

Nancy called the sheriff's nonemergency number that afternoon. The employee who answered the phone said it wasn't a high priority, but they would help if they could.

However, the police were not needed Monday afternoon— because when Nancy and Trey arrived, they didn't even enter Pfister's driveway. They could see that Pfister's handyman Merlin still had his trailer parked there from Saturday, and all they really wanted was to take the U-Haul moving truck to the storage units so they could unload their belongings. Each day they kept the truck was more money they couldn't afford. When they arrived, though, they found that someone had parked behind the U-Haul. They assumed it was a cross-country skier's car, since that was a popular spot for skiers. But the car was so close that Trey couldn't back the truck out, and there wasn't enough room to drive it forward. The Stylers waited for more than an hour, hoping the car's owner would return, but no one ever came.

***

Not wanting to be late for their next appointment, they drove straight from Buttermilk to Basalt to see Alice Pendleton's two-bedroom house on Frying Pan Road. Pendleton had advertised it for $2,200 a month, and the Stylers felt they could swing that—if they could sell Nancy's $30,000 diamond ring. Their good friend Patrice Melanie knew it was available and encouraged Nancy to rent the house. She even put in a good word with Pendleton, whom she knew personally. Nancy fell in love with the area, with its tall, rocky cliff side and another gorgeous view around every turn, when they drove up the narrow, winding road. They spent more than an hour looking at Pendleton's place and by the time they left, everything seemed perfect. Afterward, Nancy thought Pendleton seemed agreeable to having them as tenants. Maybe things *were* looking up. She began feeling better, less stressed. As they started back down the mountain, Nancy noticed it was 5:45 p.m. She realized she hadn't heard from their son, Daniel.

"Did you talk to Daniel today?"

"No," Trey said, maneuvering the Jaguar around a curve. His voice sounded scratchy and Nancy looked across the seat at him. A shadow crossed her face when she thought back to their tour of the home. Trey had been coughing and shaking and had to excuse himself and use the bathroom, where he threw up. He was in there for several long minutes. Nancy worried Trey was getting sick because he had been out of some of his meds for the last several days. Since his disease drained him of energy, Trey took an amphetamine to boost his energy level (without it, he could barely move, let alone function); Effexor XR, an antidepressant for his depression; Clonazepam, a strong sedative to help him sleep at night, since the disease also caused him to twitch a lot; and thyroid medication.

With her medical background, Nancy knew it wasn't safe for him to stop the antidepressant cold turkey, but even though their HMO, Kaiser-Permanente, had mailed all the drugs from Castle Rock, they hadn't yet arrived. Nancy wondered what else, in addition to the vomiting, her poor husband would have to endure. She just prayed Trey could hang in there until the meds arrived.

They had nowhere else to go, nothing to do, so they drove back to the Aspenalt. It was a few minutes after 6 p.m. when Nancy's phone began buzzing with an incoming text message from Daniel.

"How goes?" Daniel texted at 6:10 p.m.

"Hanging in and hanging out at the motel, waiting," Nancy texted back at 6:14 p.m.

They spent the rest of the evening in their room, but at 10 p.m. Nancy remembered she hadn't thanked Patrice. She quickly typed out a long text, feeling like Patrice was responsible for reviving her hope that things would work out for them.

"We met with Alice. She is beautiful. The house would be so perfect for my sewing equipment and she is having to outsource her upholstery work which I do. The house would be so healing for us and the frying pan is so beautifully peaceful. She had some other people looking at the house after us but she said that she would let us know. There is also the possibility of renting the other part of the house if she gets the job in New Zealand. She also said we could do the spa thing in the house. We love it. Thank you for the glowing recommendation. The frying pan is not nearly as winding or steep as I had thought. It is so beautiful. I hope and pray that she chooses us. The layout of the space is so perfect for our needs. I had a glimmer of hope for the first time today after meeting Alice and seeing the house. Know that you are one of my angels and I appreciate you so much. Thank you."

It was 10:15 p.m. when Nancy sent the message, but Patrice was already in bed.

CHAPTER SIX

THOSE SQUATTERS STOLE MY EXPENSIVE ART!

On February 25, a Tuesday morning, Nancy awoke wondering how the rest of their move would go, and if today would really be the end of their dealings with Pfister. *I hope so*, she thought.

Between packing, rearranging Pfister's house to its pre-Australia state, trying to load everything into the U-Haul and Merlin's trailer, and cleaning Pfister's house until it was spotless afterward, the last week felt like it had dragged on for one very long month. Nancy wanted it to be over with, and to never hear from or see that crazy woman again.

She was doing her hair when she found Patrice's text message.

"That's great news!!! :) if this is 'your' home/meant to be . . . It'll happen! Keep the faith! Sending love- xxoo." The time stamp said 8:57 a.m.

***

Trey told Nancy the three workers they had hired to help unload the U-Haul were waiting outside their motel room. Nancy explained she needed help from local law enforcement, which confused the Hispanic men. "Our landlord's been acting a little crazy lately, so we'll feel better if we have some witnesses there," she explained to the men.

It was 11:38 a.m. when Nancy called the sheriff's office to request a standby. Danielle Madril took the call. Thomas Wright logged it. Madril's notes read: "Heading over there now. Would like an officer to call. Nancy Pfister is the property owner."

Nancy Styler was making small talk with one of the workers when her phone rang. It was Deputy Dustin Grey, asking if they still needed his help at Pfister's house.

"We're on our way there now," she said. "I won't know until we get there, but we don't want any more trouble from her."

"I understand. Well, if you get there and need me, just call and I'll come up," the deputy said. Nancy thanked him, hoping at the same time that Pfister wouldn't try to make their life any more difficult than she already had.

***

When they arrived at Pfister's, it was early afternoon and the day was off to a bad start: Trey had gotten the U-Haul hung up in the driveway. He wrestled with the vehicle for an hour but it wasn't until a neighbor with a Bobcat stopped by to help that they were able to free the big truck from the pile of snow.

Afterward, Trey left on a post office run, telling Nancy he couldn't find Pfister, who wasn't sleeping in her bedroom.

"Well, we don't need the deputy then," she said.

One of the workers handed her a sign they found on the door. "Nancy is sleeping," he said in broken English. Since the men knew Nancy Styler was wide awake, they grinned sheepishly, after taking it down.

Just then, Merlin showed up. Not just Pfister's friend, Merlin was also an electrician who had done small odd jobs at Pfister's home while she was away, like replacing the hot water tank when it went out. In the process, he and Nancy had gotten to know each other. Merlin didn't know Trey as well, since Trey either kept to himself or was always playing on his laptop. Saturday when it looked like the U-Haul truck wasn't going to be big enough, Nancy had called Merlin, asking if they could borrow his trailer. He had agreed and had dropped it off later that day.

"Hi, Merlin," Nancy said, explaining that Trey had just run to the post office to get his meds that were coming from Castle Rock.

"Is Nancy Pfister home?" he asked.

She shook her head. "Trey said he went upstairs and checked and she's not at home."

Merlin followed Nancy into the house, but the second they entered, Gabe came running and jumped up on Merlin, peeing all over his leg.

"Whoa, little fellow. You're excited," Merlin said.

That's when Nancy realized why. *Trey didn't mention this!* She first smelled, then saw, piles of poop and yellow puddles all over, including one big pile at the bottom of the stairs. She grabbed some paper towels and began cleaning up the poop. She didn't want the movers to track it all over.

"What's wrong with your mommy, to go away and leave you cooped up inside?" she said, petting Gabe. Then she saw the dog's mess. Miso paste, oranges and avocados, as well as a box of Kleenex, were strewn all over the living room and kitchen. Nancy cleaned it all up, noticing what she thought was an odd smell. She wasn't sure where it was coming from, but chalked it up to Gabe being locked inside. Nancy checked Gabe's food and water, noticing that someone had replaced the container that usually stored the unused portion of the puppy's food with a large blue cast-iron Dutch oven. It had a heavy, Gabe-proof lid, which Nancy believed someone had carefully placed on the hearth. That seemed a little odd, unlike Pfister. Gabe's regular food bowl held water instead of food and sat next to his water bowl. Both were half empty.

Merlin told Nancy he'd be back to get the trailer later that day or the next, whenever he finished the electrical jobs he had lined up. "I can take it right to the storage unit for you," he said.

"Thanks, Merlin. That would be great."

After he said his goodbyes and left, Nancy checked her cell again. The beeping noise meant Daniel had texted her again.

"I hope you're asking a cop to be present at the move-out. It's only defense against 'Those squatters stole my expensive art!'" It was sent at 11:31 a.m.

***

By the time she finished cleaning up after Gabe, Trey was back. Nancy mentioned the odd odor to him but she knew he couldn't smell anything because of a decades-old accident that had left him with a broken nose. "It must be the feces," she said.

Nancy sent Kathy a text message saying Gabe was left alone inside and she was worried that Pfister wasn't around. While Pfister was in Australia, she and Kathy had talked about something Pfister repeatedly said: "I don't want to live without money." They had also discussed their concern that she could accidentally kill herself, considering she regularly consumed a handful of pills with her alcohol. Even though Pfister had been a real pain, and they had all joked about how great it would be if something happened to her, those were just jokes. They didn't mean anything—so Nancy felt a twinge of worry for the woman.

Clearly a person had to be very unhappy to drink that much. She and Trey had discussed it at great length, saying how happy they were neither of them had gotten caught up in the lure of alcohol or painkillers. Especially with Trey's illness, it would have been so easy. But he refused to take narcotics for that very reason. To remind himself of how addictive they were, he carried a prescription for OxyContin in his wallet from 1999.

After texting Kathy, Nancy went to join the movers. She and Trey were so busy helping the men load the truck that they didn't notice when another vehicle pulled up. But when Nancy started inside and saw a man walking down the stairs, she was a little taken aback. Then she recognized him. It was Pfister's friend Patrick Carney. For a split second, she decided Pfister and Carney must have been together, and that's why Pfister hadn't returned any of Trey's calls. But that idea soon vanished.

"Is Nancy here?" he said.

"No. I thought she was with you."

"No. She called me yesterday and asked me to come pick her up. But I broke my collarbone skiing and was in the emergency room and didn't get her message," Carney said. "Then when I tried to call her back, her phone went directly to voice mail. That's why I stopped by, to see if she's here."

"That sounds painful," Nancy said. "Yeah, we've been trying to call her too, because we had problems getting all of our stuff out by the time she got back Saturday. But we never got to her at all. Her phone wouldn't take calls."

"That's strange," Carney said. "Well, that's Nancy."

"Yeah, she must be out doing her own thing. That would explain why Gabe was out of water and there was poop all over the place when we got here," she said. "We've had some problems and we're moving out. I haven't seen her since she went to Australia."

Patrick left then, and Nancy didn't give him another thought. She took a lamp and a fan from the garage and carried them back into Pfister's bedroom. Because of the dog poop odor, she plugged it in, put the lamp where it had been before Pfister left for her trip, and plugged it in, too. Trey had taken pictures of the house before-hand, so they could ensure everything was back in its place when Pfister returned. Nancy used the pictures to remind her where each item belonged. Trey often joked that she was obsessive-compulsive, but Nancy liked having clean, neat surroundings. She hoped Pfister might appreciate how much time and effort she had taken, and stop giving them a hard time.

It was only as she plugged in the two electrical cords that Nancy realized something was amiss. She looked at the bed again and real-ized what it was: except for one pillowcase that covered a pillow, the clean sheets with an elephant pattern she had made up the bed with for Pfister's return were gone. But the duvet was pulled up to the top of the bed, neatly made. *That's weird. I don't think she's ever made a bed in her entire life.* Thinking back to Saturday, Nancy remembered follow-ing Pfister's instructions to the letter. She made up her bed exactly as she asked, and left her Champagne on ice. Trey even told her it wasn't necessary, but Nancy disagreed. "I'm not doing it for her. I'm doing it for me. Because it's the right thing to do."

Looking around the bedroom now, Nancy saw clothes and other personal items on the floor and all around the bed. It looked as if Pfister had stepped out of her clothes and gone to bed. Yet, the bed was made. And there was no sign of Pfister at all.

Something was amiss, but Nancy had more to do, so she went back downstairs. That's when she noticed one elephant pillowcase in the living room, laying on the window seat. *Now that's odd.* Nancy shook her head, knowing she had more important things to do than worry about Pfister's linens. For all she knew the woman hadn't even slept in her bed, but on the couch. That would explain everything—well, everything but the missing sheets.

Trey yelled, saying the movers were finished and they were ready to head to the storage units. "I'm coming," Nancy yelled back. She closed Pfister's front door and went outside. "We still have all this trash to get rid of," she reminded Trey.

"We can come back tonight or tomorrow and get it," he said. A few minutes later they drove away from 1833 West Buttermilk.

They unlocked the unit at 4:28 p.m., and by 5:44 p.m., the truck was unloaded. They figured the remaining items left behind at Pfister's would only involve one more load, the next day. Trey and Nancy thanked the three men for their help and hard work, and took them back to Basalt.

***

When Nancy knew Kathy was off work, she called her friend. "Hi Kathy, did you get my text about Gabe?"

Kathy said she had, and the two women again discussed how odd it was that Pfister would leave her beloved pooch alone—especially when she knew that Kathy would take him in a heartbeat, as she usually did when Pfister went somewhere.

"And the house—you should have seen it," Nancy said. "Gabe pooped and peed everywhere."

Kathy agreed it sounded weird, but then both women thought of other times when Pfister had just picked up and left, without a word to anyone. She even did it when her daughter was small.

"Did she take off the elephant sheets?" Nancy said, referring to the patterned sheets she'd noticed were missing from the bed. "Maybe they weren't to her liking?"

"The sheets weren't on the bed?" Kathy asked. "What? How?"

"I don't know. I thought maybe she wanted different ones, but the bed was made, too. Except there was just one pillowcase and pillow. I found the other one in the living room."

Kathy was silent. "That is odd." Another pause. "I spent the night and slept there with Gabe."

"Oh, you did?" Nancy immediately began to worry. She wondered if Kathy had avoided drinking, or if Pfister's influence led her to fall off the wagon again.

"Yes, she asked me to because she got drunk on the plane and fell and hurt her shoulder," Kathy said. "She said she needed my help."

"Oh my goodness," Nancy said. "Now I'm really worried, Kathy. What if something happened to her?"

"I don't know, but you know how she is when she drinks and takes those pills. Maybe—," Kathy stopped.

"Maybe she overdosed?" Nancy asked, finishing Kathy's unspoken sentence.

"I don't want to think that," Kathy said.

"Me, either. But what else is there?" Nancy asked. She told Kathy she would check on Gabe when they returned for their final load Wednesday. "But if she isn't back by the time you get there after work, take him home with you."

Kathy said she would.

***

The text that excited Nancy more than all others that day came earlier that night, from a woman who was interested in her seamstress services. Nancy felt a small sliver of hope that she and Trey could still start over in Aspen.

"Hi Nancy, I met Kathy at Alpine Bank today and she talked very highly of you . . . She mentioned that u work with leather and we would love to see if you could sew for us . . . check our website out www.purezh.com . . . Hope to hear from you- Best, Zia." It came at 6:32 p.m.

Kathy texted her too, at 8:10 p.m., asking if it went well with Zia. Nancy replied at 9:24 p.m., thanking Kathy for referring Zia to her and telling Kathy her plans for the next day: "I met her and her partner this summer at the farmers' market in Aspen and we took a picture because I was dressed in purple and their card is white and purple," Nancy texted. "I will meet with them in Brush Creek soon. I told them at the time that I would have my machines in Aspen as soon as we moved to town if they needed help. She remembered me. Thanks for the referral. Small town. I'm glad that I don't have NP's reputation. You need lashes and hair. You are a walking billboard and I haven't been keeping up with you. I'm going to try to get a lash fill in Glenwood. My lashes have never looked so bad and we have to return the truck tomorrow to Glenwood so maybe I will luck out. The nightmare is almost over xo."

Nancy's hope was growing even stronger as she and Trey entered the homestretch. She believed that would finally free them from everything connected to Pfister. But it wasn't only that: Nancy knew how much potential she could offer Aspen residents, with her talent to make women like Kathy glow so much they felt as beautiful inside as they did on the outside.

Not long after, Nancy remembered she'd forgotten to reply to Daniel's text.

"How goes it," Daniel had texted at 5:17 p.m.

She sent off a quick text back at 11:06 p.m., reassuring him all was well: "The attorney told us to take pictures of everything and to have a peacekeeper sheriff there during the process. She is not here right now and the sheriff is on call. I'll keep you posted luv u."

Not long after Nancy went to bed, Daniel texted back. By then it was just after midnight.

"K. Definitely keep the sheriff involved," he said at 12:06 a.m.

CHAPTER SEVEN

WHAT IS THAT SMELL?

Wednesday morning after breakfast, two of the three movers from Aspen Workforce showed up at the Aspenalt to help the Stylers finish up at Pfister's place and take the last of their belongings to storage. They took the Jag and the truck and by 10:30 a.m. were at 1833 West Buttermilk. Again, Gabe's water bowls were dry—and again, he had pooped and peed all over.

But whereas the day before the odor was just faint, at noon on Wednesday the house reeked. Especially the bedroom, where Nancy went to look, trying to see if Pfister had slept there the night before.

"Oh my God, Trey, it didn't smell like this when we slept here," she said, feeling almost sick to her stomach. "What is that smell? Is it from Gabe?"

"Nance, you know I can't smell anything," Trey said, "so I'm afraid I'm no help at all."

Turning, he left the room as Nancy spoke. "That smell is nasty! And I'm starting to really worry now. Why would she go off like that and not make sure Gabe had water?" But Trey was out of earshot.

Nancy looked around the room, hoping for some small sign that Pfister had returned. But nothing was different. Pfister's bed was just like Nancy had left it on Tuesday. Even the fan was still on, for all the good it did.

Knowing Kathy would be on her lunch break, Nancy dialed her number. "She hasn't been here. There's not been any action here at all, and it stinks really bad. I guess from Gabe being locked up in here the last two days."

The two women talked for a few minutes, wondering with growing worry where Pfister was, before Kathy began making a rasping sound.

Nancy spoke up. "Kathy, what's wrong!"

"I'm so stressed," Kathy said, "I'm having trouble breathing right now."

"Don't go there, girl! We don't need you to end up in the hospital again," Nancy said. "I'm sure she'll show up somewhere. Maybe she went to her sister's." Even Kathy knew that was a low probability, but Nancy felt compelled to try to make her feel better.

"Do you know any other friends of hers?" Kathy asked.

"Really, I met you through her, and Patrick and Merlin. I met people at the party, but no one I can claim to know well," Nancy said. "Maybe she called Bob Braudis, since she hurt her shoulder and needed some help."

"I'll call Patti and see if she went there," Nancy said. Kathy sighed. Patti Stranahan was godmother to Pfister's daughter, Juliana. "Well, just take care of Gabe," Nancy continued. "Make sure he's cool." Kathy said she would get him after work.

"I'll call and just tell her I'm coming to get Gabe," Kathy said. "I'm not going to tell her that you told me she hasn't been there and Gabe was alone. I'm just going to call and tell her I want to take Gabe for the night."

Nancy told Kathy they were leaving Pfister's as soon as they had the last load out. That happened at 12:51 p.m., when she texted Daniel. "One load out with no trouble."

His reply came back one minute later. "Sheriff present?"

Six minutes later, Nancy replied. "We are out of there, there is just the snowblower and some trash to dump congrats on your paper. She has been gone for 3 days and left Gabe locked up alone. I had to clean several messes but at least we didn't see her. She is not answering emails or phone. It goes right to voice mail. I'm stocked," Nancy said, evidently meaning to write "shocked."

Daniel sent two texts right back: "Wow," and "That's animal cruelty." Both arrived at 12:58 p.m.

At 1:01 p.m. Nancy replied: "Like miss piggy Kathy is picking him up after work today so he will be okay. She is really pissed that

[Pfister] would do thAt. She left her kid with a babysitter and didn't come back for. 2 weeks. Social services stepped in Nd someone Took guardianship of the daughter so I'm not surprised that she would do this to Gabep."

A few minutes before replying to her son, Nancy sent one more text—part of which would later find its way into the search warrant affidavit used to arrest her and Trey. It was 12:56 p.m. on Wednesday, February 26, when Nancy texted Kathy: "We just left the house we will come home later to get the trash tonight and the snowblower Gabe is locked in I opened a window because it is warm, we got her car in the garage and the furniture put back we are out of there. I cleaned up the Gabe mess of miso paste and Kleenex and put her dishes in the dishwasher. So if anything is out she has been there keep me posted and I'm glad that you are getting Gabe. I can't believe she left him alone for that long our poor baby xo."

The van and their Jag were loaded up with everything they had needed to start their life over when they drove it all to their storage units. Nancy felt deflated, but she was glad their dealings with Pfister were behind them. Trey was simply happy that Pfister hadn't been around to keep them from getting their spa and sewing equipment.

***

Kathy's conversation with Nancy had her so rattled she found it difficult to concentrate on her work. When she didn't have customers, she scrolled back through her old text messages from the weekend, looking for clues. *Maybe I missed something. Maybe she tried to tell me she had plans and I just wasn't listening.*

But Kathy didn't discern anything unusual. There were dozens of calls between her and Pfister all weekend, but Pfister's only text message came in Sunday evening, while Kathy was buying groceries for her friend.

"Kathy darling please give me a call when you get a chance I'd love it if you could get me some Epsom salts and so could massage cream maybe some coconut oil or something I don't know such whatever you think my skin is so dry okey-dokey darling I'll see you at the sappy or wheneveryou get here I hope you come before you go to Snowmass Snowmass Snowmass I love you!!!"

There was one other, that Kathy had sent earlier that morning, after repeatedly trying Pfister and only getting her voice mail: "Hi, did u get my msg about Gabe? Where are you? Xo."

Kathy put down her phone down and helped a waiting customer. As the customer turned to go, Kathy saw Patti at a nearby teller window. *Thank God! Now I can ask her in person!* Kathy raised her hand to wave at Patti, hopeful she would see her and come over. Not ten seconds later, the woman whose life had become entwined with Pfister in a very personal way, twenty-eight years earlier, was standing in front of Kathy's window.

***

By the time Patti Quinn moved to Aspen in 1972, she later told police, "Nancy was already a legend." Patti met and married George Stranahan, of Stranahan's Colorado Whiskey fame, in 1978, and years later the couple became Juliana Pfister's godparents.

Patti didn't know Pfister in those early days; she was closer with her sister, Suzanne. And at the time, Pfister was away in Nepal and Africa. But after her return, Patti got to know the legendary Pfister sister. In fact, Pfister was pregnant with Juliana in 1985 when the two women went cross-country skiing behind Patti's house in Wood Creek.

"Would you like to be Juliana's godmother?" Pfister had asked Patti.

"Oh, okay," she said, a little taken aback. It was a question she didn't even know how to say "no" to.

Later, Patti learned from Pfister's mother, Betty, that her daughter had "asked everybody to be the godmother. You're the only one that said 'yes.'" So what Pfister may have intended as a joke took, and Patti became the baby's real godmother when she was born in January 1986. It was a job Patti took seriously, so they held a christening for little Jules, as she later came to be called.

Patti took it so seriously, in fact, that when Pfister decided one day just to take off halfway around the globe, her preschool daughter went to live with Patti and George. No one heard from her for weeks. When Jules turned twelve, the Stranahans welcomed her into their home permanently. There were whispers around town that the authorities took the little girl from Pfister, but no one really talked about it openly. However, even Juliana herself acknowledged that her mother "was a bad mom" because she didn't know how to handle life's responsibilities.

Regardless, Juliana's love for her mother never diminished. "My mom had the . . . biggest, shiniest heart in the world, ever," she said.

For Patti, saying yes to Pfister's request that day in 1985 when the world all around them was blanketed with white ended up being a blessing for her family. "We've been in each other's lives for . . . these twenty-eight years through thick and thin and laughter and tears and family celebrations with funerals for both [Pfister's] parents," Patti said.

***

Patti volunteered at the Thrift Shop of Aspen, which donates its proceeds to community nonprofits. It's located on East Hopkins Avenue, one block away from Alpine Bank, where Patti went on Wednesday, February 26. After making a deposit, Patti waved at Kathy, who asked if Patti had time to talk.

"Is Nancy back yet?" Patti asked as she approached Kathy. She knew Pfister had returned, but was just making chitchat.

"Yes," Kathy said, adding that she was concerned.

Patti immediately thought she meant Pfister's drinking. "She has been drinking a lot and seemed to be taking more pills than usual," Patti said.

From behind her teller's window, Kathy explained that wasn't the problem. She told Patti she had helped Pfister unpack, like she usually did after a trip, and even spent the weekend with her. "But ever since Monday morning she hasn't answered my texts or emails," Kathy said. She told Patti that the Stylers went Tuesday to get the rest of their belongings, and they found Gabe locked inside with a dry water bowl. They filled it and then contacted Kathy because they were afraid that Pfister had gone off somewhere and left the dog alone.

"It's not like Nancy to leave the dog. You know she adores that dog, and I'm a little worried," Kathy told Patti.

"When you left Monday morning, did she say what she was going to do that day?" Patti asked.

"Well, she said she wanted someone to pick her up and she told me she called Patrick," Kathy said. "But he hurt his arm, so he couldn't get her."

The two women talked some more, but decided Pfister had simply taken off without telling anyone. It wasn't unlike her, after all. Neither woman suspected foul play, although Patti could tell Kathy was becoming more worried that might be a possibility.

"Do you mind, since she's not answering my emails or texts," Kathy asked, "do you mind trying to make some calls to [see if anyone else has heard from her]?"

Patti agreed, and Kathy told her if Pfister still hadn't been found by the time she got through with her shift, she was going to get Gabe. Patti returned to the thrift store, and the afternoon grew so busy that she didn't have time to call anyone except Pfister. No one answered. "Welcome back, let's get together. Call me," she said, leaving a message.

By the time she arrived home, Patti had completely forgotten about making any other calls.

CHAPTER EIGHT

YOUR LANDLADY DOESN'T OWN THIS MOUNTAIN ANYMORE

The Stylers left 1833 West Buttermilk with their two hired men just before 1 p.m. on Wednesday, February 26. Nancy was so relieved when they pulled into the Subway parking lot a few minutes later and bought themselves and the hired men a late lunch. Merlin had used his truck to haul his loaded trailer to their storage area for them so the men could unload it. Nancy offered to buy his lunch, too, but Merlin declined because he had other jobs to do.

At 12:48 p.m., Nancy sent Kathy a text, telling her she washed the few dirty dishes so if there were more when Kathy arrived, that meant Pfister had returned. She also said they locked up Gabe, so not to dawdle when getting him or there would be more messes to clean up.

There was one other item to attend to, she told Kathy; they had to leave behind nine or ten bags of trash and an old, broken snowblower that Merlin promised to haul away, but they would return for the trash that evening. Just thinking about the trash reminded Nancy, yet again, of how entitled—and "terminally cheap"—Pfister was. Before she left for Australia, their landlady took Nancy down and showed her all the large trash and recycling bins at the ski resort; she said that's where the Stylers were to bring their garbage. But the one time Nancy tried to, an employee stopped her before she could dump all the trash from Pfister's November party.

"Ma'am, you can get ticketed for this," he said.

Nancy was immediately apologetic. "My landlady told me this is where I dump my trash. I had no clue."

He had given her a sideways look. "Your landlady doesn't own this mountain anymore and no, you can't put your trash here."

"What do I do with it?" Nancy asked.

"You get a Dumpster," he said, "just like everyone else."

***

Later that afternoon, Kathy and Nancy spoke again; Kathy told her she spoke to Patti, who hadn't seen Pfister, but would make some calls. She asked what time the Stylers would be back for the trash. Kathy also said she could get Gabe and help them if it was around 6 p.m. That way, they would have two cars to haul it away.

But Nancy said it would "probably be around 8:30 by the time we get back," since they had to go to Glenwood Springs to return the U-Haul and Nancy wanted to get her eyelash extensions refilled at a salon there.

"I don't want to wait that long," Kathy said.

Nancy didn't mind. "I understand. Just go and call me when you get Gabe."

***

Driving the thirty minutes or so it took for the Stylers to make the drive to Glenwood Springs, Nancy waited for a call from Kathy. It never came.

After trying to reach her friend repeatedly, with every call going straight to voice mail, Nancy feared the worst. She knew Kathy and Pfister had a history, often a violent one. Both women joked about it together when they told Nancy some of the stories, playing down what were apparently serious altercations. But after Pfister flew to Australia and Kathy and Nancy grew closer, Kathy shared more details about those fights. She told Nancy she had to get out from under Pfister's thumb if she wanted any long-term chance at sobriety. It was one or the other: stay friends with Pfister or stay sober. Kathy told Nancy she couldn't do both, because Pfister was an alcoholic, too, and Kathy couldn't stay sober if she was around someone like her. In confidence, Kathy had told her, in detail, the problems she and Pfister had had.

* * *

Pitkin police reports for both branches of law enforcement, city and county, tell the tale: on December 29, 2009, Pfister called the sheriff's office for help. She said Kathy was trying to break into her bedroom and she thought she was having a "mental breakdown." When deputies arrived, they found Kathy not only drunk, but also quite belligerent.

"She's been using me and I'm tired of it," Kathy yelled. She threatened to punch the deputies and tried to rush past them like she was going to try yet again to get into Pfister's bedroom. They arrested Kathy and took her to jail.

Seven months later, deputies were again called to Pfister's home after Pfister said she saw Kathy take "what looked like a handful of pills." The officers found three prescription bottles in Kathy's purse and became concerned because Kathy was losing consciousness. But Kathy denied trying to kill herself and instead kept screaming at Pfister, "I hate you!"

Then there was the August 25, 2012, DUI incident in Glenwood Springs. Garfield County Communications received a 911 call from the front desk of the Hampton Inn and Suites; the clerk who called said two people outside were arguing and one of them was drunk.

According to Officer Drew Hatch's report, the clerk said the two people left in a white Toyota Prius. But when Hatch and two other officers arrived at the motel, he saw a white Prius trying to leave the parking lot. So he stopped the car, and found a woman at the wheel. Officer Hatch asked the driver to identify herself and she did: Nancy Merle Pfister. When Hatch asked what had happened, Pfister said her friend Kathy, who was in the backseat, was intoxicated and Pfister was afraid of her. But the officer didn't see or hear anything from Kathy to indicate she was aggressive. He did, however, smell alcohol on Pfister's breath. He also noticed her glassy eyes and slurred speech. Pfister told Hatch they were going home.

Hatch asked if she had been drinking.

"I had two glasses of Champagne," she said.

The officer also noticed that Pfister had two pairs of eyeglasses hanging around her neck. "Ma'am, do you have any eye problems?"

Pfister said "No," and Hatch asked if she was ill. "No," Pfister said again.

Hatch asked her to get out of the Prius, where he performed a field sobriety test, which she failed. He arrested Pfister for driving under the influence of alcohol, handcuffed her, and told her she had the right to choose between a blood and a breath test. At first, Pfister told Hatch she would have to ask her "private pilot," but she eventually agreed to take a blood test.

As Officer Hatch was placing Pfister in the backseat of his cruiser, she told him she "shouldn't be arrested" and that she was "good friends with Bob Braudis." Nonetheless, she was arrested, and her car was towed away to be impounded. Another officer interviewed Kathy, so Officer Hatch's report doesn't note what happened to her. However, the impound report said no police hold was placed on the vehicle. Whether that was due to Pfister's close ties to the law enforcement community is unknown.

***

Just thinking about the story that Kathy had shared with her gave Nancy reason to be alarmed. But she wasn't yet frantic with worry. Still, she sensed something was amiss. First Pfister disappeared, then all communication from Kathy ceased. *Has something happened to her, too? It isn't like Kathy to not call or text me back.* Especially not when Kathy knew that Nancy was already worried about Pfister's disappearance.

Suddenly, Nancy had a terrible thought: what if Pfister showed up when Kathy went to get Gabe, and Kathy gave her the news—that she was cutting ties with her? Successfully moving on from Step Four in AA, which involved letting go of past resentments, meant she had to. Nancy didn't know for certain, but she believed a stressful situation like that had the potential to end badly for both women. Most likely for Kathy, who had respiratory problems and who was far weaker emotionally and physically than Pfister.

Those thoughts chased each other around in Nancy's mind as she entered the salon to have her lashes done. That's when she decided to call Kathy's friend, Susan Waskow, who had helped Kathy and Nancy pack boxes the day Kathy hurt her shoulder. Susan, sixty-eight, had wild red hair that seemed to always be in her face. She had been in a bad car accident in 2012 that left her with a traumatic brain injury, from which she was still recovering. Nancy knew her memory wasn't the best, something Susan herself freely admitted, but she was a nice friend and she, Trey, and Kathy had celebrated Valentine's Day with Susan and her boyfriend, Jay Leavitt.

"Hi, Susan," Nancy said. "I've been trying to reach Kathy but can't find her. Have you heard from her?"

"No, I haven't," Susan said.

Not long after, Nancy found an urgent message from Susan while the stylist finished up her eyelashes. Susan sounded frantic, and begged Nancy to call her. "Call me right away! Jay was driving by to bring me my contact lenses and he saw five sheriff's cars and two police cars and an ambulance at the bottom of Buttermilk on Owl Creek Road!" Susan practically cried into the phone.

As soon as she heard the distress in Susan's voice, Nancy hit redial, fearing the worst. In her mind, all she could hear was how worried Kathy sounded at the bank when they last spoke, and what she said about having trouble breathing. Nancy pictured Kathy having another attack and not getting help in time—and Pfister finding her body too late. Or . . . that other, darker, scenario resurfaced, but Nancy refused to go there. She didn't want to think any further than she already had.

Dragging herself away from her thoughts, Nancy tried to listen to Susan. "I can't find Kathy and I'm really worried," she said.

"I am too, now, because she's usually so good about calling when she says she will," Nancy said. "Let me call her mother and see if Kathy's there. Maybe her phone died or something."

The Stylers had met Kathy's mother, Chris Carpenter, in January when Trey took Kathy to the emergency room with breathing problems. Nancy really liked her. She had even made some little outfits for Chris' dogs, since Chris sometimes helped take care of Gabe for Kathy. But the call to Chris was a disappointment.

"Chris, have you heard from Kathy recently?" Nancy asked.

"I can't talk. I can't talk," the elderly woman said, sounding breathless. "I'm on the other line. Hang on."

Nancy waited and waited, growing more worried because Chris didn't sound well. In fact, it took Kathy's mother so long to come back on the line that Nancy thought they had gotten disconnected.

"Is Kathy okay?" Nancy didn't want to mention what Susan had told her; she didn't want to worry Chris. What if it turned out to be nothing? A false alarm, or something totally unrelated to Kathy or Pfister?

Chris paused for a second or two. "I don't know. I'll call you." Then the line went dead.

Nancy looked at the phone in her hand. *That was strange. Something is definitely wrong. I just hope it isn't Kathy!* She immediately called Susan back, telling her what Chris had said.

"Boy, that doesn't sound right," Susan said. The two women continued chatting, agreeing something was very wrong on Buttermilk Mountain. First Pfister disappeared, then Kathy. And Kathy's mother didn't even know anything, which was a bad sign.

Susan said, "I'll call you back."

Waiting for Susan's return call, Nancy wondered if anyone had been in touch with Sarah, Kathy's AA sponsor. If Kathy was in trouble, Sarah was the one person she would want by her side. Nancy had never spoken to Sarah herself, although she had been with Kathy many times when the two women were talking on the phone. Once, Nancy even told Kathy, "Tell Sarah if I had to do what you do for Nancy Pfister, I'd drink, too." She and Kathy laughed, as Kathy repeated Nancy's words to Sarah.

As she waited for Susan to call back, Nancy told Trey she hoped Kathy and Pfister hadn't argued. In the past when they got into one of their famous fights, it usually involved police coming to the rescue. Before Nancy could ponder that scenario any further, her cell phone rang.

"I have news," Susan said. "They found Nancy. And Kathy is okay. She's in good hands."

Nancy let out a long slow breath she didn't realize she'd been hold-ing as Susan continued. "Kathy was admitted in the emergency room and of course they don't tell you anything."

Finally, we know something! Nancy figured Kathy was in the emer-gency room and her mother was frantic because Kathy had more pul-monary problems.

"Do you have Sarah's number?" Nancy asked Susan, who gave it to her.

After they hung up, Nancy called Sarah. When her call went to voice mail, Nancy left her a polite message. As she got ready for bed, Nancy replayed Susan's words over in her mind. She knew Kathy was safe, but what did "they found Nancy" mean? She had her suspicions, and they were based on Pfister's own words: she overdosed.

That's why Gabe was out of water, and all alone.

*   *   *

During the investigation, police later retrieved a copy of that voice mail. It confirmed what Nancy told police herself, that she was con-cerned for Kathy. In that recording, it's obvious Nancy had no idea Pfister was dead—or that Kathy had found her body.

"Sarah, my name is Nancy Styler and I'm a friend of Kathy Carpenter's, and we've just learned she's in the emergency room. We really don't know much about it and her mother doesn't know much about it and I thought I'd let you know. If I know more, I'll give you a call. I know how close you are to her. My number is 970-111-0000. Please feel free to call me anytime. We're going to try to get more information. Thanks, bye-bye."

*   *   *

By the time they were back in Basalt after their trip to Glenwood Springs, Nancy was so upset and exhausted she knew that she, at least, wasn't up to joining Merlin for live music. The day before he had invited the Stylers to join him at Heather's; he said the little Basalt restau-rant just around the corner from their motel would be a good place to relax. Nancy said it sounded like fun and she would check with Trey, but otherwise, they would meet him there after they returned from Glenwood Springs. She hadn't been able to reach Merlin to tell him otherwise.

Trey agreed. "We need to make sure Kathy's okay, and see if she needs our help," he said, parking across the street from the restaurant. Nancy ran inside to tell Merlin their change of plans. She also told him that Kathy was in the hospital and Pfister had been found. Merlin asked Nancy why she was worried about Pfister, considering how much trouble she'd given them.

"I don't know, but I'm really concerned," Nancy said. "Susan said 'they found Nancy.' What does that mean?"

Merlin didn't seem worried. "Everyone in this town expects her to drink herself to death," he said, shrugging. He tried to convince Nancy that they should join him so they could eat, if nothing else, but Nancy said they ate in Glenwood Springs.

"Well, go home and get some sleep and try not to be concerned," Merlin said, giving Nancy a hug.

Back inside Room 122, Nancy and Susan spoke one last time. "Have you heard anything else?" Susan asked.

"No," Nancy said. "Have you?"

"No," Susan said, asking Nancy to call me "any time of the day or night if you do." Nancy promised she would.

Even though her mind was awash with worry, when Nancy went to bed just after midnight, her energy was so depleted she fell asleep almost immediately. She might not have slept a wink, had she known Kathy was far, far from being all right.

In fact, given Nancy's close attention to Kathy's health and the deep friendship formed between the two women, it's entirely likely she would have gotten dressed and had Trey drive her to the hospital. But by that time, Nancy was barely able to function herself—a fact that Merlin would later share with police.

CHAPTER NINE

MY FRIEND IS IN THE CLOSET DEAD!

Since that day, Kathy Carpenter's 911 call has been broadcast around the world. But on Wednesday, February 26, 2014, only the killer or killers knew what awaited Kathy when she went to check on Pfister and Gabe.

***

When Kathy didn't hear back from Patti saying she'd found Pfister, she knew she had to go there straight from work. Better than anyone else, she knew Pfister's normal routines, and she hoped to spot clues that would tell her something about what was going on, such as whether Pfister had left with another person, been attacked, gotten drunk, or overdosed. Kathy stopped there. She knew if she continued, she'd end up unable to breathe.

Kathy parked in Pfister's driveway and went inside just before 5 p.m. What she noticed first was the smell: if it was coming from Gabe, he had eaten something rotten. But then Kathy realized—the closer she got to the bedroom, the stronger the stench. Worried, Kathy called her mother. She didn't want to feel all alone in the house, so they talked while Kathy did a walk-through, looking all around for answers. By the time she hung up ten minutes later, Kathy knew something was very wrong. She immediately called Patti.

Kathy sounded breathless. "Something's wrong. Gabe is out of water and things don't look right."

"What do you mean," Patti asked, "'things don't look right'?"

"I've looked, but I can't find the sheets anywhere—the sheets that were on Nancy's bed when I left here Monday morning," Kathy said. "But the bed's made, and that's not like her to make her own bed. And all her pills are gone, but the purse she carried them in is still here." Kathy made an odd sound like a moan. "If she went somewhere, she would have used that bag for her pills. She always did. And there's a weird smell in the room."

Patti was confused. "What kind of smell? Like a cleaning smell?"

"No, like—, I don't know, just a weird smell, and the key's gone from the closet," Kathy said. "It's always in the door and it was there Monday. I'm, I'm starting to get nervous."

"Then get out. Get out right now."

"I have another key at home," Kathy said.

***

The big closet in the master bedroom had been a source of contention between Pfister and her past tenants, since she always insisted on keeping it locked. But this time, Pfister told Nancy Styler she could put her clothing on a portable rack and store it in the master closet. Then she changed her mind at the last minute, telling Nancy she couldn't; Nancy could only use the smaller bedroom closet, but she would have to first move Pfister's belongings from there and into the master closet. She told Nancy to put the portable rack in the bedroom, rather than the closet.

Pfister left the key with Kathy for that purpose, and also in case the Stylers needed to store anything else of Pfister's, to make room for their own belongings. But Kathy lost the key the day she and Nancy stored Pfister's liquor and artwork away. Both women searched but couldn't find the key, so the closet door remained unlocked—until Kathy called a locksmith to change the locks.

The Stylers didn't care one way or another. After the problems with Pfister began, they were glad that Kathy, Nancy, and a friend of her's from Denver had locked up their landlord's valuable artwork inside the closet right after she left.

During late October, Pfister had asked the Stylers to do several things for her during her absence. Among them, Trey was to write a book about her life, using the personal journals and files she said he would find on her computer, and Nancy was to obtain appraisals for and sell Pfister's artwork, antique dishware, and other valuables. When Nancy and her sister Cindy later talked, Cindy advised against it. "Please tell me you're not going to do that. That just sounds crazy!" Cindy said.

Listening to her older sister, Cindy realized Nancy was again failing to show discernment, as she often did when dealing with people and life situations. Some people would call that naïveté, but Cindy affectionately calls Nancy a "shit magnet." That's her way of saying Nancy "loves people and a good story. She sees the good in everyone (and) is too trusting." Cindy attributes this quality to their mother, Tess.

"We were raised by a woman who truly made us feel like we could do anything," Cindy said. "Because of this, I think Nancy believes everyone is capable of greatness and thinks she can cheer them on. She's a rescue ranger."

Which explains why Nancy's bio in her high school yearbook said, "she makes the most of all that comes and the least of all that goes."

Even over the telephone line, Nancy could hear the worry as it traveled all the way from Boston, where Nancy's family lived.

"I don't know. I guess because I gave her my word, I should do it," Nancy replied. "You don't know this woman. She won't do anything for herself, except cook. She wants everyone else to be at her beck and call."

But Nancy took Cindy's advice and decided, like everything else Pfister had asked of her, that it wasn't worth the risk.

Nancy wanted the closet locked—and told Kathy to take the keys with her.

"I'm not going to use that closet," Nancy said. "There's too much liability there, especially given how she's been acting lately. No, thank you! I'll do with what little closet space I already have."

***

Until that Wednesday, Kathy hadn't had a reason to even worry about the key. Now, though, she did—and worried she was—because when she left Pfister's home Monday morning, the key had been there. Right in the lock, where Pfister herself left it, as she always did, after returning from her trips. *Why isn't it there now?*

With a start, Kathy realized Patti was on the other end of the line. "Kathy? Kathy!" she said. "Why don't you go get it, then come back and call me when you get there?"

"I'm getting really scared." Kathy suddenly gasped. "What if, what if they did something to her?"

Patti was beginning to feel a pang of worry that no one had found Pfister, either, but she couldn't fathom why Kathy should be so upset. "Look, I really think you're overreacting. Nancy's fine and so are you."

Kathy said Patti was probably right, and she would go get the other closet key. The minute they hung up, at 5:37 p.m., Patti texted her cousin, Bob Braudis. He was tight with Pfister, so perhaps he knew something. "Hey cuz, you have any idea where Nancy might be? She hasn't been heard from since Monday morning and she left Gabe alone in the house."

***

Kathy left to retrieve the spare closet key, but called her mother again, hoping it would help her calm down. She told her how worried she was, and then hung up, calling her close friend, Susan Waskow. But Susan didn't answer. By then, Kathy was back at Pfister's house, so she tried to steel herself from being overly anxious as she made her way back to Pfister's bedroom. Suddenly, as she was bent over looking at the neatly made bed, Kathy saw a small smear of something on the headboard. She immediately called Sarah, her AA sponsor, as she walked a few short feet to the closet. It was 6:02 p.m.

Kathy inserted the key into the lock and Sarah picked up just as Kathy screamed. A strong stench poured out of the closet, hitting Kathy full in the face. She was gasping and crying and trying to talk, but all Sarah could make out was, "Nancy . . . dead . . . Wrapped up . . . closet . . . ," before Sarah broke in, cutting Kathy off.

"What is wrong, Kathy?"

But Kathy was too horrified to tell her. "What if they come back?" she finally managed to say, her voice almost a wail.

Apparently, Kathy hung up on Sarah without realizing it as she fled the house, so rattled she nearly forgot to take Gabe. Jumping into her car, she locked all the doors and then shoved the gear shifter into reverse, before flooring the accelerator and tearing down the driveway. She didn't know how fast she was going, or even which direction she was headed, when she finally thought to call 911.

Kathy's nearly eight-minute ~~minute~~ call came from a woman so frantic, so hysterical, she at times sounded like a wounded animal. Even the dispatcher couldn't make out her broken, stuttered words.

***

"Oh my God. Oh my God. Oh my God. Oh my God," Kathy cried.

A female dispatcher replied, "What is the address of the emergency? What is the address of the emergency?"

"1833 West Buttermilk Road," Kathy said, barely coherent.

"Is that a house, business, or apartment?"

Kathy was still wailing, but her voice dropped as if she couldn't get enough air into her lungs to speak. "It's a house. It's Nancy Pfister's house. My friend—."

The dispatcher asked why Kathy called 911. "Ma'am, tell me exactly what happened."

And that was when Kathy Carpenter—who had just found her best friend wrapped up inside a bedroom closet—lost it.

"My friend had, my friend had—," she said, pausing to draw a ragged breath. "I found my friend in the closet—she's dead!" The last word came out as a long, anguished cry, born of such intense pain it was evident in every syllable.

"Ma'am, tell me exactly what happened," the dispatcher tried again.

In one long rush of air, Kathy's words came out so quickly they were difficult to hear. "My friend, Nancy Pfister, came back from Australia and she had some people living there and she pissed them off and made threats to them about owing money and," Kathy continued, with phrases like "she was missing" and "I went to get the dog," until her words trailed off.

"Ma'am, I need you to tell me what happened."

"I can't. My friend is in the closet dead," Kathy said, her voice raising several decibels, clearly in anguish.

***

Meanwhile, when Patti Stranahan didn't hear back from Kathy or Bob, her own worry intensified. "I'm getting worried, George," Patti told her husband. She dialed Kathy's number, but it went straight to voice mail.

A few seconds later, Bob answered Patti's text, and she had to steady herself with one hand when she read it. "Oh, my God! George!" Patti screamed. "Nancy's dead." She could only think of Pfister's daughter, Juliana. How would they break the news to their goddaughter?

Patti immediately called Bob, who repeated what was in his text message. Bob was at a social function at Sheriff Joe DiSalvo's house, along with several other people, when the 911 call came over DiSalvo's police scanner. He told Patti that Pfister's body had been found, and she had apparently committed suicide. (Braudis later told police he thought that because of the way the transmission came over the radio.)

But to Patti it made no sense.

"The closet door was locked when Kathy called me, so how could it have been suicide?" she asked the retired sheriff.

CHAPTER TEN

MENTALLY DISTRAUGHT . . . AND MEDICATED

Kathy Carpenter attempted to explain the reason for her distress to the 911 female dispatch operator. The nearly eight-minute conversation was wrought with Kathy's hysterics over the discovery of Nancy Pfister's body. The dispatcher finally instructed Kathy to pull off the road and wait for first responders. She did, and a county-wide alert went out in response to Kathy's 911 call. Unfortunately, the female dispatcher thought Kathy said "blood on her forehead," when what she really said was "blood on her headboard." That error eventually wound up being erroneously transcribed into a written document of the entire 911 call. Prosecutors would later use this incorrect yet significant detail in their argument that Kathy Carpenter was a participant in Pfister's death.

Deputy Jeff Lumsden and numerous other officers immediately headed out for "an attempted suicide or possible murder" at 1833 West Buttermilk Road. When he learned Kathy's vehicle was near the Kingdom Hall of Jehovah's Witnesses on Lion's Creek Road and that Aspen City Police officers were going to check on her, Deputy Lumsden was diverted to Kathy's location along Pyramid Road. Once there, he found Deputy Ryan Turner and Aspen City Police Sergeant Seamans with her.

Lumsden observed Kathy as she stood beside her gold Subaru station wagon. She was barely able to stand, and periodically needed to use a large rock to sit on or lean against, as if to steady herself. Kathy was "extremely distraught and loudly sobbing," Lumsden wrote in his report. She vomited, said she felt faint, and was so sick Deputy Ryan Turner had to help her inside Seamans' patrol car, before they continued talking. They needed to pass along any information she would give them about whatever crime she witnessed to the deputies who were en route to West Buttermilk. Kathy's distress didn't lessen and she was so breathless it was hard for her to speak. The officers finally learned Kathy had gone to Pfister's house to feed the dog she had in her car, and when she unlocked a closet, she found a body inside. Because she was traumatized, the officers called an ambulance to take her to Aspen Valley Hospital.

Kathy's car was considered part of the crime scene, so officers secured it with tape and arranged for it to be towed. Gabe, still in Kathy's car, later went home with Sheriff DiSalvo. Afterward, Lumsden went to the hospital to check on Kathy and to take her to the Pitkin County Courthouse, where Detective Brad Gibson waited to interview her. By then, medical staff had evaluated and treated Kathy, and given her clean clothes to wear. Kathy's mom, Chris, had arrived and was waiting to see her daughter.

***

While those officers responded to Kathy, several others rushed to the crime scene. They cleared the house, making sure it was safe for medics to enter. After finding Pfister inside the closet, medical personnel were told the victim was dead and they weren't needed. Bright yellow crime scene tape came out and a perimeter was established outside, so no unauthorized persons would enter and contaminate the area.

Detective Brad Gibson had responded to the call, too. Lately, the detective had been doing more paperwork than usual. He was still on light duty after catching his foot in a bear trap during a 2013 investigation and suffering health complications following the injury. Although Gibson knew who Pfister was—like everyone else in Pitkin County— he had never met her or been to her home.

Even so, based on what he heard about Kathy's 911 call, when he arrived at 1833 West Buttermilk shortly after everyone else, he was surprised to find the house neat and clean. Even Pfister's bedroom, the crime scene, wasn't particularly messy.

"It was a very clean crime scene . . . there wasn't blood everywhere," Gibson later said. "Somebody contained the crime scene very well . . . The body was wrapped up so blood couldn't get out. There was no DNA, no fingerprints, no nothing. Somebody was very careful to leave no evidence."

But Gibson had another, bigger problem with the room and what he saw there. "[W]hen we went into the closet, I knew there was a body there but . . . I was literally standing six inches away from the sheets that were covering the body but I couldn't see it. Until Undersheriff Ron Ryan said, 'Brad, the body's right next to your foot.'"

Gibson immediately wondered how Kathy Carpenter could have known it was a body when he didn't. "You could not tell that that was a body," he said. Gibson never did see Pfister's body, because once he left her home he was stuck at the courthouse, writing reports about the homicide.

**

Eric Hansen was a Pitkin County coroner who worked on a rotating shift basis with three other coroners. The position of coroner was not a law enforcement position. It wasn't full time, either, so Hansen also worked as a paramedic and for ski patrol. Pitkin County Medical Examiner J. Stephen Ayers, who was appointed by the sheriff, supervised their work. Sometimes that wasn't much, but in 2014, it was: there were four deaths a month—the most in a year since a Gulfstream jet had crashed on March 29, 2001, killing all eighteen people on board.

Deaths in Pitkin County came about in a variety of ways, but Hansen said in 2014 two or three people tumbled off a mountain, there were one or two drownings, a couple of people were buried by an avalanche, and "four people slammed into a tree" while skiing. Given that Aspen is known for its world-famous ski slopes, that isn't unusual. Every year, hundreds of thousands of visitors take to the town's slopes. From that number, it's unfortunately understandable that roughly four would meet bad ends.

In addition to the risks germane to outdoor activities there, law enforcement officials faced cases of suicide—which was how the news of Pfister's death was first reported to law enforcement. Pitkin County has a suicide rate about twice that of the entire state, and triple the U.S. rate. That's from a 2009 article in the *Denver Post*, which said Aspen had 31 suicides per 100,000 people—compared to 17 in Colorado and 11 nationally.

Hansen disagreed. "The numbers get counted against us. This year we're at zero." He said the Aspen suicide rate was skewed, since many people who plan to take their own lives don't want to do it near their loved ones. So people who own second or third homes in Aspen have in the past, he said, flown there, gotten off the plane, and jumped off a bridge not long after.

***

The night Pfister's body was mistakenly reported as a suicide, Hansen was on duty. His pager went off at 6:40 p.m. and he was on the scene fifteen minutes later. But he couldn't do any work on Pfister's body that night because local police were waiting for CBI to process the crime scene. Hansen realized it was going to be a while before they arrived, much less finished their investigation of the crime scene. So when he was paged again not long after, this time for a man who'd been found with a fatal gunshot wound inside a vehicle at Snowmass Village, Hansen left Pfister's house at 8:20 p.m. so he could attend to that body and prepare it for transport to the hospital morgue.

Initially the law enforcement community began to think there had been a murder-suicide, since, as Hansen said, it's unusual "to have two deaths same night an hour or two apart." But after he arrived, authorities realized the second death "was completely unrelated . . . it was an apparent suicide."

Ironically, though, that victim—like Pfister—had a history of alcohol abuse.

***

Meanwhile, by the time Gibson began interviewing Kathy down at the courthouse, police knew Pfister's death was not a suicide. Obtaining a statement from Kathy immediately could be crucial, given the possibility of a murderer on the loose.

"We brought her over here to the courthouse for just a brief interview," Gibson later said. "I know the doctors gave her some kind of medication to calm her down, but she was just so . . . mentally distraught, we didn't keep her there very long."

While talking to Kathy, Gibson surmised, "she was definitely panicked after making that 911 call." In fact, one reason the interview didn't continue any longer than it did was because, he said, "she was so mentally upset [and] medicated, so doing an interview with somebody at that point really isn't very truthful."

The interview, which was audio recorded, was done just to get the basic facts from Kathy. During the time Gibson conducted it, he said Kathy did not run her hands through her hair as she described what she saw. She did so in subsequent interviews, though, which would lead investigator Lisa Miller and Gibson to both say it indicated Kathy's involvement in Pfister's murder.

Gibson wasn't the only officer to interview Kathy that night. Sheriff Joe DiSalvo, who was personal friends with Pfister and her family, took an immediate interest in the case. DiSalvo also spoke with Kathy that same night, but no one would say for how long or what about. Deputy Grant Jahnke reported that he heard DiSalvo say "he had just spoken with Kathy in the hallway outside the sheriff's office, [where she told DiSalvo] she had seen the Stylers driving out of Pfister's driveway [earlier that day], as she entered the driveway just before finding Pfister's body in the closet."

What happened next is hard to comprehend: Based on the statement of a traumatized victim who was heavily sedated, Sheriff Joe DiSalvo contacted law enforcement agencies throughout the Roaring Fork Valley, asking for their help. Later, numerous witnesses and a trail of purchases would soon confirm the couple had been in Glenwood Springs when police claim Kathy saw them leaving Pfister's house— but which even Kathy's own police interrogations contradicted—officers were dispatched to find, surveil, and bring in Dr. William and Nancy Styler.

CHAPTER ELEVEN
YOU ALWAYS LAWYER UP

On February 27, 2014, less than twelve hours after Pfister's body was found, police had the prime suspects in hand. It was the perfect slam dunk. Or was it?

Nancy and Trey Styler, both in their sixties, were arrested and interrogated separately—Trey for upward of twelve hours that day. Even though they had been apart from each other since the police entered their motel room, waking them from a sound sleep, when prosecutors later looked at their interviews, they found their stories matched. Neither Styler made an inconsistent statement, or said anything against the other one. Nor did they say anything against Kathy Carpenter. Although police said the couple wasn't officially under arrest, every action police took that day indicated otherwise. They were escorted from their motel room in handcuffs, they were not allowed to leave the building, and their personal possessions—including all their money and credit cards—were confiscated and not returned.

In fact, it seems police believed when they entered Room 122 that morning that the Stylers wouldn't be going back to it—but instead, husband and wife would be behind bars by day's end.

Nancy was shocked the police even wanted to talk to her and Trey, because they were the last people who would have known what happened. After three days, Nancy still didn't know where Pfister had gone or why, much less why she hadn't heard from Kathy since 3 p.m. on Wednesday. Regardless, Trey was grilled by Sheriff Joe DiSalvo, CBI Agent John Zamora, and, later in the day, Detective Brad Gibson, for somewhere between twelve and fourteen hours. According to Gibson, Nancy spent four hours being calmly questioned in a Pitkin County Sheriff's Office conference room. It didn't feel like an interrogation at first because her conversation with Detective Gibson was friendly and easy. The effervescent cheerleader in Nancy came to the fore easily, even at times like these, but she had to admit to being nervous as the interview began.

***

Only later did Nancy realize she had been in a state of shock that day—over both her naked photos and the way the police had burst into their motel room at such an ungodly hour.

"Mrs. Styler, you don't have to answer these questions and you are free to leave at any time," Gibson said after introducing himself. "Like I said, you're not under arrest . . . but since we did kind of ask you to come to our office, I do have to go through your Miranda rights. If you can't afford a lawyer, one will be appointed for you before any questioning, if you wish. Do you have any—,"

"Should I get a lawyer?" Nancy asked.

"That's up to you," he said.

Nancy looked confused. "I mean, I didn't do anything wrong and I'm happy to answer your questions."

"I can't advise you either way," Gibson said.

Nancy thought about that before replying. "I mean, if I just tell the truth and whatever, then like there's no issues." She suddenly decided. "No, I want to help."

Gibson nodded, pleased. "I think it's going to take us a while, because y'all have been living at [Pfister's] house for a while."

"About three months," Nancy said.

"Yeah, so let's start at the beginning." Gibson asked if her husband went by William or Trey. She explained that his given name was William, but he was the third one in the family, which was how he earned Trey as a nickname.

Next, Gibson wanted to know where she and Trey came from, which launched Nancy into a fascinating story about their entire life up until that moment. Considering the length of the narrative, it's possible Gibson wondered if Nancy was trying to stall with her constant chatter.

But the truth was, Nancy Styler was like a lot of brilliant people, and there's an old saying that sums up her conversation style: "You ask a man what time it is and he gives you the history of the watch."

***

Nancy and Trey met in 1979, she told Gibson, at the University of Colorado Medical School; he was a resident and she, his anesthesiology instructor. They married the following February, and Trey eventually became chief of anesthesia at St. Joseph's Hospital, where his colleagues and patients loved him. They bought a big, unfinished house in Greenwood Village that Nancy designed inside and out, and where they lived for the next twenty-eight years. She told Gibson about their family trips to the Amazon rainforest to harvest the Victoria lily, the flower that had become her second passion in life, after her family.

Then "fourteen years ago he kept breaking his foot. And we thought it was stress fractures," Nancy said. But a nerve conduction study led a fellow doctor to diagnose Trey with a neurological disease, "and then they started giving him all kinds of meds for it," she said.

Trey lost his job because he was on so many medicines for his own condition that he could no longer practice safely. Eventually, due to his illness and a corrupt attorney who bankrupted Trey's trust fund, they lost their home in March 2013. "It was a $2.2 million [house] but sold for $840,000," Nancy said. "And between retirement plan A, the house falling through, and then the lawyer taking all of our money, we're flat busted."

In addition, they also lost their health insurance. "We had to start a business to be able to get health insurance," Nancy told Gibson. "He's not insurable with his disease."

They started a printing business that involves complex printing on ceramic and glass, Nancy said, because Trey's really good on the computer. "And he's a smart guy. He was valedictorian of his medical school class and the smartest resident I ever had."

Meanwhile, while they waited for their house to sell, they moved to a beautiful house on the top of a hill with gorgeous views on Happy

Canyon Road, above Castle Rock and south of Denver. "We thought it would be a great place to kind of catch our breath and recuperate," Nancy continued, making sure Gibson knew the entire story.

It was August 2011 and they wanted to run the printing business from there, but something went wrong. Whenever Daniel visited them from college, he noticed changes in their personalities—especially his father's. At first, he thought it was Trey's illness, but when his mother began acting different, too, Daniel called their family doctor. "My parents are getting stupid," he said.

Nancy was so overwhelmed with taking care of Trey and picking up the slack on the bad days when he couldn't help out, which was almost every day, that it never occurred to her that they were being poisoned. By then, Trey was in bed and "so weak in that house and we'd go to the doctor every week and say 'he feels sleepy and stupid. He's weak. His face is red.' I'm in medicine, too," Nancy explained, "and I thought he had a fever. Or the progression of his disease, which can go at any rate, any time."

During this time, no one connected the dots between the hot water and their growing health problems. Nancy said the water came out of the spigot black, so the landlord at first thought it was a bad hot water heater. But then, she boiled cold water just so she could take a hot bath, "and I'm feeling a little woozy. I think it's because I haven't had a hot bath in a while; maybe I overdid it." And because she didn't have her electronic hearing aids in during the bath, Nancy said she couldn't hear the loud sound in the house.

But when she got out of the bathtub, Nancy told Gibson, she felt "really woozy, I'm really wiped out." That's when she heard it: "in the bedroom, a carbon monoxide detector going off."

She grabbed the detector and, not thinking clearly, took it outside. Every time she opened the door, the alarm would stop; but every time she brought it back in, it went off again. Nancy told Gibson that she opened all the windows, turned on the fans, but alarms were still going off. That's when she figured it out—and called 911. It was 10 p.m.

"I've got carbon monoxide," she said.

Before paramedics and firefighters arrived, Nancy tried to get Trey out of the house, but "he's like dead weight and stupid." She was still trying to drag him out when they showed up and helped Trey and

Nancy out of the house and into their RV, which was parked in the driveway. They fell asleep until 4 a.m., when firefighters told them it was okay to go back inside.

But still no one could figure out where the carbon monoxide came from, causing them to wonder if the carbon monoxide detector was a fluke. It was easier to blame the meds for Trey's continued deterioration. So the Stylers continued to live in the house—even after Nancy called 911. "He said 'Every time I come home, I just feel weak; I can't handle this,'" she told Gibson. He grew so ill that she finally "thought that was the end, that I'm going to lose him here and we went to the doctors and tried to change medication. We had no clue."

It was only after they had moved and were out of the poisoned house that Nancy could see it all clearly: "I was cleaning soot up every day," she said, but she thought it was just dust blowing through the open windows—never realizing the "dust" was actually soot.

By December, she said she "would walk down to my mailbox and pass by the gas meter and I would smell gas." When she tried to tell people she smelled gas near the meter, no one listened. Nancy told Gibson, "They just had the attitude of 'you're a blonde' and 'it'll be okay, little girl.'"

Other people tried to tell her, "Oh, you must be real sensitive," she said. Even Daniel and her sister, Cindy, couldn't smell it the different times they visited. Finally, on New Year's Eve, Trey told her he couldn't take it anymore. "I just feel so sick and I can't stay here, sorry," he said.

They put all their clothes in the RV and slept there until the Best Western down the street had a vacancy the following day. They "both stumbled over and we checked in and called our landlord [and said they weren't going back until the problem was fixed]." He ultimately let them out of their lease, Nancy told Gibson.

Meanwhile, because of how sick they both were, the printing business died and they eventually lost $60,000 worth of inventory. One month after going to the hotel, they moved into a house in Castle Rock, which turned out to be a pit stop on their way to Aspen. Nancy was so worn out and tired from caring for Trey that she didn't see what was really going on at the time.

However, in hindsight she felt terrible. Nancy even felt bad as she told Gibson the story, and very guilty, because the symptoms were right in front of her and yet she missed them. Trey "was cherry red and," she told Gibson, "if someone [came to ER] and I saw that, I would say carbon monoxide."

The eventual involvement of Black Hills Energy officials and the Stylers' next door neighbor, an engineer, led to the discovery of the problem: propane and natural gas were connected to a generator next door, so the gases mixed and the pressure forced the gas to flow backward from the generator through the shared regulator lines and into the house.

"For a year and a half, we were burning a mixture of propane and natural gas without knowing it. We were getting gassed with carbon monoxide," she said. So, for the entire time they lived there, the Stylers were being poisoned.

Nancy finished telling Gibson the story about them being poisoned, saying that the experience damaged Trey permanently. "We were dazed—my husband more than I was, but it's hard to believe that that's a brilliant man there," she said. "He's got the highest IQ of anyone I know other than my son."

***

By then, several hours had passed, and Nancy began telling Gibson how they ended up in Aspen. Essentially, she said, it all went back to Trey's illness.

"That was when I decided to go back to work. I hadn't practiced for twenty-eight years, but I had always done facial aesthetics," Nancy said. "I was a makeup artist when I was sixteen and . . . put myself through college and medical school."

Nancy thought Aspen might be a great place for the spa, since they planned to offer services that many Aspen residents would appreciate, like Botox injections, fillers, and facials.

Rita Bellino, owner of the Queen B, one of the town's hair salons, also taught cosmetology. In June, Nancy took classes from Rita so she could become certified; Nancy passed all the exams and she and Trey began making trips to and from Aspen, trying to see if Aspen was a good fit for them.

"The woman at Queen B said, 'Come up here, when it gets busy I can really keep you busy doing eyelash extensions and things like that,'" Nancy said.

And since she was also a seamstress, Nancy spoke with Monika Olinski at Faboo on Mill Street, who said she had extra work and could use some help with alterations. That was in July. Nancy thought that between those two businesses, she could find enough work to keep her busy until she and Trey got their spa off the ground. Then, in late August, Nancy made two new friends, Patrice Melanie and Purl Shirley, at the Aspen farmers' market. After years of feeling like no one would listen to her, or to Trey, when he tried to use the legal system to fight to get back what was theirs, Nancy felt like she could really talk to Patrice and Purl. She opened up, telling them her and Trey's entire story, from his illness on. They were empathetic and attentive listeners, and Nancy fell in love with them right away. Both women were dog lovers, so Nancy gave them each some of the dog clothing she had made. They told her that she and Trey could make it in Aspen, and that's when the couple decided to relocate there.

By August they were looking for a house to rent. They looked from August to October. One place after another didn't work, though, usually because of Trey, who was "deathly allergic" to cats, Nancy explained, in addition to having difficulty walking up and down stairs due to his disability. When they saw Pfister's October 16 newspaper ad, they answered it. The woman who answered Nancy's phone call was out of breath. "Hello," she said, trying to talk. "Oh, sorry; I was just in my greenhouse watering."

"Oh, what do you grow?" Nancy asked.

"I grow organic vegetables for some of the restaurants in town," the woman said.

Nancy taught organic gardening, so her interest was piqued right away—and the thought of having a greenhouse was heaven to her. It carried her back to the days in her own beautiful garden at Greenwood Village.

"Well, hurry up and come up here because there's another couple coming with a realtor and they have a kid, and a small dog, and I would much rather rent to you," she said. "So get over here as soon as you can."

"Okay, my name is Nancy. Nancy Styler."

"So is mine," said the woman. "I'm Nancy Pfister. This just has to be karma!"

***

Trey and Nancy drove straight to the address Pfister gave them. The first thing Nancy noticed was the mountain peaks. They surrounded the house on three sides. She and Trey knocked on the red door, just like Pfister told them, but no one answered. They banged and banged but nothing. Just silence. So Nancy called Pfister from her cell phone.

"Oh, just open the red door and come upstairs," she said.

Once inside, the house seemed perfect, especially after Pfister suggested they open their spa right there, saying she wanted to invest in it with her mother's inheritance after she returned from Australia. Nancy explained, telling Gibson how warm and friendly Pfister had been, how it seemed like an answer to their prayers. She spoke about how taken they were with Pfister's generosity. That Trey had even returned to their motel room that night and written four pages about how fortuitous meeting Pfister was, how gracious she had been. They were dazzled by Pfister's larger-than-life persona, and Trey thought it was "serendipity."

After agreeing to rent her home to them, Pfister specified she wanted the money in cash, since the house was part of her trust fund. The rental term would be from November 22, when she left for Australia, to May 22, when she returned. Then Pfister suggested they could move in immediately, and live there rent-free for one month—if they would help her "pack and do things around the house."

But the best part of the deal was Pfister's enthusiasm for their proposed spa. She even offered to share her wealthy connections with Nancy, to help her get the business off the ground. Nancy said she was thrilled when Pfister seemed so gracious and willing to help them. They offered to let her play a role in the spa, thinking that it might be good for her, too. Pfister loved the idea.

Before the spa could even get up and running, though, they ran into problems. Not serious ones, just Pfister's frequently odd behavior that made Nancy feel like a servant. For instance, she told Gibson,

Pfister often walked around the house naked, even when they were there. Once she even walked around naked for almost four hours when the personal organizer she hired came over to work on Pfister's bedroom closet. "I was never so uncomfortable," Nancy said the women later told her.

And Nancy said she felt even weirder when Pfister asked her to look at her groin, to see if she had a pimple. "I'm thinking, 'Oh, my God!'"

Horrified, she told Trey, "This is a reality show! They're having you rent a house, and there's going to be this crazy lady who does all this stuff . . . it's a reality show. Let's look for the cameras."

Other details, like strange men joining Pfister in her bedroom every week, were not something Nancy and Trey expected, but they didn't feel like it was any of their business. It wasn't their house, and they were seldom there in late October and early November, given how much time they spent going back and forth to Castle Rock, in preparation to move their personal belongings into Pfister's place in November.

Tensions mounted when the Stylers were in the home with Pfister, especially when it came to finances. For instance, Nancy told Gibson, Pfister asked Trey to buy her several cases of her favorite pink Champagne when he went to Denver, so Trey did. When he asked for Pfister to repay him, she refused. "That's your donation for my party," Pfister said.

Then she hired Nancy, who was also an accomplished seamstress, to custom design some clothing, including a wetsuit and a replica in organic fabrics of an Armani jacket that Saudi Arabia's Prince Bandar, the former Saudi ambassador to the United States, once gave her. After Nancy spent more than $500 to buy the fabric and notions to construct the garments, she tried to get Pfister's measurements, but Pfister kept putting Nancy off. She kept telling her she'd rather keep her money. Nancy was appalled. "I already bought the fabric and I can't take it back."

And even though Nancy gave her their airline points, enough for a round-trip ticket to Texas, because Pfister insisted she had to fly first class, Pfister then expected Nancy to pay for other items she wanted, such as a caterer for a party she threw in November—and the cost to clean up afterward.

Pfister soon grew to expect Nancy to do her hair and makeup, something Nancy at first offered to do in an act of friendship and appreciation for Pfister's offer to let them put their spa in the chalet. But Nancy grew annoyed when Pfister demanded it, as it interfered with Nancy's ability to take care of important matters for herself and Trey. Pfister also expected Trey, a nondrinker, to take her around town, serving as her designated driver so she could drink when she went out, just as she expected them both to rub her shoulders or her feet, anytime she asked. By the time Pfister left the country, Nancy said she and Trey had become Pfister's entire staff: chauffeur, seamstress, organic gardener, biographer, hairdresser, and aesthetician. If she tallied up the money Pfister "owed" them for everything she promised to pay for but didn't, Nancy said, it would come to a few thousand dollars, easily.

The problems grew much worse, though, less than two weeks after Pfister left for Australia. For some reason they couldn't fathom, she became nasty and demanding, and threatened to have them evicted for not paying rent—even though they had paid Kathy as Pfister had directed, and Kathy, in turn, had deposited the cash into the safety deposit box she and Pfister shared at Alpine Bank. Ultimately, the tension was so bad, Pfister so unreasonable, that the Stylers decided to move out. There was simply no way to make it work—and they agreed that putting their spa in Pfister's house would end disastrously.

***

Gibson asked Nancy to tell him about her conversations with Kathy Carpenter.

"I told Kathy I had never been so disrespected by anyone in my entire life and I'd like to strangle her. But I never meant it literally. Besides, Kathy said the same thing. She was Nancy Pfister's slave. She worked for her for eight years and never got paid, and all Nancy did was put her down and poke fun at her."

"What was Pfister like?" he asked.

"Contentious," Nancy said. "She always wanted to argue, about every little thing, about things that shouldn't even matter."

Gibson nodded as he took notes. Nancy didn't mind the questions; they weren't difficult and they seemed fairly innocuous. The hours passed quickly. Finally Gibson announced it was time for lunch. He offered Nancy a Diet Coke and sandwich.

After lunch, the tone of the interview changed: Gibson wanted to know about Nancy's whereabouts the day before. She explained, again in great detail, how the Aspen Workforce employees helped them move from 10 a.m. to 2 p.m. on Wednesday, before she and Trey went to Glenwood Springs. He drove the rental truck; she followed in the Jag. They dropped off the U-Haul, then went to Nancy's salon appointment at Lovely Nails in the mall. But they were an hour early and hadn't eaten dinner, so they went in search of food. The mall lacked a food court, so they went to eat at a nearby Dairy Queen, before returning to the salon.

During the ninety-minute appointment, Nancy told Gibson, her phone kept buzzing. Since her eyelashes were being refilled, though, she wasn't able to take any of the calls. After leaving the salon, Nancy looked at her phone. Susan Waskow, a friend of Kathy's, had called repeatedly. Nancy told Gibson about Susan's frantic voice mail: how she'd said, "they found Nancy, and Kathy is okay. She's in good hands," as well as how Susan also told her that Kathy was being treated in the emergency room. When Nancy dropped by Heather's to cancel on Merlin, she told him the news, but he didn't know anything, either. That was all she knew when she went to bed Wednesday night.

Nancy sat there shaking her head. "And the next thing I knew was you guys coming in." She rattled on, about how surreal it was when the police busted into their motel room just a few hours after falling asleep, how the medicine "Trey takes makes him too groggy to think, and he can't wake up for an hour."

Eventually, Gibson got to the meat of the interview: he asked Nancy if she and Trey were together all day Monday.

"Yes, on Monday we were," she said. But Nancy probably didn't realize she was so brain-weary herself, so traumatized from being photographed naked in a room full of men, that she forgot Trey went out without her to rent the storage units while she slept in Monday morning.

"But on Tuesday he went, while I was loading up stuff with the guys, he went to the Aspen post office to get his medication," she said, noting he was gone when Merlin dropped by Pfister's place. Otherwise, she and Trey were together the rest of the day—except for when he ran out to the store late that night. But he wasn't gone very long.

Gibson asked if she had ever been "involved in anything like this before."

Nancy was adamant. "Never, never ever. This is freaky to me."

Then, hours into the interview, Nancy asked him if police knew when "the event happened," which seemed to indicate she was still unaware that Pfister had been murdered. But Gibson lied, when he denied knowing anything.

"I'm in the dark like you," he said.

*　*　*

Nancy next told Gibson about a weird comment Susan Waskow made the day before, when she called Nancy about the ambulance and police cars headed to Pfister's house. "She said, 'My son thinks that [Pfister] is going to try to set you guys up for something and put you through hell to get even with you,' and I said, 'Oh, come on now, you're watching too many shows.'"

Gibson seemed to understand what Susan was saying. Yes, even the sheriff knew Pfister and "he's made a couple comments" about her, he said.

Nancy said so many people in Aspen told them to "run!" when they heard about the Stylers renting from Pfister. So, while she didn't seem popular, "I can't tell you that anyone would want her dead."

Gibson asked if Nancy ever heard any bitter comments about Pfister.

Yes, from everyone, she said. "Pfister did this . . . she did that . . . she's crazy . . . and just watch out."

Nancy then related something Pfister had told her. "She told me her sister Suzanne should have a broomstick to ride around on. She said Suzanne was a witch, and they didn't get along at all," Nancy said, adding that Pfister told Nancy she had sued Suzanne a year or so ago, over the road that connected their two properties.

Almost as if talking to herself, Nancy said she didn't know what had happened to either Pfister or Kathy.

"Me either," Gibson said, then mentioned the fact that someone was dead. "I know he has a body up there . . . but that's all I know," he said, referring to the coroner.

Although that was the first reference to death or "a body" during the entire interview, it was not the first time Nancy had heard it. That happened when police first forced their way into Room 122, earlier that morning.

"At the house?" Nancy asked Gibson in disbelief.

"Yes, know who it is?" Gibson asked.

"No," she said with a gasp.

"Neither do I," Gibson said. Another lie.

"It had to be found—," Nancy began, seemingly reasoning to herself as much as speaking to Gibson, "we left there at 12:48 yesterday. And we were going to go back at night to get the garbage, but when we started hearing all these stories [about emergency vehicles] I said, 'I'm not going anywhere near that place.'"

What she didn't say but perhaps thought was that Pfister had already told the local police that she and Trey were ripping her off by not paying rent, and Nancy was suddenly afraid that Susan's son might have been right—what if Pfister did try to set them up for something she did?

When Gibson remained silent, Nancy became speculative. "We'll find out tomorrow" what happened, she said.

Gibson agreed. "I'm waiting for confirmation, too."

"So if I were to guess," Nancy said, "the sister is the one that, I hate to say it, but her sister is the one that she had the most venom for."

***

It was four in the afternoon when Officer Gibson announced it was time for a break. Nancy stood to stretch her legs, remembered their motel room, and felt a flicker of panic. The last thing she and Trey needed was to lose that, too. The Aspenalt was $89 a night; every other Aspen hotel cost between $300 and $600 a night. As it stood now, Nancy knew they barely had enough money for one more night. *If that happens, we'll be out on the street for sure.*

Nancy asked if she could call the motel to reserve another night. He said sure and pushed his cell phone across the table. Then, for some reason, Gibson left the room.

After calling the motel, Nancy instinctively dialed Daniel's number. She told him he wouldn't believe what had happened to them, as if it was an everyday occurrence. Daniel immediately grew worried and told his mom to get an attorney. When she balked, he asked her if she was in shock.

"You don't seem upset, Mom."

"Why should I? It's all some ridiculous mistake. Besides, I haven't done anything. We didn't do anything."

Daniel immediately recognized that tone: it was his mother's objective, clinical researcher's voice. What he didn't know was that for Nancy, the thought of getting another lawyer after their last horrible legal experience wasn't the least bit appealing. She hadn't even considered it. Nor did he know what happened in their motel room that morning, how traumatized she was over being photographed naked in front of a group of strange men, having swabs taken from her mouth and under her nails, and paraded out in public in orange inmate's clothing.

Of those indignities, the nude photos were the worst. Nancy wasn't a prude—she had gone to nude beaches before—but what did bother her was the fact that everyone in the room saw her deformed breasts. The double mastectomy happened more than twenty years ago, leaving her with such little upper body strength that Trey became her pectoral muscles and did all the heavy lifting. In return, years later when he grew ill, she became his legs.

Although the breast reconstruction was well worth it, it hadn't been foolproof. Nancy had two leaks from her implants, and more surgery down the road to remove and replace those implants. Since they were located under the pectoral muscle, in a little "pocket" of space created for the implant to sit in, whenever Nancy tightened her pecs, the implants would move under the skin, sliding across and into her armpits. It was terribly embarrassing, knowing everyone had seen that Thursday morning, but Nancy didn't feel like telling Daniel about it.

Instead, she just said what made the most sense. "I know I'm innocent, so why do I need to do that? They aren't doing anything to me other than just talking. They're just getting background information so they can figure this out."

"Mom, you get a parking ticket, you get a lawyer. You always lawyer up." Several hours away, Daniel began to pace back and forth in the living room of his apartment. Somehow, in spite of her initial objections, he managed to convince her to ask for an attorney.

Daniel's advice came just in time—Gibson said he was about to ask Nancy if she would agree to take a polygraph exam.

***

After she hung up, Gibson came back into the room and Nancy said her son told her to get an attorney. Gibson didn't seem upset, nor did he mention the polygraph. Instead, he left the room and said he'd be right back. When he returned, he told Nancy she was free to go.

"Where's my husband?"

"He's still being questioned."

Nancy looked unsettled. "I'll need a ride home."

"You probably remember Officer Nelson from this morning. We're sending her with you to go buy some clothes so you don't have to walk around in these jail clothes. Maybe by then your husband will be finished, too. Wait here and I'll be right back."

When he returned, he handed Nancy a navy blue hoodie with the words "X Games" on the front. Nancy wanted to laugh at the irony, since the X Games, which the Pfister family often hosted on Buttermilk Mountain, had just concluded. But she was afraid once she started, she wouldn't be able to stop laughing—giving police the perfect excuse to cart her off to the loony bin. "I borrowed this from one of the secretaries. You can put it over the inmate's shirt, if you want."

***

Across the hall, Trey was still being questioned. Not simply questioned, either: he underwent an intense interrogation—and an extensive polygraph exam. Sheriff Joe DiSalvo, a personal friend of Pfister's since 1987, had even dropped by to ask his own questions. However,

DiSalvo's method of questioning Trey was blunt and he even accused the doctor of murdering Pfister.

DiSalvo and Gibson, who later joined the interrogation after he finished talking to Nancy, pointed to a plastic bag on the floor. Without showing Trey its contents, they began harassing him. "We have evidence in here that proves you did it," DiSalvo said. "Wouldn't you say you were guilty of this murder if we had your DNA in this bag?"

"It would look very suspicious if you had my DNA there. But you don't, because I didn't do it."

DiSalvo leaned over until his nose was mere inches from Trey's. "Well, then, your wife did—and you're trying to cover up for her."

"No, she didn't do it."

"Yes, she did! You flunked the polygraph, Trey, so we know you did it. Or she did it. Or you both did!" DiSalvo practically hissed the words, spewing tiny particles of spit in Trey's face.

"And we know how, too." The sheriff's voice had begun soft but was now increasing in volume. With each syllable, his accusations grew louder and angrier. "You bashed in her skull with a hammer because you didn't want to pay her—and the two of you wrapped that poor woman in plastic bags and sheets and dragged her lifeless body into the closet. Then you both flipped over the mattress to hide the blood, didn't you, Trey? Your wife had to help you, because you're too weak to do all that on your own. Aren't you, Trey?"

"We know your Nancy," Gibson said, "told Kathy Carpenter how much she hated Pfister and wanted to kill her, so which was it—did you plan to kill her for your wife, or did she plan it and ask you to help?"

The incriminations continued for hours as DiSalvo and Gibson trotted out various theories. But it did no good. At the end of the day, Trey still insisted he was innocent—and so was Nancy.

***

While the deputies continued questioning Trey, Officer Nelson walked across the street with Nancy. Even though the hoodie covered the bright orange top, it did little to hide the sloppy-looking orange pants. As they walked along the street, she imagined everyone who passed by was staring at her. A proud woman known for her classy fashion sense, Nancy was mortified. She hated knowing the people who saw her believed she was an inmate—a criminal. And she was still wrestling with why the police had made her strip naked earlier that morning. None of it made any sense, and she felt herself growing furious.

The first store they entered wanted a hundred dollars for a sweat-shirt but even though the county was footing the tab, Nancy refused. "No way. It's criminal to pay that much." They continued looking, until they found more affordable clothing at the next store.

Nancy selected a turquoise shirt and slacks, disappeared into a dressing room, and peeled off her jail outfit as fast as she could. Then she peered at the mirror, glancing at her reflection one final time. Her hair was messy and her teeth hadn't been brushed, so she felt grungy—she never left her home without perfectly coiffed hair and makeup. *At least I'm dressed in turquoise*, she thought. It was one of her favorite colors.

Nancy managed a slight chuckle as she checked out her huge sneak-ers, the only county-issue clothing she hadn't been able to replace. *I look like something right out of a circus.* Heather paid with a county credit card and together they left.

Back at the sheriff's office, Gibson met her inside. "If you want, you can wait for your husband in the room we were in."

***

Suddenly overtaken by exhaustion, Nancy took her earlier seat, lying her head down on the table. She realized how uncomfortable it was, so she got down on the floor and pulled the hoodie up over her head, trying to fashion it into a pillow. She slept until she awoke with a start, to find a cleaning man standing over her.

"Am I all right to stay in here?"

"Yeah. I was just worried," he said, smiling. "You see someone lying on the floor and their head's all covered up, and . . . " His words trailed off, but Nancy knew what he meant.

"You think they're dead," she finished for him.

***

Since the wall clock was broken, Nancy lost all concept of time and fell asleep again. When she awoke, she heard Trey calling her name.

"Nance? Nance?" An agitated hand shook her shoulder. Nancy opened her eyes to find Trey leaning over her, his face full of fear. "I hardly recognized you. Where'd you get those clothes? Your feet are so much bigger and I couldn't see your hair," Trey said, kneeling down and hugging her tightly.

"The floor was so hard I had to tuck my hair up into the hoodie to make enough of a cushion for my head."

Nancy could tell Trey was shaken as she reached up to comfort him.

Gibson appeared at the door. "Mr. and Mrs. Styler, we'll take you back to your motel now."

By the time they were released and returned to the bedroom community of Basalt, it was early evening. Nancy and Trey had been in police custody for almost fourteen hours. Back in Room 122, their growling stomachs reminded them that they were starving. But they had no money, no credit cards, no cell phones. Nothing. And along with all their personal items, the police had carted off their iPads and Trey's laptop.

CHAPTER TWELVE
NANCY TAKES THE WHEEL

Room 122 was a far cry from the wealth, accommodations, and meals the Stylers had enjoyed in the months prior. Their financial situation during their stay in Pfister's chalet was certainly less than ideal, but they had maintained a comfortable standard of living. Pfister's extravagance and overindulgence offered further contrast to the Stylers' way of life, before and after their stints in police custody. Pfister used every occasion as an opportunity for celebratory food and drink.

Back in November 2013, Nancy got an education in how dramatically different Pfister could be, as if she were two different people. Nancy noticed this on one particular occasion when Pfister was very drunk. She and Trey had sold their only remaining stocks to pay Pfister half of the $12,000 they owed her. After getting her first $6,000 payment, Pfister offered to take Nancy to the nearby Redstone Inn. It was mid-afternoon when the two women arrived, and they were alone in the restaurant. They sat down for lunch; Nancy ordered a cheeseburger and a Diet Coke; Pfister ordered wild-caught fresh salmon and quinoa and a glass of pink Champagne. As they sat there chatting, Pfister suddenly had an idea: she told Nancy she *just had* to have her hair colored at a little salon in Carbondale that Pfister liked. But there was no cell signal, so Pfister asked to use the house phone. Coming back to the table, Pfister said she'd taken care of it. "You have an appointment in two hours." Nancy was appreciative of Pfister's gesture and felt like the two women were becoming friends.

As they were eating, two men came into the restaurant, and Pfister immediately invited them over for a drink. "My father built these mountains," she said, introducing herself and Nancy to the men, and then ordering a bottle of Champagne. Before long both men knew everything about Pfister, including the importance of her family name in Aspen. The younger man, about thirty-five, was an art attorney, the older, forty-nine, an insurance executive; they told the two women they were visiting from New Mexico and planned to pick up another friend who was flying into Aspen from Montreal. While Nancy and the attorney, John, discussed art, Pfister and Mark slipped away outside to smoke a joint and flirt.

"Nancy Pfister said she has some Gormans and other artwork she'd like to sell," Nancy told John. "She asked us to help find buyers for her while she's away."

"I'd like to see those," John said. "I could determine their value." That was the extent of the conversation because Pfister and Mark returned and Pfister suggested they come see her home and hang out until it was time to go to the airport. The men agreed, so all four left the restaurant together. Nancy left a $20 bill on the table, and noticed that Pfister, who had stuffed the $6,000 cash from Nancy into her purse, only left a $100 bill. Having seen the menu, Nancy knew that wasn't enough to pay for what Pfister had ordered.

Nancy added more cash to the pile, thinking that Pfister had probably been too distracted to realize she hadn't left a tip. Outside, the two men got into their Audi and Pfister asked Nancy to drive her Prius.

Nancy hesitated, knowing she didn't want Pfister behind the wheel. "I don't usually drive," she said, "and I've never driven a hybrid before."

Pfister laughed, clearly tipsy. "It's easy. Nothing to it."

Nancy slipped into the driver's seat and followed Pfister's directions about turning on the little car. The drive from the Redstone Inn to the hair salon was nothing like Nancy had experienced before: Pfister was hanging her hands and feet out the window, texting and flirting wildly with the younger man in the car behind them. It made

Nancy even more nervous as she tried to navigate the little car along unfamiliar roads. "She was acting like a teenager," Nancy later said.

When they arrived at the salon, Pfister took the two men and together the trio slipped into a Mexican restaurant a few doors away. "We'll have a few drinks, and then be over to get you," Pfister called out as they walked away.

Inside the salon, a young male stylist, Beau, asked Nancy who referred her. When she said Pfister, he asked if Nancy knew her well. "Not really, but we just rented her home and are planning to open a medical spa in it," Nancy said, sitting down in the stylist's chair.

"The last time she was here, she polished off an entire bottle of wine and got wasted," Beau said. "We offer our clients a glass—by the way, what would you like?"

Nancy waved her hand, indicating she didn't. "I'm the designated driver. Besides, I don't drink alcohol. I never liked the way it made me so tired."

"Are you a weed person, then?" he said.

Nancy shook her head. "Yes, I prefer marijuana, but I never work or drive after using. I don't like to drive anyway, so it's not a problem."

"Honey, have you come to the right place," Beau said. "Everyone in Aspen smokes it."

Draping a robe over Nancy, he continued. "Well, anyway, as I was saying, she drank the entire bottle. And girlfriend, let me tell you, was she plastered!" Tilting her chair back so he could wash her hair, Beau gave Nancy a pointed look. "Then, when another stylist sprayed her client's hair, she had a fit. 'You can't spray that stuff around me!' she screamed. Honey, it was nothing but high drama here that day!"

Nancy rolled her eyes, and wondered—not for the first time—if she and Trey would be able to last until November 22, when Pfister was to leave for Australia.

Her hair was colored a lovely ash blonde and styled in the long bob she preferred by the time Pfister and friends showed up. "Shit-faced," Beau whispered under his breath, winking at Nancy. She smiled. "Beau, thank you for doing such a wonderful job. Here's my card." While he had been doing her hair, they had discussed Nancy's plans for the spa. Beau said he'd like to team up with Nancy, since she was interested in providing quality services for people. "I'll call you," he said, as Nancy paid and left.

***

Outside in the cold winter air, Pfister's footsteps were weaving and Nancy hoped she didn't fall. Looking at John and Mark, Nancy could tell they were equally wasted. She worried as John slipped into the driver's seat of his luxury car, but she couldn't do anything about it—she had to drive Pfister's car. Nancy hoped she wasn't as googley-eyed on the way home as she had been earlier. If anything, as they drove along the winding road back to West Buttermilk, Pfister was even worse. She kept barking slurred commands at Nancy, trying to tell her how to drive the hybrid, ordering her to, "Do this!" and "Don't do that!"

Nancy tried to tell Pfister to be quiet, but the woman wouldn't listen, instead slurring commands at Nancy the whole drive back to the house. Finally Pfister lunged, grabbing at the steering wheel. *That does it!* Nancy saw a sign for El Jebel, a small town a few miles from Carbondale. She took a right, then slammed on the brake as she parked on the berm. "Either shut up or I'm going to walk home," Nancy said. "Or I'll take a bus. You cannot wrestle the steering wheel away from me. If you keep it up, you're going to cause an accident." Pfister looked surprised, like she wasn't used to being talked to that way. "Okay," she mumbled.

Just then, the two men came up to the passenger side of the car. "Hey, honey," Mark said to Pfister, "we'll have to take a rain check on that drink at your place. We need to get to the airport."

"Oh no! Please don't go!" Pfister said, looking like she might cry. The men insisted. "Tell you what. Come to my going-away party. It's in a couple of weeks," she said.

They promised they would. After giving Pfister a big kiss, Mark followed John back to the Audi. They pulled back onto the road and with a final wave, were gone. "You shoulda' seen what they had in their trunk," Pfister said, laughing like it was the funniest thing in the world.

Nancy didn't care what was in their trunk. She just wanted to make it back alive. And they did. They made it home without further incident because even in her drunken state, Pfister must have realized

Nancy had reached her limit, so she sat silent in the passenger's seat all the way back to the chalet. But that day the dynamic changed between the two Nancys, whether due to Pfister getting her money, or because Nancy stood up to her—something very few people, especially other women—did. Even though Pfister befriended all kinds of people, experiences from her personal life indicate she believed most people were there to serve her. However, Nancy Styler was—in terms of her intellect, her medical education in France, her stature in the Denver community as a prominent doctor's wife, her upper middle-class income, and finally, as the founder of the Victoria Conservancy—in every way Pfister's equal.

Or was she? Drunk or not, it's possible that was the day Pfister looked at Nancy Styler with fresh eyes and saw not just an accomplished, brilliant, successful woman with aspirations, but someone Pfister knew she could never be.

***

Not long after, Nancy saw another side of Pfister that worried her. Pfister, who had a lifetime membership to the Maroon Creek Country Club, told Nancy and Trey they could use the club anytime. They met Pfister there for lunch one day, planning to work out afterward. But the manager told Pfister her guests weren't allowed to use the facilities, unless she wanted to pay for them to do so. Pfister wasn't willing to do that, but she did take Nancy to the women's locker room so Nancy could hang a notice on the bulletin board advertising her spa and sewing services.

Once inside the locker room, Pfister took an entire container that held tea, juice, toothbrushes, shampoo, and soaps and dumped it into a bag. She did the same thing with energy drinks from the fridge. Then she told Nancy to carry the bag.

Nancy was embarrassed. "I don't need these."

"I don't care," Pfister said. "They pissed me off!"

That was when Nancy remembered seeing similar items from hotels in Pfister's suitcases, when she returned from her Houston trip. Nancy realized then that Pfister apparently believed she was entitled to anything she wanted—even if it didn't belong to her.

***

But it was the "bathroom incident" that really blew Nancy's mind. It happened just before Pfister flew to Houston, in late October, the day the Stylers stopped by and found her upstairs in the master bath.

"Nancy?" she called from the first floor. The front door was unlocked, as always, and everyone knew Pfister's open door policy. The first time they met her, Pfister told them to just walk right in whenever they arrived. They were, after all, going to be roommates for a month before she left for Australia.

"I'm up here," Pfister called out. "Come on up."

Trey and Nancy went up the stairs, slowly, since Trey's leg muscles, weakened from disease, made stairs difficult for him. Nancy entered the bedroom first. "I'm in here, in the bathroom. Come on in," Pfister said.

Nancy looked at Trey. "My husband's with me," she said.

"Oh, that's okay. Come in here," Pfister said.

Trey hung back, unwilling to go any further, but he heard the two women's exchange.

"Open that drawer; there's a vaginal cream applicator there I need," Trey heard Pfister say. He could just imagine the look of horror his wife had to be hiding from Pfister. If she even could.

"Is this it?" Nancy asked.

"Yes," Pfister said.

"I'll just wait out here until you're finished," Nancy said.

"Oh no. I need you to throw this away first," Pfister said, apparently handing Nancy the used applicator.

Afterward, when they were driving away in their Jaguar, Trey caught the look of disgust on his wife's face. "Oh my god, Trey! What's wrong with her?" Nancy asked. "She actually handed me the used applicator and expected me to throw it away. Which I did, because I was too shocked not to."

"We both know she's an odd one," he said.

"Odd?" Nancy said. "That's gross!"

CHAPTER THIRTEEN

CELEBRITY CHEF CATERS A-LIST PARTY

The cheap yet relatively insignificant acts Nancy first saw in Pfister turned a bit darker when the Stylers' landlady began planning a party to introduce them to her friends. Conveniently, Pfister wanted it to double as her bon voyage party, and initially said it would be an elegant dinner for a dozen people.

"I'm tired of meeting everyone at memorials and life celebrations," Pfister told Nancy, saying she would invite all her "A-list" friends, people in the community who would gladly open their doors wide to the Stylers and their new salon, "Mountain Oasis Spa."

The Stylers and Pfister were still friends then, although the dynamic of their friendship was slowly changing. Some people might say—and rightly so—that the friendship was slowly eroding. Others might say Pfister used the Stylers for her own ends and then, having gotten what she wanted, had no further use for them. Maybe, but maybe not. It's possible that Pfister's on-again, off-again, or hot-cold-hot behavior was due to something else entirely. Something much more serious.

Regardless, the party was planned for November 16, and between the time the idea was conceived until it was carried out four weeks later, it evolved from a small dinner affair to a blowout party of about thirty people. When the night of the party arrived, it had become a lame excuse to raise money for a "tsunami relief fund" for orphans in the Philippines.

When Pfister first told Nancy she wanted it to be completely organic, they were having lunch in the Hotel Jerome's J-Bar. Pfister asked Brenda, the bar manager, if she would cater the upcoming party. Pfister said that Larry, a Hollywood producer, was footing the bill because he hoped to find financial backers for his next movie.

"I'm going to invest my mother's money with Larry. Then Jules can have an acting job," Pfister told Nancy and Trey. "It will give her something to do."

When Brenda asked Pfister about her budget, she said there wasn't one.

"I want it to be all organic and have plenty of pink Champagne," she said.

"I think I need to bring Jimmy Nadell onboard," Brenda said.

Now, Nadell isn't just any chef: he has his own TV show, *The Bravo Kitchen Show*, making him a celebrity chef, and he was formerly executive chef of the Caribou Club in Aspen. He's catered for foreign dignitaries and celebrities alike.

Then Brenda told Pfister it would cost $105 a plate. Pfister said she didn't want to pay that much. Not long after, Nancy heard Pfister fighting with Larry about how much money she was going to invest in his next movie herself, when she received her mother's insurance money. Nancy was embarrassed but couldn't help overhearing, since Pfister insisted on using speaker phone whenever she talked to her callers. Nancy could tell that Larry was as angry as Pfister; the screaming match was punctuated with swearing. By the time the call ended, Larry told Pfister to count him out—he wanted nothing to do with her money or her party.

Pfister grew so worried about the party's costs she told Nancy she would pay for it by calling it a fundraiser to help orphans from the tsunami in the Philippines. She immediately asked Jimmy to cater the party for less money, too. "If it gets any cheaper, it will be hamburgers and hot dogs," Nancy said he told Pfister.

Still, she convinced Jimmy to bring his new sushi bar to the party, saying Nancy could decorate everything and Trey could take photographs that Jimmy could use to help market the new equipment. Jimmy agreed.

Pfister and Jimmy went shopping Friday, November 15, to buy fish and other foodstuffs for the party. When they returned, Jimmy told

Pfister she had to at least pay the sushi chef a fraction of his regular fee and to reimburse him for the extra food she insisted he buy while shopping. Pfister agreed.

During the days leading up to the party, a quiet neurophysiology professor named Lee had come to Aspen to visit Pfister. She had met him during her trip to Houston in October and invited him to stay with her. But when he showed up, Pfister changed her mind and booked a suite for him at the Hotel Jerome. Lee wined and dined Pfister, taking her out for lunch every day he was there. He seemed completely smitten with her. During that time, Nancy took over Pfister's duties, preparing for the party.

The night of the party, the eclectic mélange of invitees included four medical doctors, at least three attorneys, law enforcement, musicians, and local celebrities. Two of Pfister's newest friends traveled there from New Mexico—John and Mark, the men she and Nancy had dined with at the Redstone Inn. They brought a third friend along, a fellow with long braids and someone they called "The Doctor," supposedly because he made such delicious hash.

Nancy mingled with everyone at the party, and when he wasn't busy, she offered to show John, the art attorney, the Gorman paintings Pfister owned. He had expressed interest in seeing them when they all lunched together, so Nancy wanted to be hospitable. John looked at them and Nancy pointed out that they were signed "To Art and Betty Pfister." At the time, she still planned to help Pfister sell them, as Pfister had asked her to, so she asked John how much he thought they were worth.

By the end of the evening, Nancy was having second and third thoughts. But by the time the party ended, she had gotten a glimpse of Pfister when she was very drunk, and at her very worst. Tripping all over herself, Pfister, who had already fallen down once during the party, was sitting on men's laps and cuddling up to them. That's when she decided she needed to rethink any "business deals" she agreed to help Pfister with.

Looking around, Nancy saw that the tsunami orphan-relief flyers Pfister had asked Kathy Carpenter to make were still in the same piles where Nancy had placed them, untouched. Not a single person had contributed to "the orphans." Jimmy and his staff left just before midnight because November 19 was a day when Aspenites could ski for free, and they planned to partake in the activity. Nancy told Jimmy she would take care of putting the food away for him. Pfister demanded Nancy help pay for a cleaning crew to come in. That's when Nancy told her she had never hired anyone to clean for her even when she could afford it, so she would take care of everything herself, the food and the cleanup work.

Pfister then turned to Lee. "Tuck me into bed," she demanded.

He followed Pfister to her bedroom, but before long she was screaming, "Help!" At first, Nancy didn't know what to think. Then, when the screaming continued, she went to check—and found Lee standing at the doorway, looking helpless.

"I thought she—," he began. "She told me she wanted me to—," he stopped, looking embarrassed. From her bed, Pfister yelled at Nancy, telling her to "get him out of here." That scene was repeated at least ten more times that night: each time Pfister would call the man into her bedroom and they would start to make out, only for her to change her mind, screaming for Nancy to come get him out again.

She and Lee spent the rest of the night in the kitchen, where he helped her wash, dry, and put away all the dishes that had been used for the party. As they cleaned up together, he confided in Nancy, telling her how confused he was. He had sent Pfister flowers, and given her other gifts, and flown into town just to see her, because she gave him the idea she was interested in him.

Nancy tried to explain, best as she could without being disrespectful to Pfister, that her friend had a drinking problem. Lee agreed, and at 4:30 in the morning, after they finished cleaning the kitchen, Nancy showed Lee to the guest bedroom. She had made it up in advance, in case anyone was too intoxicated to drive home. By then Pfister was so soused she had been asleep for hours.

***

Sunday afternoon after skiing, Chef Nadell returned to pick up the sushi case and leftover food. Nancy recalls him handing Pfister a bill for roughly $550. But Pfister balked when she saw it, and told Jimmy that he should "write-off" his catering services as a donation to her "fundraiser." Nancy watched as they went back and forth, squabbling about the bill and Jimmy's services, when Nancy spoke up.

"He's worked his ass off. Why don't you pay the man?" she asked Pfister. In the back of her mind, she remembered that Pfister had told her about an anonymous donation of $100,000 for the party.

Still, Pfister wouldn't budge. Nancy was so embarrassed by then that she gave Jimmy $600 herself. Jimmy thanked her and left.

"That takes care of the clothes and boots I charged to your credit card," Nancy told Pfister.

***

For the next few days, Lee stayed at Pfister's chalet, while Trey and Nancy returned to Castle Rock to move more of their belongings to Aspen. When they returned after a few days, Lee felt like he could confide in Nancy. He told her that Pfister "had been out of it" for the entire time they were gone, and he was really glad they were back. He said he only came to visit because Pfister made him believe she liked him. Trey agreed to drive Lee to the airport and he tried to talk to Pfister before leaving, but she blew him off. She barely looked up from where she stood, packing her own suitcase, as Lee stood there trying to tell her goodbye. Nancy felt sorry for him.

Neither Trey nor Nancy ever heard from Lee again.

CHAPTER FOURTEEN

I LOVED HER FROM A DISTANCE

W hat the Stylers, and apparently many other people, experienced with Pfister could be summed up with three words that are found in the fifth edition of the *Diagnostic and Statistical Manual of Mental Disorders*: borderline personality disorder. Pfister's habit of befriending complete strangers, blowing hot and cold, making promises and then breaking them, turning on people in anger and making empty or even intentional threats, was not so much from the alcohol and drugs as it was from a mental illness.

In fact, Christina (Pfister) Smith, the youngest sister of the three, said Pfister's drinking problem was her way of self-medicating, trying to fix a problem she'd had since she was a teenager.

"I was afraid for my life as a child," Christina said. "I went and put myself into boarding school at age thirteen, and there was a reason I did that."

Talking to police investigators, Christina implied the reason she left home as a young teen was because of her older sister. "I skipped seventh and eighth grade and went around and found a place that could take me. She had the capacity to be a little scary."

Even after the sisters became adults, Pfister's behavior didn't change. If anything, it may have grown worse. "I've heard her yell and scream at my other sister," Christina said. "You know, use the C word, stuff like that."

Christina was so shaken by Pfister's tendency to go off on people without any warning that she sold her share of the family property and moved to Denver—and Christina had not given Pfister her home address for the last fifteen years, because "Nancy had a borderline personality disorder and she could twist up at any time and . . . I wouldn't expose myself or my children to that."

Pfister's autopsy results add weight to Christina's words: the forensic pathologist found that after death, Pfister still had traces of Ativan, commonly used to treat anxiety, and Meprobamate, which is also an antianxiety medication (as well as a sedative), in her system.

There were really three Nancys, Christina said. The one who "picks up people all the time," a habit "she's gotten away with . . . for a really long time." Then there was the Nancy who "went off on somebody . . . that was bigger and scarier than her," the one with "a horrific temper" who might antagonize someone and, if she did, "often got more than she expected in return." That behavior, Christina said, was why Pfister "drank and drugged so long . . . to medicate that."

Because that's how she was, Christina said the best she could do was give Pfister "as much time on the phone as she needed." For the last few years, the two sisters talked several times a month on the phone as Christina gave Pfister financial and investment advice because her older sister wasn't good with money or handling her own finances.

As a result, Christina said Pfister, who received "a very small stipend, to maintain the house . . . was very, very poor at doing math," so the attorney for Pfister's trust fund took over the responsibility of upkeep on the house. Pfister wasn't even told about her mother's insurance money until a few months before she was murdered, Christina said, because of Pfister's inability to hold onto her money.

So Pfister was constantly worried about her financial situation, and was even "paranoid" about the people hired to help her manage her money. She was afraid her trust fund would go dry, or she wouldn't have enough money to care for the upkeep on her house—the house Art Pfister built for his middle daughter because "of Nancy's alcoholism. And he wanted a roof over Juliana's head."

Not long before Pfister went to Australia, Christina advised her to steer clear of Richard, her Aussie playmate who Pfister met on Amtrak about a year earlier, because he wanted Pfister to invest money in some project or another. "He gave me the heebie-jeebies," Christina told Nancy. "This guy is not for real."

But money issues weren't Christina's only complaint. For years the three sisters had fought, and the younger two were estranged from the eldest, Suzanne. Christina grew worried when Pfister sent her an email saying that Suzanne was bullying her "big time. Please . . . help." Suzanne, Christina explained to police, was trying to sue Pfister "for [Pfister's] lot rights."

* * *

Then there was the third Nancy. Christina said that one "just didn't have an edit chip or anything," calling it her sister's "biggest gift and her biggest flaw . . . that was just the joy of Nancy. That was who she was."

In the interview, Christina sounded wistful, and wished they had had more time together. "I always wanted to be the [one] that would be there with her when she decided to get sober," Christina said. "I was starting to love her, but it would have taken a long, long time." But because she could "probably never trust her," Christina said she had to put a wide berth between them. "I loved her from a distance."

CHAPTER FIFTEEN
CRIME IN THE ROARING FORK VALLEY

Surrounded by the majestic Rocky Mountains on three sides and the Roaring Fork River on the fourth, Aspen sits so high in the sky it looks heavenly. Filled with aspens, those regal white trees scarred with black slashes as if from a swordfight, the tiny town named for them—with a population of less than 7,000 in 2014—is also full of scarred people. Still, it can rarely claim a murder. And yet, when they do happen, they happen in a very big way: every murder to occur there in the last several decades—including that of Nancy Pfister—has had celebrity connections. Think of famous ski racer Spider Sabich, who competed in the U.S. Olympics and the World Cup, and whose ex-girlfriend and starlet Claudine Longet (and ex-wife of famous crooner Andy Williams) shot him in the back in 1976 while he was at home in his bathroom, preparing to shower. Longet served just thirty days in jail.

Then there was the 1983 "Dr. Feelgood" murder, involving the fatal shooting of Michael Hernstadt, a rich Aspenite who loved to party. Keith Porter, who ran "Dr. Feelgood's," a shop that sold drug paraphernalia, murdered Hernstadt. Porter, a former Vietnam sniper, shot and killed him with a high-powered AR-15 rifle after the two argued and came to blows in Porter's apartment.

Not even a year later, Steve Grabow, a local drug kingpin, was blown to bits by a pipe bomb not long after he finished a tennis match

99

at the Aspen Tennis Club. His murder occurred within one month of federal agents seizing his home, cars, and $1.4 million in cash.

And what would Aspen be without momentarily housing one of the most notorious serial killers ever: Ted Bundy, who in June 1977 escaped from the second-floor window of the Pitkin County courthouse—until he was recaptured six days later. At the time, Bundy was awaiting trial in nearby Glenwood Springs for the murder of Caryn Campbell, who was kidnapped from a Snowmass ski lodge and whose body was later dumped along Owl Creek Road. Bundy's Aspen escape wasn't his last; he was returned to the Garfield County Jail, from·which he escaped again, going on the lam and murdering several more women in Florida.

Nonetheless, residents have grown accustomed to feeling secure enough that many of them leave their doors unlocked at night. But security isn't enough, because for all its ability to provide its residents with designer clothing, five-star cuisine, and multimillion-dollar homes, Aspen seems unable to supply one particular element: peace of mind.

Aspen has long been known as a hedonistic playground for the rich and famous, who come here to ski, to shop, to get away. They can stay at the St. Regis or Little Nell, where three nights of lodging costs just under $18,000 in peak season; pay $10,000 for a sixty-minute massage; or, like former president Bill Clinton did, get a $4,000 haircut. The quaint little town has locally run businesses but also high-end, Fifth Avenue shops. Shoppers can buy jewelry, a fur, a Ferrari. Perhaps not surprisingly, given Aspenites' penchant for desiring a healthier lifestyle, there is only one fast-food restaurant: McDonald's.

At the intellectual and creative end of the town's spectrum, Aspen is also home to the Aspen Institute and the Aspen Music Festival, a magnet for politicians, prominent thinkers, and musicians from around the world who are or once were child prodigies. Silicon Valley and Big Oil executives, like Enron's Kenneth Lay, and famous politicians, like former vice president Dick Cheney, come to visit but not be seen; celebrities like Miley Cyrus and Kim Kardashian choose to shop in full view of the public. Some—like Kevin Costner, Goldie Hawn and Kurt Russell, and David and Victoria Beckham—build homes and even choose to live among the locals. Many of the über-rich come to Aspen to build their second or even third homes, knocking down older $3 million dwellings to construct $15 million mansions complete with dumbwaiters, elevators, butlers, nannies, and entire paid staffs.

That's where people like Kathy Carpenter come in: the rich and famous buy their services, depending on the longtime local residents to cater to their every whim.

***

It wasn't always this way. In fact, before 1879, Aspen didn't even exist. It still wouldn't, if not for the tenacity of a small band of miners who, ignoring Governor Frederick Pitkin's pleas to leave the area, persisted in digging for silver long after he ordered them to stop. The following year, 1880, Aspen became the most productive silver-mining area in the country. However, the Panic of 1893 led to an economic collapse and the silver mines eventually closed down, leaving residents longing for another source of revenue. Given the annual record snowfalls that occur there—an average of 170 inches a year—the tiny town of Aspen, once word got out, simply had to whisper, "White is the new silver." The town had turned into a popular ski resort by the middle of the twentieth century, first attracting ski enthusiasts and later, hippies, with their accompanying cornucopia of drugs.

Buttermilk Mountain is one of the town's three internationally famous ski resorts and home to ESPN's X Games since 2002. Early founders Art and Betty Pfister had family land that helped create the famed ski area, which eventually became part of the Aspen Skiing Company.

Buttermilk Mountain looks like it would be just the place to escape to, if one were looking for a panacea of sorts. Yet even there, peace can be elusive. Nancy Pfister, the couple's wild middle daughter, seemingly enjoyed little peace. After she was murdered in 2014, even the people who truly liked her told police she had a drinking and drug problem. And it was no secret that Pfister was also at war with her trust-fund attorney: she told everyone she met he was stealing her money.

Nor did her former—and final—tenants, Trey and Nancy Styler, find peace there. The couple had practically been considered royalty in Denver's medical and horticultural circles. There, Trey, a prominent anesthesiologist, had chaired that same medical department at St. Joseph's Hospital, while Nancy, who had once been Trey's colleague, researched, lectured, and hybridized the giant Victoria water lily that hails from the Amazon. Nancy provided seeds to the world from the Victoria Conservancy, a nonprofit they founded. The Conservancy was so successful that it provided water lily seeds and plants to more than sixty botanic institutions around the word.

By the time the Stylers met Pfister in October 2013, their once grand lifestyle lay in ruins. Trey's neurological disorder, a series of bad business moves, and a nasty brush with carbon monoxide poisoning and another with Powell, Trey's corrupt Denver attorney, had just about finished them off. They were barely treading water when they moved to Aspen, after several local residents convinced them they could start over there. Trey and Nancy knew it was a gamble, but they believed the odds were in their favor, and they hoped that last-ditch course correction would allow them to recover financially.

Not long after meeting them, Pfister introduced the couple to Kathy, her friend and personal assistant. Then a full-time teller at the Aspen branch of Alpine Bank, Kathy, a single mom trying to put her only son through college, didn't have great wealth. Like many long-time residents in the nearby bedroom communities of Basalt and Carbondale, she lived in company-supplied housing and served the wealthier citizens of Aspen. No doubt she found the luxuries of the rich desirable, and people who knew both women say being Pfister's friend gave Kathy the opportunity to indulge in them.

But what Kathy lacked in assets she more than made up for in her friendliness and desire to please. However, along with the Stylers and even Pfister, Kathy too was finding peace elusive. And she had a drinking problem—but, unlike Pfister, when Kathy met the Stylers, she was trying to get sober and regularly attended Alcoholics Anonymous meetings.

***

One reason Nancy Styler was considered a suspect so quickly after Pfister's body was found was because of the animosity between the two women. Nancy tried to keep quiet about her negative feelings, but when

Pfister began defaming her and Trey on Facebook, Nancy was more vocal with her own views about Pfister. But something she said about her landlord—an everyday, common phrase most people say in a variety of situations without ever meaning it—did pique police interest.

"I said I'd like to kill her," Nancy Styler admitted to police on February 27, when they asked her about her feelings concerning Pfister. However, Merlin Broughton, the local electrician who had harbored a crush on Pfister in eighth grade, who often helped her get home safely after she'd been on a long bender, and who had also helped the Stylers during their stay in Pfister's home, defended Nancy, saying that's not what Nancy meant. "She said she hated [Pfister], not that she had a hatred for the woman but she hated all of the things that she had put [her] through," Merlin told investigators Zamora and Miller.

As it turns out, the list of people who said those very same words— that they hated or wanted to kill Pfister—was very long. Is it possible one of them actually did loathe the woman herself, rather than her behavior? Many people told police that Pfister's irresponsible, flighty ways caused them to give vent to the same feelings Nancy expressed. So many people, in fact, said they "could kill Pfister" that it would have taken police several weeks to interview everyone who made such a comment—which meant they wouldn't have arrested anyone for her murder until at least early April.

Whether the collective words were simply spoken from a place of frustration or true hatred, accompanied by an intention to make good on such a threat, eventually, in February 2014, one of those people carried it out. Was it someone she knew? Someone who voiced the same words Nancy Styler did? Or was it perhaps a professional killer, hired by the person (or persons) who had millions to gain—or lose, depending on the outcome of the February 28 property sale Pfister was so worried about? Was it one of her many ex-beaus, some of whom threatened her at one time or another? Or was it, as police and the district attorney's office have maintained since March 2014, a conspiracy between the Stylers and Kathy?

CHAPTER SIXTEEN
PLEASE COME TO BOSTON

Back in Room 122 Thursday night, Nancy was trying remain as stoic as she had throughout the entire day. Although she was determined to believe the entire surreal experience was just "normal" police questioning, the minute she unlocked the door to Room 122, Nancy lost it.

The room looked like it had been ransacked, thanks to the officers who served the search warrant at 5:30 a.m. "What is wrong with them?" Nancy yelled. "Do they honestly believe we're criminals? How on earth could they ever think we would murder someone? Don't they know we called *them* for help, so we wouldn't have any problems with her? Are they crazy?"

"Well it is a small town and the Pfister name does hold sway here," Trey replied.

"And we don't even have any money to buy dinner, or food to eat," she said, suddenly at the mercy of her growling stomach and the tears she'd bottled up all day long. "You'd think they could have left us a little money, for crying out loud. They must think we're going to run off into the night—like we have anywhere to go! Look at what they've done to all our things, to my clothes and makeup and—," she couldn't even finish, gesturing at the disaster the officers had made of her carefully organized belongings. By then, Nancy was sobbing.

***

Cindy McDaniel was 2,000 miles away in Boston when her cell rang at 10:30 p.m. that night. She had just fallen asleep when she realized her nephew, Daniel, was calling. He knew Cindy's early morning work schedule meant she went to bed early, so the late-night call immediately worried her. There was only one reason he would call that late.

Oh, my God, it's happened. This is the phone call I have been dreading.

For years Cindy had harbored a silent fear, one she never shared with her sister: Trey was going to kill her sister and then himself. Cindy and Daniel did discuss it. "Do you think your father has ever physically abused your mother?" she had asked her nephew a few years ago.

"Not that I'm aware of," Daniel said, "but he is controlling, and that's a form of abuse. And you already know about his temper." Daniel and Cindy discussed the way Trey had so ingratiated himself into Nancy's life that she couldn't function on her own anymore.

"She won't even drive herself places, and he has to always be with her, whatever she does," Cindy said.

Daniel thought a moment. "Of course, she would say she hates to drive, and enjoys having him chauffeur her around. And he doesn't exactly join her; he just waits in the car until she's finished. Then he brings her home."

"Yeah, he's been doing that for years," Cindy agreed.

* * *

The first time Cindy saw her brother-in-law's temper was in Denver in 1990. Trey was installing a big-screen TV in the family room, but to make it fit, he had to knock out a wall in their garage. He was moving the woodpile stacked inside the garage for their fireplace when he dropped a piece of wood on his foot.

Cindy remembered that incident clearly. "It involved a hammer," she said. "He swore and flung the hammer and it went right through the drywall in the garage." Daniel, then nine, was nearby and watched it happen: he was terrified.

She quickly went over and bent down to the little boy. "It's hot out," she said, anxious to reassure him. "Daddy's having a bad day."

That was the only physical outburst she recalled seeing, but other episodes of verbal anger occurred more often. Cindy saw those because, prior to her 1987 graduation, she lived with them for three years during her college years. Daniel had bad allergies and once Trey asked her to "bring home some Dimetapp." When Cindy bought the generic brand, Trey "flipped out."

Then there was their visit to Disneyland. They were en route to the amusement park as Nancy tried to help Trey navigate through the heavy city traffic. She told him to take a left when it should have been a right, and "Trey was all crazy about it," Cindy said, "screaming, 'Jesus Christ, Nance, can't you read a fucking road map!'"

Nancy tried to make light of Trey's frequent rants, but Cindy insisted "there was no downplaying it."

So while Trey was never physically violent toward her sister, Cindy believed he was possessive, and for a long time she feared he was the type of man who, if he couldn't have Nancy, wouldn't want anyone else to have her, either. Which is why, when Trey came up with his famous October 2013 suicide plan, supposedly designed to help make Nancy's future secure, *both* Nancy's sister and her son couldn't help thinking that he would take Nancy with him—and so Cindy kept wondering when she would get *the* phone call.

***

When she answered Daniel's 10:30 p.m. call, he could hear the distress in her voice.

"They're both okay but—," were Daniel's first words. "The woman they're renting the house from was found dead."

"Oh, thank God," Cindy said, feeling like her heart was going to burst from relief. Then she realized what she'd said. "Oh, my God, I didn't mean that," Cindy said. "Was it an accident?"

"No, she was found dead in the house."

Cindy's first thought was the same one Nancy had, when no one could find Pfister, because her sister had told her about the drinking and drugs: *She overdosed.*

"They were brought in for questioning," Daniel continued.

"Have they been released?"

"Yes."

"Where are they?" Cindy asked. Daniel gave her the name and number of the motel, but he didn't know their room number.

***

Back in Basalt, Nancy was making sandwiches for her and Trey. After getting her crying under control, she went to the front desk and asked Lucia, the night clerk, if there was anything left from the motel's continental breakfast that they could have for dinner.

"We're the criminals in Room 122," she tried to joke, hoping if she made light of it all she'd feel better. Her entire family—she, her sister, her mother, Daniel—all had that dark sense of humor. It was a family trait.

She told Lucia that the police took everything, including their money. "We have no credit cards, no cash, and no food."

Lucia was sympathetic but said there wasn't anything left. Then she offered to go to the convenience store next door and get some foodstuffs for them. When she returned with a bagful of snacks and sandwich ingredients, Nancy was overwhelmed with emotion. She hugged Lucia tightly. "You're my angel," Nancy said. "Would I be allowed to make a quick call to Boston to tell my family what's happening?" Lucia let her use the phone and Nancy dialed her mother's number.

When her mother, Tess, answered the phone, Nancy broke down and started crying. She tried to explain everything, but it was difficult and she didn't want to take advantage of the motel so she didn't talk long. Back in the room, as she gave Trey his sandwich, Nancy felt her tears well up again. She was trying to eat her own sandwich when the phone rang.

When Nancy answered, Cindy could tell: it was obvious her sister had been crying. "Hey Nance, what's going on out there?" Cindy asked.

"I don't know. They found a body and—," Nancy said. "How did you know to call and on the motel line?"

"Daniel called me," Cindy said.

Nancy began explaining, or trying to explain, and Cindy said it sounded like "she knew but she didn't really" know what happened. Nancy knew Pfister was dead, Cindy could tell that by her sister's words and confused tone of voice, but that was all. Cindy couldn't help herself, and she began laughing. The entire idea of the police thinking they might be murderers was just so foreign to her, so bizarre—so preposterous! Then she heard Trey in the background. "Just hang up," he ordered.

"Stop, I need this!" Nancy yelled back at him.

Cindy began pelting Nancy with questions. But her sister had very few answers. In the middle of it all, Nancy cut Cindy off, telling her everything she and Trey had gone through—the police busting into their room at 5:30 a.m., the naked photos during the frigid morning air, the baggy orange jail outfits and clown shoes, everything.

"They think we had something to do with this, Cindy," she said. "I know they do."

"Nancy, none of this makes any sense. Of course they questioned you. They should; you lived in the house. They don't know you," Cindy told her.

"I don't know," Nancy said, sounding uncertain.

"I mean, I've seen you get pissed off, but I've never even seen you lose your cool, let alone kill anyone," Cindy said, trying to reason with her. "Look, is there anything online about it? I'll bet there isn't. It can't be that big a deal."

"How would I know? They took Trey's computer. But I looked on TV and didn't see anything there."

"Hold on a minute," Cindy said, putting down the phone so she could get online. After a brief pause, she picked up her cell. "Hey Nancy, they towed the Jag."

"No, they didn't," Nancy insisted, walking over to the window. She opened the curtain and that's when she knew: they did tow the Jag! And she saw the police car parked not far from their room.

"Trey, they towed the Jag," Nancy said, sounding deflated. "And they're watching our room." She told Cindy about the two officers sitting inside the police vehicle.

"Look, Nancy, I think they're going to find out she overdosed. It's going to be okay. This is just ridiculous." Cindy felt like she had just tumbled two steps backwards, after convincing Nancy it was nothing to worry about. "You know what, Nancy? If you go to jail, you'll make a good prison wife because you make such a nice bed."

The dark joke broke the tension enough and they both laughed.

They talked for several more minutes, until Cindy was certain she had convinced Nancy there was no way the police were looking just at them—they were only two of the many people they had probably done that same thing to, in their quest to find the real killer, so the Stylers could be ruled out as suspects.

"The Aspen police can't honestly believe that a couple of doctors in their sixties would do this," Cindy said, finally getting through to Nancy.

"Yeah, especially when they're as crippled as we are," Nancy said with dry humor.

It was the first time since Daniel had called her an hour earlier that Cindy actually felt like everything was going to be okay. When she hung up from talking to Nancy, she called her closest friend, Donna.

After describing everything that had happened out in Colorado, Donna spoke up.

"That sounds terrible," she said. "And you know your sister better than anyone, so I know you're right. No way did she have anything to do with that woman's death."

Cindy and Donna chatted some more, and the conversation ended with an inherent truth about her sister. "She couldn't do it. It's not in her DNA," she said. "Besides, there was never a second of violence in our family."

CHAPTER SEVENTEEN

YOU'RE BULLETPROOF. YOU'VE GOT THIS.

After talking to her sister, Nancy reached out to someone a little closer: one of her new friends in Aspen. When she dialed Kathy Carpenter's friend Susan Waskow's cell number, though, Susan didn't answer. In her message, Nancy explained in great detail the long and grueling ordeal she had gone through at the hands of police:

"Susan, this is Nancy. We spent all day, we got busted in on in our room at 5:30 in the morning with Pitkin County sheriffs and the Colorado Bureau of Investigation telling us that there was a body at, found at [Pfister's] house. And they stripped us, handcuffed us, took pictures of us naked in every position, and took us down and we spent thirteen hours at the courthouse today. We were out in prison clothes and they were dragging us around Aspen in orange jumpsuits, orange prison garb. They took all of our computers, they took all of our phones, they took our money, and we are in this motel room at the Aspenalt, and boy, did your son [get it right]. We don't know what happened to [Pfister], they haven't told us anything about what happened, and I guess they haven't released it to the press.

"And at first we didn't know if it was Kathy or [Pfister], they wouldn't tell us. And when finally it came out to be that [Pfister] was dead, but they had Trey as the prime suspect, so they hunted down the Jaguar, they busted into the room and they questioned me for, I don't know what time we got down there, but I got done about 5:30. And we left, they busted in at 5:30 in the morning, so I don't know how long it took to get down there. But anyway, give me a call. We're at the Aspenalt Lodge. My number is 970-927-3191 and we're in Room 122. Like I said, we have no phones, no iPads, nothing to communicate with except this phone, so gimme a call. Love you. Bye."

***

Nancy's message was two minutes long and it was 8:46 p.m. when she finished leaving it for Susan. What she couldn't know at that moment was that Cindy had been wrong. The actions of the Pitkin County Sheriff's Office, with some assistance from the Aspen police and CBI, had ensured that the town's residents were now thoroughly frightened by the Stylers. Many people, even people who knew them well, as it later turned out, were duped into believing that Trey and Nancy were hardened killers. But Nancy didn't know that then, and when Susan returned her call, Nancy just attributed the dismay she heard in her friend's voice as peculiar to Susan.

In particular, Susan stated her son Sam had never said "that." Nancy wasn't surprised, though; she knew Susan's memory was unreliable. *Her cognitive difficulties from the car wreck probably make this a challenge.* But Nancy remembered clearly the day she, Kathy, and Susan had gone to lunch together in Glenwood Springs not long before Pfister flew home.

"My son Sam said if anything goes wrong with Pfister's place she will blame it on you," Nancy said Susan had told her and Kathy.

But the evening of February 27, Susan sounded afraid. "I don't know what you're talking about," she said. Then she hung up without saying goodbye.

Nancy tried not to let the fear she heard at the other end of the receiver upset her; it was Susan, after all. She tried to give others the benefit of the doubt, and she didn't plan to stop doing that now. *If I'm wrong, I guess I'll know when we go out in public.* The thought made her smile wryly.

Nancy's level of concern may have been much higher had she witnessed the scene playing out eighteen miles away in Aspen. She no longer would have wondered why the officers who busted into their room that morning had dressed them in orange, as if they already were inmates.

* * *

Sheriff Joe DiSalvo had already purchased four big bottles of liquor, which he planned to take to the office to commemorate the team's quick work. All he had to do was wait for Pitkin County District Judge Gail Nichols to sign the arrest warrant that would let his deputies transport the Stylers not back to their motel room, but to jail. However, DiSalvo's celebration plans were a bit premature: Nichols, known as a "fair, but pretty conservative" judge, refused to sign the warrant.

Instead, the Stylers were released and taken back to their motel. At 8 p.m. Thursday night, though, Judge Nichols did agree there was good cause to sign a warrant allowing police to search the Stylers' two newly rented storage units in Basalt. Deputy Jahnke and two other officers opened the units and, based on the contents inside, verified they belonged to Trey and Nancy. But the units were too large to search with just three men, so they returned to Aspen empty-handed.

* * *

The Aspen-Pitkin County Airport is twelve miles southwest of Snowmass, where Pfister had lived at 1833 West Buttermilk. Juliana Pfister's plane probably flew right over her mother's home Thursday night. Given the family tragedy, coming home must have been difficult for the young woman, but since her maternal grandmother, Betty, had been not only an aviation mechanic and a flight attendant but also a WWII aviator who later raced Galloping Gertie, her little P-39 fighter plane, all around the country, she must have felt a sense of pride when she thought of her family's heritage.

Nothing could make up for the huge loss of her mother, with whom she was trying to rebuild a relationship that hadn't existed since she was a little girl. Juliana wasn't sure what it was that her mom lacked— sometimes she thought she "had too many genes"; other times, too few. Juliana had been resentful for years and still struggled to understand her mother. In spite of her loss, Juliana, or "Jules" to her loved ones, had only one thought: she had to call Joe DiSalvo, or Joey, as her mom called the sheriff.

Jules had to wait hours longer than she wanted to before she could make that call. There was a snowstorm, so her plane was forced to return to Grand Junction to refuel. Instead of landing at 5:30 p.m., her flight arrived two hours late. Her godparents, Patti and George Stranahan, endured the same two-hour wait, but at the airport where they went to pick up Jules. During the delay, Patti was shocked when Kathy Carpenter approached her from behind. Patti turned around to find Kathy with Gabe, Pfister's dog. At first Patti didn't know what to say; Kathy was so emotionally exhausted she "looked like she was a hundred years old," and it was clear to Patti that Kathy was heavily medicated. She could only worry about why Kathy was there—had she somehow learned about Jules' flight? *The last thing I need is more chaos for Jules.*

"What are you doing here?" Patti asked.

"We came to get my son. Michael's flight gets in at nine," Kathy said. "I'm here with my mother. We're picking him up."

"Oh, where's your mother?" Patti asked, more to determine if Kathy was being up front with her than anything else. But Kathy introduced her to Chris and then mother and daughter sat down next to the Stranahans to wait. Suddenly, Kathy began sobbing, telling Patti that the police wouldn't let her go home the night before, since "they know where I live."

"Who?" Patti asked.

Kathy told her "the Stylers. I know they did it. I know they did it."

Patti was confused. "I thought you said they took good care of the dog."

"Yeah," she said, still crying, "but later they hated her." Kathy went on to tell Patti how bad Trey Styler's temper was, and how his wife had said Kathy should let Trey get Pfister from the airport on February 22, because "she'll never make it home."

Patti had trouble following Kathy's logic. It all sounded "weird" to her, and she chocked it up to the medicine Kathy was taking. But she also knew how someone could "get exasperated with some of [Pfister's] demands." Even though she had never met the Stylers, Patti knew

Pfister well enough to believe they simply spoke in anger—without any serious intentions to harm Pfister.

***

By the time Juliana reached her Carbondale bedroom, tucked away in the lovely Stranahan home, she was exhausted. She'd spent the last eighteen months in Mexico, and had flown from a remote area to arrive back home for her mother's funeral. And she desperately longed to talk to Joe, but he hadn't been in when she called.

Back at his office, the sheriff returned her call the minute he saw her message. After sharing details of the case with her, such as why the Stylers hadn't been arrested yet, and why she couldn't see her mother's body, DiSalvo swore her to secrecy. He said she couldn't tell another soul. "Jules, I'm so fuckin' sorry," he said. "I have to go to your mom's funeral and watch these people [the Stylers]," he said, crying.

Then DiSalvo explained why he was so upset. "We took it to the judge and I had already bought four bottles of whiskey for everyone to celebrate because we've been all working our fucking faces off and," DiSalvo stopped, crying some more, "she didn't sign. She needs more forensic evidence."

Juliana tried to reassure him it would work out. Then she said she wanted to see her mother's body. DiSalvo told her she couldn't. He tried to soften the blow, saying she didn't want to see her mother like that. By then they were both crying, and the topic came back around to the Stylers.

"It might be a day, it might be a week, it might be a month, and it might be never, you know," Joe said. "They're free to fucking go."

More than anything, Juliana wanted her mother's killer or killers, to be arrested—whoever did it. She knew Joe would make sure they were. She also knew how much support he had in the community. Everyone loved him. "You're bulletproof. You've got this," she said. "Make the arrest."

***

At no point during the investigation did Juliana Pfister say or do any-thing that could have stopped or affected the sheriff's actions. Those wheels were turning before she even knew her mother was dead. Nor did she make any decisions that would have impacted the outcome of the investigation.

No, not at all. Juliana had just lost a parent and had been plunged into the same media shit-storm as Daniel, the Stylers' adult son. Like him, she was just a grieving child.

CHAPTER EIGHTEEN

LEGAL HELP ARRIVES FROM DENVER

That same Thursday evening found Daniel Styler sitting back and shaking his head. How had his parents gotten themselves embroiled in such a terrible situation? He wanted to hope their daylong interrogation was the normal way the Pitkin County Sheriff's Office conducted business, and there were several people being treated likewise at the same time as his parents—but he was too much of a pragmatist. And ever since his mother's phone call earlier that day, Daniel kept envisioning the worst-case scenarios.

Daniel Styler felt like he was born an adult; as an only child, his "playmates" were all over the age of twenty-five—primarily, his nanny, his parents, and his godparents. He was a precocious child, but not one who needed a great deal of discipline. His intellectual qualities weren't only what made him feel so grown up: it was his life experience, coupled with his emotional maturity. By the age of eleven, he was traveling the Amazon rainforest in Brazil with his parents, and by the time he was a teenager, he was more serious and introspective and, some would say, cautious, than either of his parents.

"I was the more boring of the three of us," Daniel said, summing up his self-analysis.

Being that responsible meant Daniel couldn't just sit still in his Denver apartment after his mother called him during her interrogation with police. He immediately began making phone calls and not long after, Daniel got a referral from a family friend for a high-powered defense attorney in Denver. Lisa Wayne had worked on many a complicated case, and Daniel felt confident she would do a good job. He felt he could trust her, which was good, given that after the John Powell affair, he'd lost all trust in any attorney. Even more important, Wayne agreed to take the case. No, she agreed with Daniel, they had not been charged with any crime—yet—but she felt his prudence and forward thinking were wise. She was also quite clear: she could only represent one of his parents, as it would be a conflict of interest if they were both ultimately charged with murder. In the meantime, she would advise them both, and be a few steps ahead.

Daniel, who had $1,200 to his name, set about trying to come up with her $35,000 retainer fee. Being charged with a capital crime in Colorado wasn't cheap and since he was still just a college "kid," he didn't have access to that kind of money. Neither did his godparents, as it turned out. He wouldn't ask any of his dad's former colleagues, either—even though Trey implored him to. Daniel couldn't bring himself to do so, for although they had access, the long and nasty lawsuit against his former employer, with Powell at the helm, had ostracized them all.

After several hours of reflecting on his mom's words and analyzing the situation from every possible angle, Daniel took a breather that evening, dabbling on his iPad while binge watching the sitcom comedy *Scrubs* on Netflix. It was the one sure way he could relax and take his mind off his parents.

***

Back in Boston on Friday morning, Cindy couldn't stop thinking about her sister. *This is ridiculous. Nancy's in a motel in Basalt, Colorado. She has no money, no cards, nothing.* Just thinking about Nancy's predicament made Cindy feel like she was dying inside.

Born fourteen years apart, Cindy became Nancy's living baby doll, and Nancy has said that she wanted to take care of her sister so much that she and her mother would have friendly arguments over who cared more for the infant. But Nancy went away to college in Boston when Cindy was still quite young and yet, "we've always been very close,"

Cindy said. They could go without talking for a while, but there still would be no distance between them.

"We have a very similar soul . . . like twins," Cindy said. "I know what she's thinking, if she would like a certain kind of food, because I would like it, too." And even when she and Nancy weren't physically close, "we're emotionally close. We've always had a connection. It's wonderful."

***

When Cindy tried to tell their mother, a retired social worker, what had happened, it didn't compute, even though Nancy had tried to explain the night before. "What are you talking about?" Tess McDaniel asked her daughter. So Cindy did a quick run-through of the previous day's events: Nancy and Trey had been questioned. Naturally, since they lived in the house where the dead woman was found. So it makes sense, she told her mom, not wanting to alarm her.

"Let's keep close tabs on her. If she calls collect, this is the number," Cindy wrote it down.

Throughout the weekend, Tess did call Nancy a couple of times. "My poor baby," she told Cindy, clearly worried about Nancy. "She's got no way to eat. She's hungry. How can we get money to her?"

Cindy tried to make light of the situation. "Well, Mom, if she gets up early enough, the motel has a free continental breakfast." She knew they could wire money, but since it was the weekend and banks were closed, that made it more difficult. Even if they wired money from Walmart, Nancy had no means of transportation to get it. Besides, the closest Walmart was in Glenwood Springs.

When Tess learned how Lucia, the motel clerk, had gone to get Nancy and Trey food, she called the motel to thank her.

"I never in my wildest dreams thought it was going to go any further than that," Cindy said.

***

Lisa Wayne immediately went to work on the case. Friday morning, on February 28, she called the sheriff's office, but no one would tell her anything about the investigation. Next, she called the Stylers, speaking to them repeatedly throughout the day. Finally, she called David Olmsted, a private investigator in Aspen she often worked with, and asked him to meet with the Stylers the following day. They were expecting his call, which came early the next morning.

When Olmsted arrived at the Aspenalt Lodge, it was about 10 a.m. By then, the police had already taken Nancy to the Basalt Police Department to be fingerprinted and returned her to the motel afterward. Nancy didn't have to think twice about the request. "I knew I hadn't done anything, and so it would only help to clear me," she later said.

Olmsted had been a private investigator since 1981, but he only worked for the defense. He had even investigated cases throughout the country and in foreign countries, and he was considered an expert witness in criminal investigations. That made him a great addition to the Stylers' team.

The first thing Olmsted noticed that first day of March was a sheriff's deputy sitting outside the Stylers' room in her police car. He introduced himself, told her that Ms. Wayne was representing the Stylers, and said he was there to meet with them. When Trey and Nancy let him inside their room, he looked around. It was small, with simple furnishings, and two double beds were piled high with personal belongings. In addition to clothes, Olmsted saw piles of paperwork. The physical chaos was immediately familiar to him: it was how a room usually appeared in the aftermath of a police search.

Later, Olmsted said Nancy was less concerned about the investigation—and much more worried about Trey's physical condition. Olmsted watched Trey closely. He spent almost the entire time Olmsted was there in bed, but he willingly took part in the discussion. He noticed several prescription pill bottles on the bedside table, prompting Trey to explain his health condition.

Olmsted got a better look at Trey when Nancy was searching for paperwork she wanted to show Olmsted. "Trey, can you help me?" she asked.

The PI watched Trey try to maneuver the few feet from the bed to the pile of files on the second bed. It was "very difficult for him to get out of bed and move himself," and it took several long minutes, Olmsted later said.

The Stylers told him about their relationship with Pfister and, equally important, what had happened during their arrest on Thursday.

"They said we weren't under arrest," Nancy said.

Olmsted smiled. "Yes, you were." Then he explained how the police's actions—locking them up, searching them, and taking them in for questioning—met the definition of an arrest by the legal system.

When Nancy told Olmsted about being photographed in the nude in front of several male officers, Olmsted admitted at first he "was a little suspicious that it really happened that way."

But when he later learned Nancy hadn't exaggerated, he was quite troubled by what had happened to her. "I was a cop for ten years, and . . . I've never seen that happen before. There were no women there [when the photos first began being taken]," Olmsted said. "And we've arrested women who needed to be strip-searched for some reason, but you take a female officer and [have her do it. Besides that], they wouldn't let [Nancy] go to the bathroom for half an hour, forty-five minutes. I don't think they should have done that," he added.

As a private investigator, Olmsted was used to seeing criminal suspects who were defensive, but the trauma from the inappropriate photo shoot explained why Nancy was so "animated, garrulous, and clearly anxious," as he described her, when she explained all that she and Trey had endured at the hands of the police.

By the time he left Room 122 six hours later, Olmsted was certain neither Trey nor Nancy had anything to do with Pfister's murder. He was more concerned about their mental state. "They were very scared, very confused, and disbelieving about their situation," Olmsted said, "but also very confident they would be exonerated."

He called the Stylers several times on Sunday, mostly just assuring them that he and Wayne were monitoring their situation and had everything under control. Nancy, especially, was very grateful for his help, and thanked him repeatedly.

CHAPTER NINETEEN

LEADING PATRICK CARNEY

After learning that Pfister had been murdered, several Aspen residents tried to do their civic duty. Patrick Carney was one of them. He heard that his friend Pfister was murdered not long after Kathy called 911. Patrick, in turn, called police, saying he had information that might help. An officer scheduled a time to take Patrick's statement, and CBI Agent John Zamora and DA investigator Lisa Miller conducted the interview.

During that interview, Patrick told police that Pfister had left him a message at 2:30 a.m. Monday, February 24, 2014, asking for a ride later that day. Because he was hospitalized for a shattered collarbone, Patrick didn't get back to Pfister right away. He tried to contact her Monday night.

"I sent her a text message saying I'm not going to make it. I got hurt, I'm in the hospital," Patrick told Miller and Zamora.

However, when Garfield County Sheriff's Deputy Lee Damuth used forensic software to pull all the data from Pfister's cell phone, the only call it showed between Pfister and Patrick occurred at 10:17 a.m. Sunday, when she called him. And Damuth's report didn't show any text messages between the two.

Part of the problem with Patrick's entire police statement was his memory, which was affected by his surgery. Doctors put in fourteen pins and two metal plates, and he was taking very strong painkillers.

Another problem was how Zamora and Miller conducted the interview. As with all the witnesses they spoke to, there were many times throughout when a witness, as happened to Patrick, was cut off. Or a witness cut off the interviewer.

When he hadn't heard back from Pfister by Tuesday, Patrick said, he got his car from the Snowmass parking lot so it wouldn't be towed, then went to Pfister's house to see her. But she wasn't there.

"What time Tuesday?" Zamora asked.

"I want to say one in the afternoon, but I—," Patrick began, before Zamora cut him off.

"Okay."

Patrick finished his sentence. "But don't quote me. I shouldn't have been driving. I'd had way too much hydrocodone at that point."

He continued, telling the two investigators that when he arrived, two Latino workers were loading a U-Haul, and Nancy Styler came out from Pfister's poolroom, which was the first room you enter from the front door. "But she came out, and I said, 'Is [Pfister] here,' and she's like, 'No, she isn't,'" Patrick said. "I said, 'Do you know where she is, I was supposed to meet her.'"

According to Patrick, Nancy Styler just told him Pfister wasn't home—but then he contradicted himself.

After asking where Pfister was, Patrick said Nancy replied: "[W]ell, we had some problems. I asked her to stay upstairs while we were packing, and you know how [Pfister] is, that was a problem, and I haven't seen her."

At that point, Zamora asked Patrick to repeat what he said. "So you said, 'Have you seen Nancy,'" Zamora said.

"I just said, 'Is Nancy here,'" Patrick replied.

"Okay, is she there," Zamora agreed.

Patrick replied, "That's, this is my recollection."

Zamora repeats what Patrick told him. "'Is Nancy here?' She's like, 'No, don't know where [Pfister] is.'"

Patrick continued, contradicting himself again and going back to his first story. "'I haven't seen her,' Nancy said, and then she said, 'Her car is sitting here, I don't know where she is.'"

It's entirely possible that the problem Nancy Styler alluded to, but that Patrick can't fully recall, was the rental dispute, and how bad she and Trey felt Pfister had treated them. That makes sense, given that

Nancy and Trey on their wedding day, February 21, 1982. Trey said it was the happiest day of his life.

Nancy in the Amazon in 2000 with the first and second night flowers of *Victoria amazonica.*

The Styler's 6583 East Ida home in Greenwood Village near Denver was valued at $2.2 million, before they were forced to sell it for $840,000.

Nancy (middle); her sister, Cindy (right); and Donna (left), a friend, after spending a day together building a pond in August 2015.

Pfister's bedroom the morning she left for Australia.

Pfister's bedroom closet and the scene Kathy Carpenter found when she unlocked the door on Wednesday, February 26, 2014.

Pfister's bedroom the day Kathy Carpenter found her friend's body, February 26, 2014.

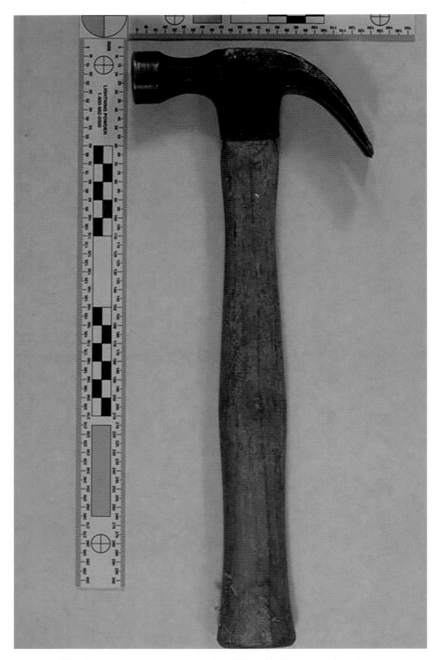

The hammer used to murder Pfister, discovered Friday,
February 28, 2014, by a city employee in a Basalt trash bin near
Alpine Bank and the Aspenalt Motel.

they were in the process of moving out when Patrick arrived and he may have asked them why they were leaving.

At that point in the interview, Zamora seemed to have taken Patrick's words out of context. And once again, Zamora ignored the fact that Patrick had already told him twice that Nancy Styler said she had not seen Pfister. Instead, Zamora honed in on Patrick's contradictions, as if that were the real story, the story the police believed.

"So when she first says, 'I don't know,' but then she says, 'Okay, we have a problem so we asked [Pfister] . . . to stay upstairs,'" Zamora continued.

Patrick agreed: "'To stay upstairs.' So I went up the stairs," Patrick said, "but she was never there. At least, I never saw her. You know, I went to the stairs, and she said she didn't know where [Pfister] was."

By then, Patrick had told Zamora and Miller three different times that Nancy said she didn't know where Pfister was. But Zamora completely ignored that part. "And when you went upstairs, where did you go?" he asked Patrick.

"I just went to the top of the stairs. I looked around," Patrick said. "To be honest with you . . . they were packing all this stuff and there are two really expensive paintings . . . by Zuniga and Dunn, and I looked to see if they were still there."

Apparently the idea that the Stylers might have been stealing Pfister's art caused Patrick to momentarily forget about his friend. Or it could have been the painkillers he was on that caused his obvious distraction.

"Ah, were they?" Zamora asked.

"They were."

"So what did you see, when you got upstairs?"

Patrick said he saw nothing. "It was completely empty, to be honest with you. There wasn't any personal stuff around at all."

Zamora, who apparently had not been inside Pfister's home, asked Patrick about the layout of the house. Patrick told him there was an island, a fireplace, a kitchen area, a living room, and "a big, ugly plant [which was] still alive; I was surprised. It looked kind of dead," but it wasn't. "I didn't go into her bedroom or anything," Patrick said.

"Could you see her bedroom from—," Zamora began, before Patrick cut him off.

"You can't see—," Patrick said, until Zamora cut him off.

"That area?" Zamora asked.

"—her bedroom," Patrick finished.

He explained why. "You can see down the hallway, and then it's back to the right. But I never even went down. I never looked. I never got to the top of the stairs. I was like right at the top of the stairs, but I never left and went into the living room."

Zamora asked if Patrick saw anything odd, and Patrick said, "Not really." Zamora seemed to take this at face value, and didn't press Patrick by asking follow-up questions.

"Did you call for her?"

Patrick wasn't sure. "I may have said 'Nancy,' but I tried calling her [from his cell] multiple times and left messages and made multiple phone calls, but I didn't, you know—," Patrick stopped.

He continued, saying he left Pfister's then. "I went outside, flipped the ball . . . with Gabe a few times, and then drove back out of the driveway." The next thing he knew, on Thursday night, a mutual acquaintance in Florida called, telling him Pfister was dead.

Patrick told the investigators about the weekly dinners he and Pfister had at L'Hostaria, and how they hung out together.

"Who paid?" Zamora asked.

"I did . . . Nancy never stuck her hand in her pocket if her life depended on it," Patrick replied.

What he didn't tell Zamora and Miller was that he was sometimes jealous when other men interacted with Pfister; witnesses for the defense spoke about Patrick's "jealous possessiveness" when they saw him in public with her.

Zamora then asked Patrick to tell them about Pfister.

"[She's] a little nuts," he said. "She smoked way too much dope. She drank Champagne from the minute she woke up in the morning until she passed out at night."

But in spite of that, Patrick said, "she was friendly, nice, sweet; never hurt a soul."

"I heard she could be kind of tough," Zamora said, "get on people's nerves if she wanted to, push buttons . . . "

Patrick agreed. "I'm sure she could." But he said she didn't do that with him. "She was apologetic . . . because if she'd get too drunk or something and say something that I thought was inappropriate, I'd say, 'That's out of line, Nancy. You can't talk like that.'"

Zamora asked "who her go-to person was," and Patrick said it was Kathy.

"Her number one person . . . I think they used to drink a lot together, and then Kathy stopped drinking." Patrick said he didn't really know Kathy; she was just a teller at his bank.

Continuing the questioning, Zamora asked Patrick if he and Pfister had a sexual relationship.

"No," Patrick said. "[Pfister] had genital herpes and I told her that was someplace I couldn't go."

For the first time in the interview, investigator Miller spoke up, asking Patrick if that was "a deal-breaker." He said, "Yes." Then he said Pfister had sex with men who didn't know that. "She's not great to tell anybody that," Patrick said. "Even complete strangers."

One would think that fact would have been important to objective, open-minded investigators who were trying to find out how large their suspect pool was. But for some reason, it was a mere footnote in the interview, and neither Miller nor Zamora thought it was important enough to discuss further. Apparently, the idea that one of those "complete strangers" would have killed Pfister didn't even cross their minds. Instead, the discussion focused on whether Pfister was a "sloppy drunk" or a "crying drunk? Like a lot of women?" Miller asked.

"No," Patrick said, "[she] couldn't talk anymore," and needed someone to drive her home and tuck her into bed.

The questioning turned to drugs next, when Zamora asked Patrick if Pfister took any medication.

"I think she took everything. She had every joint in her, every part of her hurt, and she was taking all kinds of medicine," he said. "I couldn't tell you what they were." Pfister had a lot of physical pain "broken ankles . . . and [a] screwed-up wrist," so she regularly took pain medicine, Patrick added.

Even though they were confronted with someone who drank and popped pain pills as much as Pfister did, they didn't ask Patrick any other questions that could also tell them about their suspect pool. Questions such as: did she get the pills legally or illegally? If so, who was her dealer? Did she sell any of them? If so, to whom?

Zamora picked up the interview thread by asking if Pfister had problems with anyone.

Patrick says yes. "Only her sister [Suzanne] for the road. Her sister who has the house up above," he said. "There's the road that splits and goes below . . . The sister wanted to have that become a right-of-way and they were in court and they had a mediator because they were trying, because [Pfister] thought that would devalue her land."

Patrick explained that Pfister told him it was her father's idea of a joke, to give each sister forty acres and a horse when they turned twenty-one, "but . . . they didn't speak to each other at all." He said he'd never met Suzanne, and he didn't know anyone else Pfister had problems with—except for her tenants. Pfister had emailed Patrick in early January, telling him "she hadn't gotten paid." He told her to call her lawyer, "Have 'em evicted."

Then Patrick told police what Pfister told him: "From the first day they didn't pay money."

He told Miller and Zamora that both Nancys were very nice, but he didn't really know Trey. Whenever he was around, "the other Nancy was cleaning things."

Before long, the interview went back to what happened on Tuesday when Patrick went to Pfister's house. Zamora asked if Nancy and Trey greeted him.

"It was, 'Oh, hi,' and I mean that was it," Patrick said, adding that Trey "said 'hello,' turned around, and walked away."

Although the investigators didn't ask, it didn't appear from what Patrick said that either Nancy or Trey tried to go out of their way to keep him out of the house, and they didn't try to make a lot of small talk to divert him.

Patrick said he asked, "Where's Nancy?"

Zamora asked if he was worried.

"No," Patrick said, because he "thought [she] lost her phone. Or it's dead."

"Did you have any concerns?" Zamora asked.

"None whatsoever."

Later in the interview, after trying to find evidence of the emails Patrick mentioned, Patrick said, "She was just going to let them live there and I told her they have to have a lease, so afterward she was going to get a lease . . . She's got lawyers that take [care] of everything. They take care of her life."

Zamora asked Patrick what he thought happened to Pfister, but Patrick had no clue: "I have no idea . . . I wish I could tell you," he said.

But then Patrick referred to the newspaper article he had read, about the Stylers and their car and them having "something to do with it." He only became worried when he read that.

"I never imagined that they would do something violent to her. I don't know what happened to her . . . I don't know if she overdosed or if she got beat up or what happened. Nobody in town knows what's going on. Nobody's talking, so I don't know what happened."

Patrick continued talking about an overdose. "If somebody had told me that she had done way too many drugs and overdosed, I'd say that's not outside the realm of possibility."

Zamora asked Patrick if he would take a polygraph test, and Patrick agreed. "I would be stunned and shocked if you failed," Zamora said.

Miller then redirected the conversation to Tuesday, but she was either trying to trip him up or she didn't realize what he said earlier. Miller asked him about "when you went in and to [the] top of [the] stairs."

"Correct," Patrick said.

"You didn't go—," she began.

"I never went up to the top of the stairs," Patrick said, correcting Miller.

Either Miller didn't hear him, or she wasn't listening. "When you went to the top of the stairs, as far as walking that direction as you were going up, where were [the] renters? Doing what?"

But Patrick apparently didn't catch her mistake, because that time he didn't correct her.

"She was behind me and [Trey]," Patrick said, "after I came in, had went back through the garage and into the basement part of the house."

At that point in the interview, Miller's questioning changed, as she did something called "leading a witness." For example, if Miller were being objective, hoping to learn what actually happened, she would have asked, "What do you mean she was behind you?" But she didn't. Instead, Miller led Patrick: "She's behind you, as in behind you following you up the stairs?"

Patrick agreed—even though he never said that happened earlier in his account. "Up the stairs, yeah."

Miller asked, "And what's she saying?"

"She didn't say anything."

Again, Miller led the witness, by inserting something he never said. "But she was just sticking close?"

"Yeah . . . I didn't even think about her, okay." When Patrick said this, it was clear nothing Nancy Styler did gave him cause for alarm, and he couldn't even recall what she was doing at the time. But Miller continued to push Patrick into saying things that he hadn't earlier.

"Walked in and followed you up the stairs or—," Miller asked.

At that point, Patrick told them he didn't know.

More leading occurred with Miller's next question. "Just to be with you?"

"Yeah. Could be. I don't know."

"And so when you said, 'Hey, Nancy' or whatever—," Miller began, even though Patrick never clearly said he called for Pfister. He said he might have—but only after Zamora suggested it.

But Patrick may not have realized how important that was, so he didn't clarify. "Yeah. Yeah, I, you know." Nor does Miller ask him to.

"And then—," she began.

Patrick finished: "Nancy Styler's like, 'She's not here.'"

They were rehashing Patrick's earlier statements, about telling Pfister to stay upstairs, when he added a new detail to the story. "She wouldn't stay out of the way," he said Nancy Styler told him. Eventually, Patrick circled back to the beginning, when Nancy told him Pfister wasn't there.

"Well, then I said, 'She's out. Somebody came and picked her up and she's out doing something somewhere,'" Patrick said.

Miller asked about Nancy Styler next. "How would you describe her personality and demeanor?"

"She wasn't like she was last fall when she was friendly," Patrick said. "But she wasn't mean or nasty or anything. She's just, it seemed like they were just put out that they were having to leave."

"Oh, okay. Describe him to me," Miller said.

Patrick said Trey "never said two words to me the whole time."

Miller asked, "So just not outgoing?"

"Not at all outgoing at all, none," Patrick said.

"Healthy? Frail? Something else?" Miller asked.

Patrick's answer seemed thoughtful. "I wouldn't say he was frail. They seemed certainly, she seemed less fit. He seemed more fit and like he did stuff outside, hiking and stuff," Patrick said. "No. He didn't [seem] weak or anything like that."

"Was he actually moving things? Did you actually see him—," Miller asked. When she was given a chance to learn more about why Patrick spoke of hiking, outside activities, and Trey being "more fit" than Nancy, Miller didn't pursue it.

Was this perhaps because Patrick's perception of Trey didn't fit with her theory of the crime? If so, it showed Miller's inability to be objective and it may even have showed that she had already mentally convicted Trey as the killer.

Patrick answered, "I never saw him actually carrying anything. I saw just the two guys throwing stuff into it. But he, they both came out when I pulled in the driveway, parked."

Patrick had just contradicted himself again. When the interview first began, he told Zamora and Miller that Nancy Styler was inside, in the poolroom. Now he said the couple were both outside. By then, Patrick Carney should have been considered an "unreliable witness." Instead, his statement helped form the basis of the arrest warrant affidavit.

"I talked to her," Patrick said. "He turned around and went right back in."

At that point, following Miller's early leading of the witness, Zamora introduced as fact an idea that Patrick said he was unsure about.

"So then, when you went upstairs, stopped, called Nancy," Zamora said, "the other Nancy follows you and says, 'She's not here.'"

Again, Patrick failed to correct Zamora. "Not here, yeah."

"And again, just what Lisa was saying, was it angry? Or was it, like, 'Hey, no, she's not here'?" he asked.

"No, I, I wouldn't say it was angry. It was just, she just wasn't friendly, you know." Patrick repeated what he said earlier. "It's like, honestly, she just seemed put out. Like, that they had to leave."

Zamora had another question. "Did she follow you back down-stairs or did she continue on upstairs?"

"She followed me. She went back down the stairs," Patrick said.

Miller had a question. "So when you're flipping the ball for Gabe, outside—."

Patrick cut in. "They were inside."

"They were inside," she repeated. "So they didn't follow you back outside?"

"No," Patrick said. "Because I was flipping the ball up on the hill, and can't throw it very far with my left hand. And then [Gabe] couldn't, it's the dumbest dog ever."

The Stylers "went back in that house, and I never had any interaction with them after I got in my car."

After more dog chitchat, Zamora asked if there were "anything else you think of that we should know or kind of out of the ordinary?"

Patrick said he'd been trying to think of anything else. "I can't think of anything that is, you know, like, so overt that it's like, oh, these people are bad people."

Miller asked if Nancy spoke about them moving out, but Patrick said no. "Not a word. And I didn't ask them, either."

"Did they refer to Nancy by name or did they say—," Miller began.

Patrick finished. "She said Nan—, she said Nancy, uh, she said that Nan—, it was a—I'm trying," Patrick said, clearly having trouble. "I've been trying to remember and I can't, you know. There was something about, it was, 'We asked [Pfister] to stay upstairs and it was a problem.'" Then Patrick clarified, "But I couldn't tell you the exact phrasing."

Miller said they weren't worried about that. But Patrick wanted to make sure what he said was clear. "I, I don't want to—," he began.

But Zamora cut him off. "And we appreciate you—," he said.

Patrick continued, "—put words, I don't want to put words in someone's mouth," he finished.

"And I don't want you to," Miller agreed.

"But there is, you know, and it was, like, inferred that . . . Nancy was being Nancy and sticking her nose into everything," Patrick said.

"One other question," Miller said, "and please, don't take any dis-respect, but you said you'd been taking OxyContin?"

"Oxycodone, I think."

"Oxycodone? Okay. Um, what would you, were, were you clear? Were you levelheaded?" Miller asked.

Patrick didn't really say. "I was comfortable driving. I mean, I knew that I probably shouldn't be, but honestly, I was not like, so impaired that I felt like drunk or wasted or anything like that. I was aware I had to be careful that I did not run over Gabe." He said he was taking the prescribed amount and "was clearly aware what was going on."

Miller pointed out that when "people are lightweights . . . they're [a] little fuzzy about stuff."

Patrick said he wasn't fuzzy. "But I was not, like debilitated, wasted . . . I know what I'm like when I'm like that, and that wasn't even close."

Zamora seemed happy with that, and said Patrick would know if he was mentally clear. He added that if they needed Patrick to take a polygraph, they'd let him know. But, in spite of Patrick's several contradictions, as well as having been on oxycodone the Tuesday he went to Pfister's, they never did.

CHAPTER TWENTY

THE BLUE BATHROBE SEEN AROUND THE WORLD

While Patrick was waiting for the police to contact him to take a polygraph, Olmsted was leaving the Stylers' motel room Saturday afternoon. As he did, he asked the deputy standing guard if one of their credit cards could be returned, since they had no money or the means to get food. The deputy said he would check with Detective Gibson and get back to Olmsted, who already knew the answer was no. Finally, Olmsted asked if the Stylers were free to leave their room and, theoretically, Aspen. "Yes," the deputy replied. Olmsted just smiled.

Over the weekend, in addition to Olmsted, a few brave souls went to the Stylers' aid. Nancy's friends Patrice and Purl showed up and took her out for dinner, buying foodstuffs for Nancy to take back to the motel room. Merlin dropped by, too, with a hot meal and to see how they were doing, and several motel clerks helped them out. But everyone else stayed away. It was a depressing weekend and Nancy couldn't remember the last time she had cried that much.

On Monday morning, Olmsted called and warned the Stylers that they would probably be arrested. He also explained his need to fly to Arizona for another case, but said he and Wayne had things under control. Nancy was shocked, and couldn't understand the reason for their arrest when she and Trey were innocent. Olmsted told her not to worry, and gave them tips about what to say and what not to say, in the event an arrest occurred.

Olmsted didn't know that two pieces of circumstantial evidence were found that connected Nancy and Trey to Pfister's murder. Armed with that, the results of Trey's polygraph, and the interviews of several locals who had come to know the Stylers during their four months in Aspen, Detective Gibson swore that the two affidavits containing facts about the case were accurate and true. Sheriff DiSalvo signed off, and Gibson delivered the documents to Ninth Judicial District Attorney Sherry Caloia.

Caloia, the top dog of the Ninth Judicial District, oversaw criminal cases in three counties: Pitkin, Garfield, and Rio Blanco. She was known as a micromanager who looked very closely at her team's work, so it's safe to say she was fully aware of everything that happened in the murder investigation. Thus, the DA would have been largely responsible for overseeing the facts contained in the affidavits that made their way to Judge Nichols.

Next, the judge signed the affidavits and at 4:45 p.m. officials from CBI and the PCSD returned to the couple's motel room, where they were arrested, charged with first-degree murder, and led away in handcuffs to the Pitkin County Jail. As deputies led Nancy away in handcuffs, reporters saw tears streaming down her face. Trey, who wasn't dressed when police arrived, was taken away wearing his wife's blue bathrobe. "Her, too?" Trey asked, when he realized Nancy was also being taken in. Then he softly said her name.

For the throngs of media waiting outside the motel, it was the perfect photo op. They captured a photo of the frail doctor, which they publicized hundreds of times during the coming months.

* * *

Although Olmsted and Wayne thought the arrest was probable, they didn't know it would happen so soon.

Olmsted had barely had time to turn his cell phone back on after his plane touched down in Tucson when he got a call from Wayne saying the Stylers had been arrested. Olmsted called the jail and arranged to have Nancy call him back. When she did, she was "extremely upset."

Olmsted reminded her of what he told them earlier that morning. "If you have to be in jail in America, you want to be in the Aspen jail," he told her. "Nobody will mistreat you, everybody will be kind to you, and if you have a question, ask the question," he said, "but don't whine about anything."

Before he hung up, the private investigator told Nancy he would return Wednesday, March 5, and he would come straight to the jail to see her. Two days later, he did so, but not before learning new information about the case while on the last leg of his return flight home.

Two women traveling back to Aspen sat close enough to Olmsted that he clearly heard their conversation. One sat beside him; the other woman behind him, and as they spoke, he realized they were discussing the Pfister case. "Well, I heard she was wrapped in sheets and plastic and tied up and put in the closet," one woman said to the other. It was news to Olmsted, though he was only unofficially helping Wayne on the Stylers' case because the defense team had yet to get off the ground.

By Wednesday, the Stylers were resigned: they couldn't pay Wayne's fee. Her departure left a void to gradually be filled by four public defenders: Beth Krulewitch, in private practice, was already working on Nancy's case, even though she hadn't yet been appointed to it. Garth McCarty, also in private practice, would later join Krulewitch on Nancy's team.

Colorado state law requires that defendants in capital cases, cases that are serious such as first-degree rape or murder, each have two attorneys. Where there are codefendants, like Nancy and Trey, the law requires they be represented by two other attorneys, since there is always the potential for codefendants to become witnesses against each other. Public defenders Tina Fang and Sara Steele wound up being appointed to Trey's case. And in the meantime, Wayne asked Olmsted to continue his work, helping Krulewitch get up to speed on Nancy's case.

"I didn't know that information," Olmsted said about the details he overheard on the plane about the murder victim. "But it turned out to be exactly accurate." When he told Krulewitch what the women had said, she didn't know it, either.

"But on Friday [March 7], we got the arrest warrant affidavit," Olmsted said, "and it proved to be exactly right."

Suddenly, Krulewitch and Olmsted knew the defense had a big problem: someone was leaking information about the case—and it wasn't them.

Later, the defense team figured out how this information was likely leaked. Former sheriff Bob Braudis told police about a party he was at the night Pfister's body was discovered. The party was at DiSalvo's house, and details came in over the police scanner.

Aspen is a small town. Within minutes, everyone at the party came to know the details of Pfister's body being found. And the story traveled quickly from there.

***

Cindy and the rest of the McDaniel family learned about the pending arrest when Nancy called them Monday afternoon. "It's my sister and she's crying and she says to me," Cindy said, "'Cin, you have to call Dad and ask him for $35,000. They said we're going to be arrested.'"

At the Colorado end of the telephone line, Nancy was afraid of being arrested, and of not having any money for an attorney. *What then?*

But at the Boston end, Nancy's words simply wouldn't compute in Cindy's brain. She began questioning Nancy when Trey grabbed the phone. "Cin, just do this. Do this for Nancy," he said.

Cindy was annoyed. "Let me talk to Nancy."

"Just do this for Nancy," Trey repeated.

"I want to talk to my sister," she said firmly. Trey gave the phone back to Nancy. "How do you know you're going to be arrested?" Cindy asked her.

Nancy told her that Olmsted tipped them off and they needed money to retain an attorney. Then the call ended.

"That was it. He grabbed the phone again," Cindy said. "'Do this for Nancy,' he said, like it was his last dying breath." Then Trey hung up.

Cindy immediately called Daniel. "I don't know what's going on. What's wrong with your father?" He, in turn, called the Aspenalt. "They're no longer guests here," the clerk said. Daniel had no reason to assume they would be arrested, but by the sound of fear he heard in the clerk's voice, he thought "they had killed themselves or my dad had done the murder-suicide."

Daniel then called Lisa Wayne, who called Pitkin County and learned of the arrest. She reported back to Daniel. "On what charge?" he asked.

"Well, murder one, I assume," Wayne said.

Daniel called Cindy back to tell her.

"Oh, my God! I don't even know what to do with this," she said. Then she thought of her mother: "I have to tell her."

That didn't happen until 9 p.m. Eastern time, and since Cindy and Nancy's brother Roger was out of town, Cindy had to break the news to her sister-in-law, Angie. Because the McDaniels had been separated for thirty years, Angie drove over to tell her father-in-law in person, while Cindy went to tell her mother.

When Cindy arrived, Tess was on the phone with Daniel's god-father, Joseph. "She was still in disbelief," Cindy said. *I don't even know how to do this.* "Do I Google how to tell your eighty-three-year-old mother her daughter's been arrested?" she wondered. Cindy was as worried about her parents as she was about Nancy, afraid the news might cause either one of them to have a heart attack.

"What do you mean? What do you mean?" Tess asked. "Is she okay? What's going to happen?"

Cindy told her she didn't know. Then she heard back from Angie. "She said my father was white as a ghost."

The entire situation felt surreal, so bizarre, to the McDaniels. When Cindy spoke to Roger, he suggested they wait for definite news of an arrest before they asked their father for the money.

Because of that, they never did. Roger, along with the entire family, had to take a little time to figure out what was going on. No one in the McDaniel family had ever had any experience with the criminal justice system, so they didn't know what to expect. They were as confused and overwhelmed in Boston as Nancy was in Aspen.

In fact, it wasn't until Nancy and Trey had an attorney that the McDaniels even learned the arrest had really happened. Wayne was instrumental in those attorneys being appointed to the case, and had discussed it with Daniel in the event his parents couldn't pay her retainer. Daniel spoke with Public Defender Tina Fang before she was even appointed, and he notified her when he learned his parents had been arrested.

There was a glitch, though, from the side of the prosecution. Fang sent Steele to the jail to check on her new client, but Steele wasn't allowed into the jail for more than an hour. Fang was frustrated, Daniel said, and told him to call the jail and make a formal request for his parents to have access to legal counsel.

When Daniel called Cindy with this report, she "Googled and saw my mother's mug shot." *My mother's going to die if she sees this.*

Cindy continued worrying about her mom. "My poor mother. She just laid on the couch and cried."

Tess kept repeating the same five words: "She couldn't have done it."

Cindy stayed with her, consoling and rationalizing as each new detail about the case became breaking news. Over the course of the next few weeks, she felt like a broken record, saying the same phrases over and over again. "Of course they [will find] DNA; they lived in the house." "It's going to be okay." "It's a mistake."

From time to time, a lighter moment would punctuate the darkness that enveloped the McDaniels. For instance, when Tess said, "Send your sister a TracFone, then she can call us anytime." Tess had no idea that prisoners weren't allowed to have cell phones, and they couldn't just make a phone call at will. They had to set up an account, which cost money, paid for by someone on the outside.

Or when the media called Nancy "elderly."

"Oh, your sister's not going to like being called elderly," Tess said in her thick Boston accent.

Then, because everyone in their family knew how fastidious Nancy was about her hair and grooming, came the lightest moment of all: "What's she going to do if her roots start showing?" Tess asked.

Cindy laughed, but all she could think of was the anguish she knew Nancy must be feeling—and how long it would take for her to be released. "There wasn't one second where I thought my sister was capable of murder."

***

The McDaniel family, 2,000 miles away in Boston, learned the arrest was a reality the same way the rest of the world did. The media reported it following the first news conference about the case, which was held an hour after the couple was arrested and charged with two felonies: first-degree murder and conspiracy to commit first-degree murder, Class 1 and 2 felonies, respectively.

There, everyone got into the act. Surrounded by law enforcement officers from various agencies throughout the county and the state, as well as officials from the DA's office, Sheriff Joe DiSalvo mostly spoke of how the case affected those people—not Pitkin County residents. As the *Aspen Times* reported, DiSalvo said, "[It] has been hard from the beginning on all of us, because of [its] nature . . . First-degree murders don't happen here too often [but] when they do, we take it very seriously, and we storm it. We throw everything we've got at it." The sheriff said his team worked "almost twenty-four hours a day, on little rest for a lot of people."

In response to reporters' questions about the Stylers' daylong interrogation on Thursday, DiSalvo didn't say much, simply that the DA lacked "probable cause"—a legal term meaning enough hard evidence—to arrest the couple before Monday afternoon. He also refused to say how Pfister died, even though by then the gruesome rumors about "blunt-force trauma" and finding a body in a closet had traveled all the way around the world. Nor would he discuss any evidence the police collected and then used to obtain the arrest warrant. In fact, DiSalvo had so little to say that the news conference was over in less than twenty minutes.

He certainly didn't mention the warrants police took to the court three different times, which the judge refused to sign, citing a lack of evidence. Nor did he announce that with the Stylers' arrest, the community could rest easy, which would indicate his personal views about their guilt or innocence. But then, he didn't have to. His next words reflected that loud and clear.

"My job is," the sheriff said, "for the most part, done."

* * *

Nothing in Nancy Styler's sixty-two years could have prepared her for life as an inmate. After being led into the facility in handcuffs and shackles, she was instructed to take off her clothing, one piece at a time, from the top to the bottom. She handed each item over to a female guard, who searched for any sign of illegal substances. "They took away all of my clothing, all of my jewelry, my medicine, everything," Nancy said, "and then they give you someone else's stained granny panties."

A woman for whom cleanliness really is next to godliness, and for whom style and fashion are synonymous with daily grooming, Nancy was appalled when a jailer handed her the stained underwear that looked ten sizes too large. She could barely bring herself to touch the garments—much less wear them.

"These are disgusting," Nancy said.

"This is jail, Styler. What do you expect?"

"I've gotta wear these? I don't want to wear any."

"Not an option," came the jailer's curt reply.

Nancy wasn't impressed with the generic sports bra, either, having had breast surgery twenty years earlier that meant she wore specially fitted underwire bras. "I had a double mastectomy and the doctor put the implant under the muscle. But the pocket they put it in, well, my pockets are starting to open up a little bit, so I need an underwire bra for support. It's essential."

When the guard stood there looking bored, her outstretched hand waiting for Nancy to take the sports bra, Nancy knew it was pointless. So she put the bra on, but it had absolutely no support at all. "This won't work for me," Nancy said.

"Then put on two," came the guard's reply.

After donning her county-approved apparel, Nancy was taken through the paces: bend over and shake out your hair, presumably to ensure no contraband entered through someone's tresses—or you didn't have lice. Someone then checked each ear and looked up Nancy's nostrils. The final humiliation? Once her hair was as messy as possible, they ordered Nancy to look into a camera for her mug shot. She couldn't have smiled if she wanted to—she had passed the point of utter humiliation four days earlier, while having to strip naked in front of a motel room full of armed men. Now, she simply felt dehumanized. Like an animal.

"They want you to look like that," Nancy later said, "so when people on the outside see your photo, you look like a crazy person—or the murderer they claim you are."

"Styler!" a voice rang out from somewhere down the corridor. Having also been stripped of her hearing aids, Nancy didn't hear someone calling her name.

"Hey, you, Styler!" a jailer called again.

Nancy was still in the holding cell when Sheriff Joe DiSalvo appeared, his expression more like a sneer than a smile, she said.

"I don't normally welcome people to my jail," he said, sarcasm lacing his voice, "but I'm glad you're here!" Then DiSalvo turned on his heel and was gone.

The waves of nausea, the headache, all came on soon after. Nancy suddenly realized she and Trey were in trouble. *DiSalvo's friends with the entire Pfister family—and he thinks we're guilty. He thinks we did this. He already has us convicted.* She remembered back to the day Pfister told her, in that bragging voice of hers, "Oh, Joey and I are good friends." What Nancy didn't know was that Pfister had been copying DiSalvo on all of her emails, and threatening to have her law enforcement friends evict them.

Nancy refused to give in to fear, though, and the sheriff's attitude turned her defiant. *I'm innocent. Once police get the toxicology report and realize Pfister overdosed, they'll open the door and I'll be free to go. We will be free to go.*

A friendly female guard brought Nancy some supplies—including a comb, six inches of dental floss (since any more had the potential to be used as a deadly weapon), a toothbrush with bristles that felt like wire, some deodorant, a towel, a sheet, a pillow, and enough clothing for three days. Then she led Nancy to her new home for the foreseeable future: a tiny cell with gray walls.

"You're gonna be here for a while," she said. After the door closed Nancy remembered hearing something about how she and Trey would both be in solitary confinement. Neither one was allowed to leave their cell because the jail was so small they might run into each other. And since they were codefendants, that wasn't permitted.

Without her regular medicine for the night sweats she was prone to, Nancy spent her first few nights tossing and turning, soaking her clothing and the single sheet on her bed. If anything, she sweated more than usual because for the first time in her life, she became claustrophobic. Confused and unable to sleep at night, her mind volleyed back and forth between believing the authorities were going to figure out they made a mistake to wondering how anyone could be so wrong—how the police could possibly believe people like her and Trey would ever intentionally kill someone. Or, worse yet, why they didn't realize Pfister's death had to have been a suicide.

By the next morning Nancy was still thinking about DiSalvo's arrogant comment—and she was angry. *Whatever happened to "innocent until proven guilty"? How dare DiSalvo be so rude! He doesn't even know us.*

Nancy vowed to show him. She asked the guard for some paper and something to write with, and was given a white legal pad and pen. Nancy wrote down everything she could remember about the interactions she and Trey had had with Pfister. She was awake all night writing, until the pen ran out of ink. When she finished, she had written thirty-two pages, front and back.

She would prove the sheriff wrong—and in the process, write the entire sordid story about how they came to live, and then—three months later—leave, Pfister's house.

CHAPTER TWENTY-ONE

WHEN LIFE WAS
A FAIRY TALE

F ive years before being dragged from their motel room into the cold Colorado air like criminals, William Styler, a renowned and beloved Denver anesthesiologist, and his beautiful wife, Nancy, a scientist who attended medical school in France and later graduated from the University of Colorado with a master's degree in anesthesiology, had a fairy-tale life. They owned a huge home, complete with an indoor waterfall. She drove a Mercedes convertible, Trey, a Jaguar. Nancy wore expensive diamonds and their family traveled twice to the Amazon rainforest.

The trips to the Amazon allowed the Stylers to provide more than fifty flower conservatories around the world with seeds from the rare and exotic Victoria lily that they had painstakingly cultivated along the way. Their venture wasn't widely publicized because Nancy and Trey weren't interested in broadcasting their philanthropy. In fact, they gave away most of the fruits of their labor for free. If a number had been put on their generosity, it would have easily amounted to several hundred thousand dollars over the course of thirteen years. Neither Nancy nor Trey cared, though, because Trey's combined medical salary and trust-fund money meant they lived on $250,000 to $300,000 annually. Even Daniel didn't know how much money his parents had because they never talked about it. To them, money was simply a way to live, and help others do the same.

And help others they did. The Victoria lily is a world-famous plant known for its eight-foot lily pads capable of holding up to fifty pounds. It became the focal point for the Stylers' ornately landscaped backyard, which, in turn, hosted annual class trips for local elementary students and garden tours for the public. It also provided an excellent outdoor classroom setting for college students interning at Denver Botanic Gardens. Nancy, who taught a master gardening class, provided them with first-rate instruction, with Trey often by her side caring for the more technical aspects.

"My mom was the garden's artist, he, its engineer," their son, Daniel, said.

Back then, even Daniel got into the act; it was a family affair they all loved. Even as the fairy tale slowly started to evaporate, they rubbed shoulders with owners of the Las Vegas Bellagio, who wanted the Stylers to use their lilies to help create a world-class centerpiece within the legendary hotel's own conservatory.

* * *

It took thirteen years for the Stylers' life to slowly implode. To Nancy and Trey, it seemed like only a matter of minutes for their perfect world to finally wither like a dying bloom in 2013.

It didn't come as a surprise to many they knew and loved—some of those people, people they once accepted unquestioningly as loyal colleagues and friends—had actually contributed to the firestorm that laid them low. The 2007 recession, in which many people lost equity in or even lost their homes, didn't help the couple, either. Proud people, the Stylers still had enough money to start over. Neither cared that the money, the house—their son's childhood home, the luxurious life they once shared, was gone—because they still had what meant most to them: they had each other, and they had their son, Daniel.

What more did they really need?

Once it vanished, though, how does a couple whose lives were immersed in the medical, research, and botanical worlds go from there to being reduced to peering through prison bars at that same world? How did the Stylers go from the kind of charmed existence most people can only dream about to being charged with first-degree murder in the death of one of Aspen, Colorado's, most well-known and whispered-about socialites?

Not just any heiress, either, but Nancy Pfister, whose family founded Buttermilk Mountain, home to famous celebrities who fly in from all over the world to ski, attend ESPN's X Games, and live large. Nancy Pfister, the goddaughter of literary great Hunter S. Thompson. And how did a murder happen in Aspen, anyway, when the tiny town hadn't experienced a murder in more than ten years?

Why would the Stylers even want to kill Pfister—or did they?

***

Sitting inside her cell at the Pitkin County Jail, Nancy soon filled thirty pages with all the relevant details: how they met Pfister, how she convinced them to rent her home, the way she tried to treat Nancy like a slave, and how, once they had paid Pfister and she was overseas, she claimed the Stylers weren't paying rent. The rest of the details were history—but they ended with Pfister dead. Sitting there, Nancy couldn't believe the police thought she and Trey had anything to do with Pfister's death. Or that it was even a murder. She was certain Pfister had killed herself—just like she threatened to do before she left for Australia.

Nancy could easily imagine it, too: with enough sleeping pills for a lifetime scattered around the house and plenty of pink Champagne to wash it down, it would be all too easy for Pfister to overdose, intentionally or not. She didn't know how to care for herself, nor did she want to. She told Nancy as much, when the two women first met. More important, though, was the sense that she couldn't live without money. A lot of money. The estate attorney gave her $7,000 a month, but that wasn't enough to keep Pfister happy. In fact, she complained to anyone who would listen about how much she disliked the man charged with doling out her trust-fund allowance.

***

Nancy thought back to how happy she and Trey had been, when they lived on that "little" money. It was 1982, the year they had married.

She was a faculty member at the University of Colorado in the anesthesia department when she and Trey had first crossed paths eighteen months earlier. Back then, Nancy overheard Trey, a new anesthesiology resident, comforting a patient before surgery.

"Don't worry, I'm going to be right here, I'm going to treat you as though you were my mother, and I've got a stethoscope and I've got it on your chest," Trey told the woman. "I'm hearing your every heartbeat, your every breath. I'm not going anywhere."

It was a glaring contrast from what she had seen many other anesthesiologists do, the ones who slap on a mask and tell their patients to count backwards. Trey Styler was very different. Nancy knew that. He took the time to connect with his patients. It made a lasting impression. That singular experience confirmed what Nancy soon learned herself: he was the gentlest man she knew.

They met in person a few weeks later. Trey was on call, and so was Nancy. It was November 1979 when they began chatting in a hospital breakroom. Nancy learned that Trey's earliest college days had been one big party—but even after dozens of medical schools denied him entry, he refused to give up his dream of becoming a doctor. The Oklahoma College of Osteopathic Medicine finally accepted him. Later, Trey graduated as valedictorian of his medical school class. Nancy knew from this that Trey wasn't just gentle—he was also very smart.

They talked and talked, but Trey—who thought the voluptuous Nancy beautiful—was crushed to learn she was also taken. However, she was in the final stages of an unhappy marriage, so Trey had some reason to hope she might someday be free. He left for a medical rotation at another hospital not long after they met so they didn't talk again until the following April. By then Nancy had left her husband, and when she and Trey ran into each other on April 9, 1981, he had high hopes of pursuing her. So high, in fact, that even though Nancy seemed hesitant to be more than good friends, he went home and called his mother. "I just met the woman I'm going to marry," he said.

That was, Trey said, "the beginning"—of a great friendship, of a slowly growing commitment to each other (since Nancy wanted to be sure it wasn't a rebound relationship), and finally, their marriage. Throughout the next few months, Trey began telling their friends,

"Her first husband was a placeholder," he joked, "keeping her tied up until I came along."

His fellow residents were all jealous of the bookish-looking geek's efforts to win the affections of the most beautiful woman at the hospital. When they asked how he got so lucky, Trey replied, "Her ex did me the great favor of being obnoxious, so I looked really good to her."

Nancy soon proved to be more amazing than Trey even knew. When they first met, he fell in love with her physical beauty, but during their courtship, his love deepened after glimpsing her incredible friendliness. "Nancy gets the life history of the cashier in the checkout line," Trey said. "She meets people and they immediately fall in love with her."

Trey described feeling "deliriously happy" at their February 21, 1982, wedding, which he said was "the second happiest day of my life." The first? The birth of the couple's only son, three years later.

***

During that pregnancy, Nancy found an unfinished house in Denver sitting on a vacant 1.25-acre lot. She called Trey, who said he didn't have to see it. He could tell by the sound of Nancy's voice that she had fallen in love. If Nancy loved it, so did he. "Let's buy it," he said. They did and by the time their son was born, Nancy, a master gardener, had finished the home's interior—complete with an indoor waterfall. Then she began designing the exterior gardens that would become elaborate over time.

That's how Nancy Styler gave birth twice. First she had her son, Daniel, then she "birthed," or created, her beloved garden. After Daniel was born and Nancy found out how much she enjoyed being a full-time mother, she decided not to return to medicine. Instead, she wanted to stay home and teach her son. Trey was completely supportive, and said he was happy to be the sole breadwinner. In fact, he felt proud knowing Nancy trusted him enough to take care of her financially, because he knew she was more than capable of being self-reliant. During their first few years together, Trey had grown even more in love with his wife, and she with him. She admired how dedicated he was to his patients, and knew how often patients and even other doctors put in a bid for Trey to be the anesthesiologist for their own surgeries. In addition, he was selfless and generous, often giving away many of his services to his colleagues as a professional courtesy—as well as taking on more Medicaid patients than they did, even though the fees he received from caring for those patients was less than he would have gotten for anyone who had private medical insurance.

Throughout their marriage, Trey was constantly amazed by Nancy: she evolved from designing gardens to jewelry for people and canines and clothing, including a line of doggie clothes. She often came up with the most fascinating ideas, which Trey would help bring to life on the computer.

They were the perfect couple, and they had it all.

CHAPTER TWENTY-TWO

A BIG SISTER NAMED VICTORIA

W hen Daniel was about eight, his parents planned to add to their elaborate water lily garden. The new addition came about after Daniel, then a third-grader at Greenwood Elementary, saw a turn-of-the-century photo in which a woman stood on a Victoria lily pad playing a violin. He suggested that they could grow the flowers named for Queen Victoria of England, and joked that his classmates could pay to have their picture taken on the lily pad. "We can pay for my college tuition," Daniel said.

Trey and Nancy thought the idea amusing and Daniel very entrepreneurial. They knew how much Daniel adored his third-grade teacher, Mrs. Filarowicz, who had her class construct a "rainforest" each year, using just construction paper to build the canopy, the understory, and each level of the rainforest. Each student was responsible for a plant or an animal in the forest; Daniel chose the Victoria lily. So when Daniel suggested his family grow the flowers, they didn't want to disappoint him. At the same time, they also knew how difficult it would be to cultivate the flowers, which were not even indigenous to the Western world. "It's impossible! We can't grow those things," Trey told Nancy.

Nonetheless, they wanted to let Daniel run with the idea and see what happened, deciding it would be a great learning experience for him. So Nancy sent their son to the Denver Botanic Gardens, believing the curator would talk Daniel out of the idea. Instead, Daniel came home with a stack of literature about the flower. Three weeks later, the curator called their home. "Your plants are ready, Daniel," he said.

Trey and Nancy were both pleased and proud of Daniel's early success and determination. In response, Trey began expanding their garden pond, and continued to do so every year after. It was the beginning of the entire family's love affair with the Victoria lily.

Looking back, Daniel was amazed the plants survived. "They grow in a rainforest, with hundreds of inches of rainfall a year and yearly lows in the seventies. It's the equivalent of raising a dolphin in the backyard in Denver."

He also recalled those years fondly. "As a child, I joked that I was a garden orphan or that I had a big sister named Victoria."

Nancy, in particular, found the exquisite water flower, with its eight-foot-wide leaf shaped like a pie tin, an amazing plant. With a leaf that's strong enough to hold a fifty-pound child, the lily also fascinated engineers. She fell in love with the night-blooming flower that changes from white to pink—and from female to male overnight. As a researcher, she also appreciated how, in the Amazon wild, the scarab beetle pollinates the flower, whose fragrant blossom releases an aroma of fresh pineapple and tuberose. Nancy was hooked, and once she began researching the flower, she couldn't stop. By the year 2000, she had boxes and boxes of research on the Victoria lily.

What began as a labor of love soon led the Stylers to the Amazon rainforest in 1997. Daniel took pictures of his school and classmates to show to Amazon children. Nancy, who often was a homeroom mother in Daniel's classes, helped him collect school supplies to take to those children, and while there, the entire Styler family visited a class of students studying English, showing them pictures of Greenwood Village school buses and Colorado snow on the computer (a real novelty for the students). In preparation for the trip and as a project for the third-grade class, Greenwood students asked questions on the computer and Trey filmed the responses, allowing students in the Amazon to interact with schoolchildren in the United States.

While there, Daniel took pictures of the rainforest school buildings that sat on stilts high above the Amazon River, including pictures of little dugout canoes, their "school buses," that six-year-olds manned by themselves, to show to his class when he returned home. Even though Daniel left Greenwood Elementary in fourth grade, going to a new charter school, he returned every year during Mrs. Filarowicz's unit on the rainforest, teaching the students about the vanishing rainforest. Thanks to Daniel, many of the children learned birdcalls and could speak a few words of Portuguese.

That was only one of the adventures Daniel's plant led them on: every year during the first week of September, area third-graders took an annual class trip to the Stylers' backyard, the location of a mini rainforest comprised of the snail shells, fish scales, dried piranha, and Amazon staples such as "manioc" (similar to tapioca) that the Styler family brought back from their rainforest trips. The classes toured the yard and received instruction about the exotic flora. Nancy enlisted local scientists to build several stations, allowing the children to make paper from papyrus, look at different Amazon plant seeds and dried beetles under a microscope, and finally, have their picture taken while standing on one of the Victoria lily pads. That was the highlight of the day.

Then came the grand finale: a contest in which Nancy showed the students a yardstick, for them to use as a gauge when estimating the diameter of the Victoria lily. The winners received T-shirts that read, "I survived the giant Amazon water lily," a bouquet of flowers, and the chance to lead the children in a parade back to school while marching with large papyrus stalks.

Nancy was a gracious host. She served organic grapes from her garden as part of the refreshments she prepared, and if the children knew the name of the plant, she allowed them to pick flowers to take home. The following day, Nancy and Trey delivered prints of pictures they had made of all of the kids standing on the giant lily pads.

Nancy also founded the Victoria Conservancy, which provided (often from the Stylers' own pocket) seeds and plants to famous conservatories around the world and hours and hours of training for interns from the Denver Botanic Gardens in the Stylers' backyard. Using the foundation, Nancy also educated the community about the exotic flowers. People in the botany world jokingly called the Styler home "Denver Botanic Gardens South," and by the late 1990s, Nancy was traveling all over the United States, teaching people about the Victoria lily. She eventually became a key figure in the international botanical world.

***

Education motivated everything Trey and Nancy did back then, because they loved helping people. They also enjoyed sharing their knowledge—especially with their young son. But they were also kind, humane beings who believed they had an obligation to care for the earth and its creatures.

Such was the setting one hot summer day when their pond pump died. Since it was also Independence Day, the local pump store was closed. Because the pump operated the waterfall and oxygenated the water at the same time, Trey and Nancy were suddenly faced with losing some of their family members—Japanese koi, cold-water fish known for their brightly colored scales. The large pond was filled with them, but the warmer the water got, the less oxygen the water could hold. Before long, the eighteen-inch-long exotic koi, called *nishikigoi* in Japanese (which means "brocaded carp"), became lethargic. The two doctors knew that the slower the fish moved, the less oxygen they would take in. In short, the koi were suffocating—and unless they acted quickly, their deaths were imminent.

"We poured our entire stash of hydrogen peroxide into the pond," Daniel said, "hoping the oxygen would dissolve and help. But it wasn't enough." The fish were simply too large, and they required a lot of oxygen. The amount added by the peroxide was only a temporary fix, and maybe gave the fish an extra boost of oxygen, at best.

Nancy and Daniel threw on hip waders and jumped into the pond. Trey dragged out every air stone, the type used in aquariums, he could find. While he tried to resurrect the pump, Nancy and Daniel spent hours in the pond, holding the lethargic fish in their bare hands and moving them back and forth in the air bubbles created by the air stones. Then they grabbed the next koi and repeated the procedure. The Denver sun was setting by the time Trey managed to find another pump and hook it up. As Nancy and Daniel stepped out of the pond, they were exhausted but ecstatic: only five of the twenty-five koi had died.

Ironically, the five dead fish were the biggest in the pond, and brought to Nancy's mind the saying "the bigger they are, the harder they fall." She had no idea how true those words would soon become, and she could never have imagined how she would personally be impacted.

After successfully saving the beautiful aquatic creatures, a range of emotions—happiness, joy, pride, and relief—was shared by the Styler family that night. As she got ready for bed, Nancy reflected on the wonderful men in her life. They were both brilliant men—geeks, to be sure—but more important, they were sensitive and kind and gentle and intuitive. She couldn't have asked for anything else, because she knew she had it all.

Hers was a charmed life: Nancy was married to her soul mate, she had a great son who never gave them a day of trouble, and she had a lifestyle that allowed her the luxury of spending her days exactly how she wanted to. She could craft clothing or jewelry, train interns in her garden, or conduct research on the many botanical and medical topics she found so fascinating. Because Trey made almost $300,000 a year, she had enough money to buy whatever suited her fancy. When Nancy's four hundred pairs of shoes finally filled an entire basement wall, Trey jokingly called her "Imelda Marcos," after the Filipino dictator's wife who owned more than a thousand pairs. Nancy laughed, knowing how much Trey loved her, and knowing he didn't give a whit about how many shoes—or purses and designer outfits—she owned.

***

Then, just as the family's philanthropic and educational efforts exploded in the late 1990s, they were blindsided. It began, of all things, with a broken foot. Just a little limp. Or so they thought. At first doctors believed Trey, who had high arches and walked three miles a day between hospital rounds and seeing patients, had developed a simple stress fracture. Over the course of several months, doctors learned it wasn't the foot at all.

They did a nerve conduction study on his left leg, using his right leg as a control for the test. The doctor conducting the test said it wouldn't work, because both feet were compromised. In other words, Trey had far more wrong with him than a simple fracture.

The doctor who gave Trey the diagnosis was also his friend, and Trey could tell it was hard for him to break the news. The doctor told him it was a rare illness, a nonfatal form of Lou Gehrig's disease, or ALS, and his health would continue to decline. Before long, he was a shadow of what he had once been: strong, vibrant, kind, and happy. Pretty soon Trey's other foot needed surgery, too, and within no time, he couldn't walk without some form of assistance. The worst part? There was no cure, and he would require ongoing medication if he wanted any semblance of a normal life.

Later on, after seeing more doctors, having more tests, and taking more medicine, Trey received another diagnosis: Charcot-Marie-Tooth (CMT) disease, a constellation of neurological disorders that affect the peripheral nerves that transmit messages between the brain and the body's muscles. Named for the three French physicians who discovered it, the disease leads to muscle atrophy as the nerves slowly degenerate, resulting in loss of sensation that leads to weakness. Although most cases are genetic, when Trey was tested, his apparently wasn't the genetic variety, and Trey said he didn't know of anyone in his family who could have had it.

People with CMT usually have high arches, and Trey did, which led to the stress fractures in his feet. Eventually the legs atrophy, and that, along with a progressive lack of sensation, makes the legs look like inverted Champagne bottles, an accurate description of Trey's legs. CMT is a painful disease at first, but eventually the nerves burn out, leaving only numbness. This pattern began in Trey's legs and gradually, over a period of time, moved to his hands.

Because fatigue is another hallmark of the disease, Trey's doctors advised him to pace himself. This meant that although he could stand and do hard work, moving bags of mulch or rocks in the garden, he could only do it for a short time, and would pay the price in pain later that day. Although there is no treatment, exercise helps maintain mobility and may even slow the rate of progression. Without treatment, however, all doctors can do is alleviate the symptoms of the disease, using drugs known to help other neurological disorders.

***

Nancy wasn't as devastated by the early news as Trey was. In fact, she was secretly happy that one of her dreams was coming true: she would have more time with her soul mate, the man she loved with all her heart. Until she began seeing changes in Trey's personality. They showed up sporadically at first, like the way he went from growing agitated over small matters to having a full-blown tantrum. What no one then recognized was this: not only had the disease ravaged Trey's body—it had ravaged his mind, too. Slowly, Nancy saw the signs of depression, especially when she became his caretaker. She worried, because depression naturally ran in his family. But when she and Trey talked about his mood swings, they chalked it up to the powerful meds he was taking.

Trey told Nancy that if he could be productive, he would feel better. So he tried to return to work, quite a few times, even riding around the hospital on the motorized scooter he used at home when his legs wouldn't carry him. It was a short-lived experiment, and ended when Trey realized he still couldn't perform all his duties. Some of those tasks required an anesthesiologist to be on his feet, near the patient's face and neck, which was more than Trey could do from the confines of his scooter.

But the death knell that distinctly convinced Trey his career as an anesthesiologist was over came when he was under the effects of so much medicine himself, as his illness required, that he was afraid he had forgotten to give a patient the necessary medicine in the operating room. He wasn't sure, and there was no way he could be, but he knew the error was potentially fatal. Trey decided then and there to give up his second love. He consoled himself with the thought that he still had his first: Nancy. He tendered his resignation and went home to learn how to live without his medical profession.

Before long, though, he was pleasantly surprised when his medical group asked him to come back to work in an administrative capacity. They knew Trey was a whiz with computers and that during his spare time he was envisioning and planning a piece of software that would help alleviate the scheduling nightmares for their team of fifty doctors. They said they would pay him cash, to help supplement the income replacement insurance he was getting. Trey felt like it was a dream come true, and so did Nancy—at first.

Then one thing after another went horribly wrong: the computer programmer Trey hired to help him get the software up and running was really slow, using a near-obsolete language and writing it poorly, besides.

Later, the insurance company stopped payment, saying there had been an error and Trey didn't have the right policy. Finally, since Trey had tried to return to work time and again, by the time he applied for federal disability, the agency didn't calculate his disability on his full-time wages. Instead, his most recent wages were used. But that was only a sliver of the annual income Trey earned until the illness forced him to reduce his hours.

Every little loss meant Trey had to dip into his trust fund again. For the time being, they were solvent. But when Trey kept coming to Nancy—who had paid the bills in full every single month for years, to the point where they had a perfect credit rating—asking her to write one check after another for the computer system, she began to worry.

Finally, Trey grew so angry at everyone: his former colleagues and fellow anesthesia group members (who were by then his employers), the computer programmer who Trey felt was bilking him for ever dollar he could get, and the insurer who refused to pay his claim for lost wages, that he began lawyer shopping. Which is how he met John Powell, the attorney who promised him the moon but later turned out to be the biggest crook of all.

***

It took a cockatiel named Puffball for Nancy to understand how far her soul mate—and the man who once stood as an intellectual giant in the medical community and his own home—had fallen. The ivory-feathered bird was originally Daniel's pet, but he quickly grew attached to Trey. And even though Nancy sewed little vests for Puff, she didn't think the cockatiel liked her, because he tried picking the earrings from her ears and squawked loudly for Trey from the time Trey left the room until he returned.

By the time Trey underwent two foot surgeries, Puff was his constant companion. The bird was devoted to Trey, repeating Trey's whistles and riding on his shoulder or the handlebars of Trey's scooter as Trey puttered around in the garden. Then one day in 2001, a family friend was outside in the Stylers' yard, checking out a water pressure problem they were having. He opened a steel manhole cover to look at the valves, but when he dropped the cover down, Puff got spooked and took flight from where he had been perched on Trey's shoulder. The Stylers and many of their friends searched for the bird, to no avail.

A distraught Trey spent almost the entire night driving around and whistling for Puff—until he was so exhausted he had to stop. Even though they placed advertisements for the lost bird, answered every single bird sighting, and hung flyers all around the neighborhood for more than a month, they never found Puff. Trey became depressed about the loss of his little friend and refused to give up the search. When Nancy and Daniel suggested he get another bird, he refused.

"I just want Puffy back," Trey said, quietly crying.

CHAPTER TWENTY-THREE

TRAUMA TO TREY

After the Stylers' March 2014 arrest, the world saw a frail-looking gentleman wearing his wife's blue bathrobe, and her, with tears streaming down her face, being led by sheriff's deputies to separate patrol cars.

Until that terrible day, Nancy had never been handcuffed or arrested, and she did not have a criminal record. Trey's record reflected a 1970s drug possession charge of marijuana and a citation for his involvement in a horrific car accident. However, neither charge indicated a history of malice in Trey's character. In some ways, though, it may have done as much damage to the state of Trey's mental health as everything else—the onset of a debilitating neurological disease, carbon monoxide poisoning, and the loss of his profession, reputation, wealth, and home—combined. The August 2008 accident had caused serious injury to the other driver: namely, a young teacher driving her brand-new Volkswagen Beetle to school for the first time.

Nancy's life by then was so fraught with financial and housing problems from Trey's ongoing crises that she could hardly grasp the significance of what had happened at the time. But later she remembered the details quite clearly, and believed they added to Trey's crumbling mental state, which was already quite unstable.

Trey called Nancy to tell her he had crashed on the way to a pretrial conference hearing for the software he had developed and was suing his former employers over. John Powell was Trey's attorney then, but he quit just before the hearing, leaving Trey to go it alone.

Neither Nancy nor Trey knew at first if he had sustained any serious injuries. Nancy thought his voice sounded odd over the phone, and he told her he had been briefly unconscious. Trey said he would call her after the doctors finished running tests.

The accident happened just two miles from their home, so Nancy got into her car and drove to the scene, where she found both cars very badly damaged. Trey was released later that day and when she drove him home, he told her how he had slammed into the teacher's little car, which had stalled on the off-ramp of the interstate. The driver apparently didn't know how to operate a manual transmission. Trey watched in horror as the little car spun around, and he later learned that the other car's airbags didn't inflate. Although he lost consciousness on impact, Trey knew she might die. They were transported by ambulance together and he saw the severity of her injuries.

Trey believed he had killed the woman, Nancy said, "because he saw her legs twitching, which meant she had a neurological injury." Riding in the back of the ambulance was traumatic and tortuous for the gentle doctor. He still had a hard time talking about it. And Nancy believed that watching the woman beside him during that ride reminded Trey of his brother, Bob, who had committed suicide years before.

***

Trey was the older of the two brothers by three years, but said the title of "older brother" was his in name only, since Bob was usually the leader and more daring of the two boys. His older brother role usually consisted of "running back to the house yelling, 'Mom, Bob's bleeding again.'" After being patched up, Trey said Bob "would head straight back to whatever he was doing that got him injured in the first place."

Bob began struggling with major depression while in his late teens, and after returning to live with his parents in their Tulsa, Oklahoma, home, he began seeing a psychiatrist who prescribed an antidepressant. Bob hadn't been on the meds for very long and had just broken up with his longtime girlfriend, but he seemed to be on the mend. He and Trey even enrolled in a speed-reading night class together, which both brothers enjoyed.

"Then came the day I will always regret, no matter how long I live," Trey said. Bob called, asking if he could come over and "just hang with us for a while." Trey and his first wife, Diane, were in the middle of being amorous, so Trey blew his brother off, giving him "some lame excuse," telling Bob he'd see him the next night at class. "Bob took it like it was no big deal," he said.

But the following evening, Bob was a no-show for class. On Tuesday morning, a police officer called Trey, telling him he should come to his parent's house immediately. "I sensed trouble," he said, "but still had no idea what kind."

Inside his parents' home, the officer led Trey to the breakfast area to identify Bob's body. He had taken a massive dose of sleeping pills and was writing a suicide note when he lost consciousness. In the note, Bob "expressed his misery and his sense of having failed—at everything," Trey said.

It felt surreal, to see Bob's handwriting stop and trail away, leaving only a thin line of crooked ink from the pen behind, as it ran down and off the edge of the page. Trey never forgot that scene, of seeing his brother dead.

Because their parents were away on a trip at the time, Trey had to handle everything, including funeral arrangements. But the most painful task was notifying his parents: they returned immediately, but his mother fainted in the airport and was taken to the hospital. His father came home only after she had received medical care. Everyone, including Trey's first wife, was in shock over Bob's death. "At the time, I was caught completely unprepared," Trey said, going through the motions but not really processing anything.

"We all felt we had failed him, and took his guilt upon ourselves. I'd like to think that I eventually 'got over it,'" Trey said, "or at least got on with my life."

Likely, he truly never did.

***

Mental illness had long been a problem in Trey's family. His mother had a history of severe depression and needed antidepressants and weekly visits to a psychologist for many years. She was still being treated when she died at age seventy-two. And somewhere along the way, when Trey struggled in college and "felt lost" in math and physics class, he spoke to a "shrink in student health services," who suggested Trey had bipolar disorder, then called "manic-depression." Trey researched the illness and then discussed it with his parents, who wanted him to take a semester off, get some therapy, and then return to college. The "help" came in the form of weekly visits on a therapist's couch, where he was expected to do all the talking—but seldom did. The only words the therapist uttered during each visit were: "How are you doing?" and "Our time is up."

Trey took doctor-prescribed Ritalin, but he found his work in a local bowling alley most effective. There he joined two leagues and became so proficient he toyed with the idea of turning pro. Even better, though, were the long solo drives Trey took after work. He drove out to the eastern tip of Long Island, to the Montauk Point lighthouse, where he sat on the cliff and reflected on his thoughts until dawn.

Not long after, Trey got involved in the party scene; it was, after all, the early 1970s, when young people felt they were obligated to engage in drugs, have free sex, and take part in marches opposing the Vietnam War. His marriage failed as he and Diane grew apart. They spent a short time in marital counseling, but in the end parted as friends on amicable terms. By then, never having given up his dream of becoming a doctor, Trey was working the graveyard shift as a hospital orderly, applying to one medical school after another. By the spring of 1976, forty-six medical schools had rejected him.

Then came the forty-seventh: Oklahoma Osteopathic Medicine and Surgery accepted him, in spite of his poor track record in academics. Trey finally felt redeemed when he stood up to give his speech, as valedictorian of his 1979 class.

***

During that awful August day in 2008, as Trey laid on a stretcher next to the young schoolteacher, those helpless feelings returned to haunt him again.

"It was a horrible thing, and it was horrible for him," Nancy said. "He was a mess."

Trey had a lot of headaches following the accident, but no other residual symptoms. Then two months later, their insurance agent came to their home. "I hope you have your big checkbook ready," he said.

"Why?" Nancy asked.

The young woman sued and the insurance company settled for $2.5 million, so Nancy and Trey knew she hadn't died—but they assumed she had sustained a debilitating head injury.

Trey was cited in the crash and he lost points on his license. It was the closest scrape they'd had with the police—until Kathy Carpenter found Nancy Pfister in Pfister's bedroom closet.

CHAPTER TWENTY-FOUR

ANGELS IN ASPEN

Nancy wasn't strip-searched at Pitkin County Jail, but she was immediately put into solitary confinement. And after her initial shock wore off and she overcame her strange, new fear of being in such small, confined quarters, Nancy remembered Pfister nicknamed her "Martha," after Martha Stewart, because she sewed and usually had one craft project or another underway. *I just didn't know I would be serving jail time like Martha.*

She also realized Olmsted was right: Pitkin County wasn't a bad place to be. "Pitkin was a country club compared to Eagle," Nancy said, referring to the Eagle County Jail where she was later transferred. "And the food [compared to Eagle] was a culinary delight."

Inside her cell, she found a bed, complete with a twin-sized mattress and pillow, but Nancy, who in her own home tossed out a bath towel at the first sign of a fray, was disturbed by the bed linens. When she first arrived at the jail, a male guard handed her a stack of linens, including sheets. She noticed they had stains and holes, and told the guard. "These are disgusting. They're gross."

"Lady, this isn't the Four Seasons," he said. "You've been charged with a very serious crime."

"But I'm innocent," Nancy said.

The guard looked dubious, as if to say, "Sure you are."

Like the food, the linens came from Aspen Valley Hospital, and while Nancy could tolerate the food, she called the linens "gross hospital rejects." Her cell also had a porcelain sink, a bookcase, a desk, and Velcro curtains on the long narrow window, which was blocked so inmates couldn't see outside. It opened into a dayroom where there was a table, four plastic chairs, a bunk bed that was used during times of overcrowding, a TV, and a fridge.

Another cell, a mirror image of Nancy's, opened into the dayroom opposite hers, and the entire area had the feel of a college dorm room—except for the heavy steel doors that were always tightly locked. Each door had a small glass "window" with a Velcro curtain on the exterior; every night at Pitkin the lights went out and guards would check on inmates by pulling open the Velcro curtain and shining their flashlight into the room.

Nancy couldn't sleep for the first few days, given how often the light shone into her room. Every thirty minutes or so a guard came around, checking on the inmates.

"What's that all about?" Nancy asked one guard.

"We have you on suicide watch," he said.

Nancy couldn't believe it. *Now I really feel like a real criminal.* She still wasn't sleeping as much by the time she left almost three weeks later, but the flashlight beam no longer bothered her. Sometimes she'd even wave to the guards who came around.

Much to Nancy's delight, there was also an exercise bike and yoga mats—and a really nice guard named Roger, who worked out in the gym, as the guards called it, at night after everyone else was in bed. Nancy was almost never allowed in the dayroom during the day, for although they were both confined to their cells in theory, Trey often wasn't, and was allowed in the dayroom. So Roger let Nancy work out at night when he was there.

The one downside was that she could only work out for an hour—the total time any inmate was allowed out of his or her cell each day. She loved the gym, especially after a guard took pity on her and exchanged her extra-large sneakers for a pair that actually fit.

***

Nancy was thankful to be treated with respect, but she never forgot she was a prisoner. And jail rituals ensured she felt like one during the eighteen days she was there.

Except for the nasty comment Sheriff DiSalvo made when she arrived, the only other negative experience inside Pitkin happened when Nancy thought she was suffocating and a female guard wouldn't let her out of her cell.

Room inspection was every Friday, and if an inmate's cell passed inspection, they received a bottle of Coke as a reward. Nancy loved Coke and besides, she knew how to get dirt off of anything. She was cleaning her cell and wanted to get rid of a bunch of hair in the shower drain, because when she showered, the hairball clogged up the drain and Nancy hated the idea of having standing water in the shower. It grossed her out, so she asked for some cleaning supplies. She was given a bleach solution, which she sprayed quite a bit of down the shower drain. Almost immediately, Nancy realized there was no ventilation in the tiny room. She began choking on the bleach fumes.

Nancy hit the call button in her cell to notify the guards she needed help, and Jill, a female guard with a dark bob haircut, came to the room.

"What's the problem?" she asked Nancy.

"I kind of overdid it with the bleach," Nancy said, "and I'm realizing there's no ventilation and I can't breathe."

But Jill wouldn't let her outside the cell.

Nancy begged her. "I need to get some air. Please let me out."

"You're overreacting," Jill said.

"No, I really overdid it on the bleach in there, because there was a hairball in the drain, and I need to get some air."

"Quit being a drama queen," Jill said and left.

***

That was the first time any of the guards actually mistreated her, and Jill's response took Nancy aback. Usually the guards at Pitkin came when called for, gave Nancy her medication when she needed it, and were polite and respectful, even calling her "Mrs. Styler," and, for the most part, were nonjudgmental.

"Normally they were wonderful," Nancy said.

But after that experience, Nancy did feel like a prisoner, like someone whose rights had been taken away. And, at times like that, remaining hopeful and upbeat while jailed and charged with a crime she didn't commit—could never in her life even dream of committing—wasn't easy.

In fact, three days after going to jail, Nancy knew what it felt like to die. Friends she hadn't heard from in so long that she thought them dead, strangers from around the country, so many different people reached out to her. Through cards and letters they told Nancy good things about herself, so she felt like she heard her own eulogy even though she was still alive.

"I calmed down," Nancy said, "and felt like I was being wrapped in a big, warm, fuzzy blanket of love." Those people helped keep Nancy's hope alive. Communication from the outside world became her mainstay.

And when she heard from the Duran family after three years of no contact, Nancy felt like her heart would burst. Years earlier, she and Trey had given the Latino family help when few people would. After working for the Stylers for several years, they became like family. When Daniel told the Durans what had happened, they sent money every week to help with Nancy's commissary fund, and they continued to pay for a Denver storage locker the couple couldn't afford to keep. Members of a local Aspen church Nancy had never met even brought Cokes and Sun Chips to all the inmates every week, which helped cheer her up, too.

**

For the most part, Nancy did remain hopeful—with tons of help from the outside world. Her mother, Tess, wrote her every day. (She wrote Trey almost as often.) Cindy and Daniel sent them both letters and cards with funny, inspirational sayings and advice and good news designed to help Nancy survive the ordeal.

Much of what they sent was funny, so funny that Nancy would often find herself—in spite of facing one first-degree murder charge, as well as another for supposedly conspiring to commit that murder—laughing out loud. The McDaniel family, unlike Trey, had a wicked sense of humor. It came from Tess, the family's matriarch, and Nancy had inherited more than her share of it. When Nancy returned from college, her bond with Cindy became closer than ever, and family photos down through the years showed it. There were pictures of the time the two sisters dressed up, with Nancy in her cheerleader uniform and her baby sister as the team mascot, and of them dressing up as characters in the many parodies they wrote and filmed. The photos revealed two self-confident young women who weren't afraid to look goofy or ridiculous together.

***

Nancy's sense of humor definitely buoyed her during her 108 days in jail, as did the visits she received from her Aspen friends. There were only two such visits, but each time they restored Nancy's spirits at just the right moment. Patrice Melanie and Purl Shirley, the two women Nancy had met at the Aspen farmers' market in August 2013, came to the jail bearing gifts. Both times, they brought Nancy fashion magazines, which she loved, and self-help books to read.

"Patrice and Purl are the most beautiful people I've ever met," Nancy said, "and just truly, truly, truly beautiful, and inspiring, and they believed in us so thoroughly. They were two of my angels."

During their first visit, which happened inside a little room over telephones and through a window made from bulletproof glass, Patrice put her hand on the glass and Nancy raised her own, their palms together, each on opposite sides of the glass. It was the only kind of "touch" possible for jail inmates. A few minutes later, Nancy pulled down her pants enough for them to see her jail-issued undies.

"I was showing them the granny panties and we started laughing," Nancy said. She regaled them the stories about her arrival there, with the sports bra that offered her breasts no support; the humorless guard; the stained, holey castoff hospital linens; her oversized clothing and shoes; and getting only six inches of dental floss.

Then came words Nancy couldn't believe she was hearing—and which she was so grateful for. "Patrice was on the phone and she knew that everything was being monitored, and she was saying, 'Joey [Sheriff DiSalvo], you made a big mistake here!'" Nancy said. "She said that over and over."

Patrice didn't care; she wanted her words to reach the ears of the sheriff, because she just knew he had arrested the wrong people. The couple she knew could never be killers! It wasn't in their makeup. Nancy felt overwhelmed by the conviction in Patrice's voice. Yes, there were people who believed they didn't do it.

Throughout her entire time in jail, from March 3 until later that summer, their flawless hand-designed cards, filled with precious messages of faith, hope, and reassurance, sustained both of the Stylers. But it was Nancy who came to rely on Patrice's infectious belief in their innocence, when her own hope began to lag during brief moments of darkness.

Patrice and Purl's first visit came early in Nancy's jail stay, when it was still easy to laugh then. Although still in shock over being considered a felon, she knew any day the police would realize their mistake; they would find that Pfister's death "was a suicide."

It was like Pfister herself had told Nancy when they first met. "She was broke and said she didn't want to live without money," Nancy said. "Either that or her sister killed her. She told me if she's ever found dead, to look for her sister Suzanne." Even though the two sisters hated each other, Nancy didn't really believe Pfister's sister would murder her.

What Nancy did believe, what she knew from her own past experiences in the field of scientific research is that science would prove her innocence. Before she gave up her career to rear their son, she was a highly skilled clinical and medical researcher who took emergency calls from doctors around the country about the treatment protocol for malignant hyperthermia—a deadly disease that can quickly kill patients under the effects of general anesthesia.

That's why Nancy insisted the autopsy and DNA test results, along with the absence of their fingerprints on anything involving Pfister's death—all very real, tangible scientific evidence—would lead to her and Trey's freedom.

So she told everyone—from her two angels who came to visit to her attorneys to other inmates—that. The officials would "get this right and any day they'd come in and say, 'You're free to go.'"

***

However, "any day" turned out to be a vague number that sometimes led Nancy to despair of ever seeing Trey again. By Patrice and Purl's second visit, not many days after their first, Nancy's spirits were so low that they were frightened. And regardless of what the public believed, and what people were saying, their affection and loyalty to Nancy remained unfazed.

What Nancy didn't know, because no one told her during those first few days in the Pitkin County Jail, and which she wouldn't even learn during her March 4 advisement hearing, was that the autopsy results were back, the DNA evidence already processed.

CHAPTER TWENTY-FIVE

LOOSE LIPS SINK SHIPS

T
he day Sheriff Joe DiSalvo stood in front of Nancy, gloating over her arrest, Judge Gail Nichols sealed the case file at Public Defender Beth Krulewitch's request. The next day, March 4, Nancy and Trey appeared before the judge. That was the first time the world learned, by way of the news media, that there were problems with the case. Or rather, the media lightly touched on the fact that problems existed in the district attorney's office's handling of it. The size of the cracks in the prosecution's case had yet to be discovered. That would take a while to come out, since the wheels of justice seemed to barely creep along.

The Stylers were marched outside that March 4 wearing handcuffs and leg shackles, en route to their advisement hearing. They were part of a parade of sorts, as they were made to walk or, in Trey's case, ride in a wheelchair, between the jail and the courthouse.

They passed a throng of reporters waiting to take their photos, while doing what Garth McCarty, one of Nancy's two public defenders, would later call the couple's "perp walk." As Nancy shuffled along, moving neither fast nor gracefully, she felt the weight of the chains around her waist drag the oversized pants down off what little hips she had, exposing the ugly granny panties underneath. Mentally, she felt like the entire town's eyes were on her, and another layer of shame and humiliation was heaped on the growing pile.

Garth wasn't there that day to protect Nancy from the intrusive news cameras as he later would; he was still in New Orleans for a

National Association of Criminal Defense Lawyers (NACDL) conference. But he would soon return to Glenwood Springs and join Beth Krulewitch's fight to aggressively defend Nancy's innocence.

Garth first learned about the case from Tina Fang, one of his mentors, and he was immediately interested. Fang was also a good friend, and Garth said it was "important from the very start to have a strong working relationship between the attorneys for Trey and Nancy, so the fact that Fang was Trey's attorney was a selling point for me."

Colorado courts routinely appoint public defenders, using attorneys who belong to the Colorado Alternate Defense Counsel, or ADC. However, the ADC can decide which of its attorneys are best qualified for homicide cases, since some lawyers aren't experienced or competent enough to handle cases that are tough and tricky to navigate.

"Those of us who are [qualified] usually step up and make ourselves available," Garth said. So he volunteered for the appointment, notifying the ADC that he was available by cell phone if they needed him—in spite of being out of town. Then he called Beth.

"Time is of the essence when a homicide occurs, and the defense lawyers must 'front-end' the case immediately," Garth said, "both in terms of advising and protecting the client from law enforcement and snitches, and also in terms of getting motions filed and investigators working."

And Garth said that can't happen soon enough. "A good defense attorney should jump into action less than twenty-four hours after a homicide arrest, if not sooner."

Sara Steele and Fang, Trey's two attorneys, both knew that and jumped pretty quickly—because after trying to visit her client following his March 3 arrest, Sara felt that a two-hour wait was not in keeping with Trey's rights. The March 4 advisement hearing made it even clearer: the Stylers' rights were being violated.

Before the hearing began, due to the high-profile nature of the case, Pitkin County authorities used a metal detector to screen everyone who attended the hearing. Nancy and Trey were led into the courtroom through the same door used by judges and attorneys, and not long after, Judge Gail Nichols entered behind them.

"All rise. Court is in session," a bailiff's voice rang out inside the packed courtroom. Someone overheard Trey tell Nancy he couldn't stand "for her," so he remained sitting in the county-issued wheelchair.

Those were his first words to Nancy since they had been arrested the day before, separated, and taken to different cells. She didn't need to fight to keep from crying, because the tears wouldn't come. They were frozen somewhere deep within her. Nancy's heart swelled when she saw Trey, and she felt a mixture of anger and concern, knowing that not having his prescribed medicine forced him to rely on the wheelchair.

Neither husband nor wife quite knew what to expect. Beth had visited Nancy just before the hearing, and quickly told her what an advisement hearing was: as a defendant, she and Trey would hear the DA's charges against them, the judge would advise them about the right to have an attorney, as well as tell them what to do if they couldn't afford one. Normally, the judge would set bond. However, with a first-degree, Class 1 felony murder charge, as well as a charge of conspiracy to commit first-degree murder, a Class 2 felony, there was no bond.

Nancy laid eyes on her public defender for the first time when Beth arrived to escort Nancy to the hearing. She thought Beth looked to be in her forties. She was fit, like a skier, with straight blonde hair that stubbornly fell into her eyes whenever she spoke, leading Beth to constantly brush it away with a sweep of her hand. In just a few seconds, Nancy sensed that Beth was a fighter, and someone who was direct and blunt.

"Let me do all the talking," Beth warned her. "No matter what happens, don't say a word."

Nancy liked her immediately.

***

Ninth Judicial District Attorney Sherry Caloia and Deputy District Attorney Andrea Bryan appeared in court together, representing the prosecution. According to the March 5 article in the *Aspen Daily News*, Bryan wanted six more weeks to file charges, but Nichols refused her request. She said that was too long to wait, because the Stylers were currently being held without bond. Instead, Judge Nichols set the next court date for March 17—just two weeks away—and told Bryan she would need a "very good explanation" if the prosecution filed for an extension. She said she was concerned about lengthy delays because the couple was in jail. Nichols stressed the need for action in the case, since she signed the arrest warrants believing there was "sufficient probable cause."

Oddly enough, when Judge Nichols turned to the matter of appointing the Stylers' attorneys, District Attorney Sherry Caloia quickly argued against it, calling it "premature." And that's when the news media suspected something wasn't quite right, because they later reported how Caloia's argument prompted Sara Steele, one of Trey's attorneys, to speak up. Steele told the court that she and Fang were worried that the prosecution was violating the Stylers' rights by denying them access to their attorneys and to mental healthcare. They have "mental health issues that need to be taken care of," Steele said. Area newspapers and other media outlets quickly reported on the DA's argument, and Steele's reply.

In spite of Caloia's efforts to deny the Stylers access to immediate legal counsel, and perhaps because of Steele's concern about multiple violations of Trey and Nancy's rights, Judge Nichols made it official and Beth was appointed to represent Nancy. (Steele and Fang had already been appointed to represent Trey.)

Nichols had to appoint Nancy an attorney, because that premise is one of the chief cornerstones of the U.S. justice system: defendants have a right to legal counsel, regardless of the charge against them or their ability to pay.

Every defendant also has a right to a speedy trial, but nothing about this case happened speedily. Not only were Nancy and Trey denied access to legal counsel right away, but it would also take another three days before Nancy or Trey's attorneys received copies of the affidavits and the search and arrest warrants.

***

With the first hearing behind them, the Stylers returned to their mundane life behind bars, while their attorneys went to work in earnest. Olmsted, one of the defense's three private investigators who would eventually work on Nancy's case, had realized there was a leak in the case during his return flight from Denver to Aspen on March 5.

Needless to say, the Stylers' four attorneys (by then Garth had been appointed) jointly wanted to find it—and permanently plug it.

The defense team was worried because any leaks about the case could impact their defendants' ability to receive fair and unbiased treatment when the case went to trial. And the leaks continued during the first two weeks of the case, at least. Even more troubling, the earliest pieces of leaked information proved correct, indicating that someone working on the case was talking when he or she shouldn't—if that person was a prosecutor, it would be a clear violation of legal ethics. That someone close to the case had loose lips was evident in the February 28 issue of the *Aspen Times*. It reported, "There has been considerable talk in the community about the manner in which Pfister was killed, [citing] that she was the victim of blunt-force trauma and left inside a closet."

It appeared that the leaks were coming from within the sheriff's own department—or someone very close to the agency. As it turned out, Sheriff DiSalvo had a little social gathering at his house the evening of February 26. And since he had his police radio turned on, when the 911 call was broadcast that very same evening, DiSalvo and former sheriff, Bob Braudis, who was also at the party, started following the radio traffic. Braudis thought the address sounded familiar, and checking online, he discovered it was Pfister's. Next, DiSalvo called his office and learned the victim was Pfister herself.

No one would have known who leaked the information if not for Braudis. The leaks didn't come from within the rank and file of either the sheriff's office or that of the DA. They came from the top dogs themselves. Braudis later told Agent Zamora that it was DiSalvo who shared details about the murder with several people. However, it was a case of "the pot calling the kettle black," because so did Braudis.

Other police interviews, specifically with Pfister's younger sister, Christina, and Patti Stranahan, verify this. Patti told police how she found out about Pfister's death from her cousin (Braudis), and, in her case, that might be understandable. Given that Patti and George Stranahan were Juliana's godparents, and Patti and Braudis were cousins, it seems logical that the two family members might share news that Juliana's mother (who, after all, because of Juliana, was somewhat like a family member) was dead.

In addition, Patti had called Braudis earlier that day, after she became worried about Pfister's unexplained absence. This call occurred not long before Kathy Carpenter discovered the body, so when Braudis heard the news at DiSalvo's house not long afterward, it seems only natural—and not as much of a violation of legal ethics—when he replied to Patti's text with details about Pfister's death.

Christina would disagree. She told investigators Braudis knew everything about the murder victim, and he was talking "way too much" about the crime. Christina learned about her sister's death when an out-of-state family member called her late Wednesday night, saying he'd seen a story about Pfister's murder on national news. And by 2 a.m. Christina said several Aspen friends had called, sharing specific details about the murder.

"I was furious," she said, "because my understanding is that it is an impediment to an investigation for too many people to know too much too early . . . I am very angry because Bob Braudis has told everyone from California to South America."

Ironically, perhaps because of the Pfister sisters' longtime estrangement, Christina said she never received official police notification when her sister's body was discovered, in spite of calling the sheriff to inquire about it. She implored DiSalvo to tell her what had happened, saying, "Suzanne says that you and she are very, very close . . . Suzanne's [always talking about] 'Joey, Joey, Joey.'"

Still, DiSalvo refused to tell her anything.

Suzanne Pfister was equally unhappy. The people who contacted her "practically read me the autopsy report," the eldest Pfister sister said. "It's very painful for a family member."

Because of that, Suzanne asked investigators Miller and Zamora a question. "Is [Braudis] on the sheriff's payroll?"

CHAPTER TWENTY-SIX

WHAT THE MEDIA DIDN'T KNOW

The wheels of justice rolled along slowly, preventing most outsiders from even realizing that the DA's entire argument was based on a schism the size of Buttermilk Mountain. Because Judge Nichols sealed the case immediately, the media and the general public were prevented from knowing specific details about it, including what evidence appeared so strong that the authorities could arrest and charge the Stylers with two serious felonies.

And while Pitkin County's two most recent sheriffs—who together had held the office since 1986, when Bob Braudis was first elected—spoke freely to friends and acquaintances about the details of Pfister's murder, Sheriff DiSalvo would say nothing in public. Especially not after Tina Fang attacked him in open court.

In the days and weeks following the March 4 advisement hearing, the defense, comprised of two teams, each with two attorneys, and operating separately (but still dependent on each other) and with Fang as its unofficial, outspoken leader, would accuse Sheriff DiSalvo of many things—all of which he denied. Their foremost accusation? That the sheriff, who shed tears in public over Pfister's death, and then appeared on the front page of the local newspaper the day after her body was found, posing with Pfister's eight-month-old puppy, Gabe, whom he was housing himself, was too close to the case to remain objective.

There are many historic examples of police officers and judges stepping aside from an investigation or a case where they have a personal relationship with the suspects involved, so their personal judgment doesn't interfere, and bias either for or against the suspects does not become a problem. The Pitkin County sheriff didn't do that and didn't think he needed to.

Specifically, in the February 28 issue of the *Aspen Times*, DiSalvo denied the importance of his personal relationship with Pfister and some of her family. He explained it away, saying that Aspen was a small town where "everybody knows everybody." It was especially difficult not to know Pfister, who regularly dropped by for chats with Braudis when he was sheriff, DiSalvo said. (DiSalvo became second in command the year after Braudis was first elected sheriff.)

Hoping to appear even more objective, and perhaps believing it himself, the sheriff then said that every murder victim would receive the same treatment from his office. "I will tell you this: I would put as much effort into the investigation if it were Nancy Jones, someone I never knew."

However, in the March 3 edition of the newspaper, DiSalvo's own words had some people already questioning that, as they wondered how the sheriff could possibly lead an unbiased investigation. "I loved Nancy—she was a good person," he said.

* * *

The sheriff's own comments about his earlier visit to the Stylers in jail led Nancy Styler to shake her head in disbelief when she learned about them. The account DiSalvo related to the media was nothing like she had already experienced.

The March 5 issue of the *Aspen Daily News* quoted DiSalvo, citing his words at the press conference following the couple's March 4 hearing. There, the sheriff mentioned having made personal visits to see the Stylers the Monday evening of their arrest. "I wanted to make sure their needs were met," he said. "I just wanted to tell them that they would be treated with dignity and respect, as every one of my inmates are."

However, when asked about Steele's comments during that same hearing, concerning the couple's mental state, DiSalvo's response certainly didn't show that. "I'm not a psychiatrist so I can't answer that," he said, without any indication that he was also personally concerned, as his comments to the media about Pfister repeatedly indicated. In fact, when DiSalvo confessed he had seen the Stylers in jail, saying it was "the first time that he had paid such a visit to defendants," he basically admitted his bias.

The media didn't know everything, including the fact that DiSalvo discussed confidential details of the case with the victim's daughter, Juliana Pfister, proclaiming the Stylers' guilt before they were even charged with a crime—and certainly before any solid evidence even appeared that might link them to it.

The defense maintained that DiSalvo was after their clients since the discovery of Pfister's body, targeting the Stylers because they were outsiders, because the Pfister family name holds such sway in Aspen, and because neither DiSalvo nor the investigators working the case even cared that Pfister's overseas allegations, that the Stylers weren't paying her, were untrue.

Instead, the sheriff freely disclosed his early suspicions. At the March 3 news conference, DiSalvo admitted the couple was under investigation from the start. "We all felt it was crucial . . . to keep these people within our view," he said.

Within two hours of Kathy Carpenter's 911 call, the police were dispatched to the Aspenalt Lodge, the motel where the Stylers were staying. From that time until they were marched from Room 122 on Monday, March 3, the couple was under constant police surveillance.

***

In other media, specifically social media, Pfister posted about the Stylers on her Facebook wall. Investigators later pointed to her public comments as "evidence," saying a rental dispute with Pfister gave the Stylers motive to kill her.

"Okay everyone I am still in Byron Bay I have just found most beautiful place on earth and I really want to buy it first of all I need somebody to rent my place in Aspen because the people that I was letting to did not come through they are out of there February 22nd I believe and I do not want to say much more," she said on January 21, 2014.

Then, three days later, Pfister shared more information on Face-book. "Hi everyone . . . I'd like to stay in Australia but the people that were supposedly taking care of my house are not doing what they said they would do and they're not paying rent and they haven't paid util-ities, I put the rent very very low so they would take care of my dog a beautiful [L]abradoodle named Gabe."

Those Facebook posts, coupled with Kathy's hysterical comment to the 911 dispatcher that "they did it," was enough to send the police looking for the Stylers.

And in fact, the couple had paid Pfister long before her return from Australia. As of early January, their rent was paid in full through February 22. After being left without hot water for a month, and after Pfister expected them to absorb the growing costs of caring for Gabe (who destroyed many of the Stylers' possessions), and finally, after their landlord repeatedly changed the terms of their oral agreement—since they never had a binding written one—the Stylers felt their only option was to leave Pfister's 1833 West Buttermilk home. So they refused to pay the upcoming $4,000 March rent.

Police suspicions should have been raised about Pfister's claims on social media and in her personal emails to some officers themselves—including to DiSalvo and Braudis—when they saw the contents of Pfister's safety deposit box, with proof the couple had paid her, before the Stylers' March 3 arrest.

"The evidence was all right there on the back of an envelope," Nancy said, "proving [Pfister] was lying."

However, Nancy agreed that DiSalvo got one thing right, at least when he told the media about his visit to see her. "I'll tell you this, I did the talking, they did the listening," the sheriff said during the March 3 news conference.

From Aspen to Argentina, from Los Angeles to New York City, the press published everything it could about the case, including its two defendants, the victim, and DiSalvo, who told the world that solv-ing Pfister's murder was "the highest priority for this office"—and how, with the Stylers' arrest, the case was basically solved.

***

The media wasn't to blame for getting the story wrong. Reporters simply had poor sources, some who had been so frightened by the police that they unknowingly gave the media incorrect information. Nor could the media know the only real evidence the prosecution had was a dead body, because, due to the DA's request that the case be sealed, no members of the media had even seen the autopsy results yet.

Although the media filed a collective motion to have the case unsealed, that motion was denied for several months. It wasn't unsealed until the case was over, on July 18. In the meantime, the media had no access to anything—the arrest warrants or the affidavits containing more than one hundred bulleted points, some of which were "razor thin," as Beth said, others based on lies and omissions, as well as statements given by people on painkillers, who were emotionally traumatized, who had head injuries and cognitive impairment, or who had even their own agendas. All of the affidavits came from the criminal case file, which was compiled by a staffer who was not a trained law enforcement officer. The primary affidavits—those used to arrest innocent people—were written up by a detective on desk duty who never even saw the body, who didn't attend the autopsy, and who received out-of-context information from the DA and police investigators with their own biases.

Of course, all the errors would come out in due time. But not in time to save another person from being wrongfully arrested.

CHAPTER TWENTY-SEVEN

ANATOMY OF AN AFFIDAVIT

B efore former governor Bill Ritter appointed her to the bench in Colorado's Ninth Judicial District in 2008, Judge Gail Nichols had a long career as a federal prosecutor in New Jersey. There, she took her golden retriever to work with her every day, while working for the U.S. Attorney's Office.

"She's very smart, she's very thorough, she's very careful, she's very good," Olmsted said. "I like her." Olmsted, who has testified in federal court many times and as an expert in criminal investigations, said he and Nichols bonded over their dogs when he worked in New Jersey years earlier; Olmsted had a retriever, also.

According to a recent article in the *Aspen Daily News* about Nichols' plan to retire that October, she also worked as a federal defense attorney, representing defendants who had ties to organized crime. And Nichols put in her time in private practice, even working with former New York City mayor Rudy Giuliani.

Even after working on both sides, for the defense and the prosecution for many years, presiding over such a high-profile case as the Pfister murder had to be challenging for the sixty-four-year-old judge. "It's painful" to be a judge, Nichols told the *Aspen Daily News*.

Beth Krulewitch, one of Nancy's defense attorneys, later said she thought the judge "could have held [the prosecution's] feet to the fire a little more," but overall, she was fair.

And while Olmsted believed Judge Nichols hesitated on some rulings, "by and large, she did a good job."

***

In spite of that, many people in the legal community have wondered whether Nichols would have been disturbed to know the warrants she signed in the Pfister case were based on an affidavit that contained factual errors.

It isn't just police and prosecutors who make mistakes. Anything with too short of a lead time, such as a newspaper article, is more likely to be fraught with errors than not. Usually, there are checks and balances to catch the errors. In the case of news reporters, there are proofreaders and copyeditors who serve this purpose, since an extra set of eyes is always better at catching mistakes. That way, people are less likely to end up reading online or print articles that contain errors.

For example, it was widely reported that Nancy Pfister graduated from Pratt Institute in New York City. Even the March 6, 2014, issue of the *New York Post* carried a story about Pfister's death that repeated this rumor. Someone clearly didn't check the facts, though, because, according to a clerk in the registrar's office, Pfister only attended the world-famous college for one semester in 1977. Her stay was so brief, the clerk said, that Pfister's transcript didn't even contain any information about what she did during her time there.

The same problem occurred in the affidavits used to obtain search warrants to arrest the Stylers and, later, Kathy Carpenter. However, the investigation into Pfister's murder didn't have a deadline that was as time-sensitive as, say, a newspaper that goes to press in a few hours.

If police had good reason to believe there was a mass murderer on the loose, then they would have had an overwhelming need to act quickly and protect the public. But they didn't believe Pfister's death had such implications. And if the Stylers were the killers, then they were safely tucked away at the Aspenalt Lodge, clearly not in a hurry to leave town. So there was far more reason for police and prosecutors to take their time in such a high-profile murder investigation, and do things right.

But that doesn't seem to be what happened. In fact, before Pitkin County Sheriff's Detective Brad Gibson would sign the affidavit that would be used to convince Judge Nichols that enough evidence existed to arrest the Stylers on March 3, Nichols signed an earlier affidavit.

Deputy Grant Jahnke requested the "Application and Affidavit for Search Warrant" that Nichols signed at 7:50 p.m. on Thursday, February 27, giving him permission to search the Stylers' two storage units, numbers 371 and 396, at the Storage Mart located on Park Avenue in Basalt. The warrant said police were specifically looking for not just personal belongings of the Stylers, but also "D. Any and all human remains; E. Any bodily fluids, saliva, semen, and any DNA evidence in the form of skin cells, hairs, fibers, or any other transferable DNA; F. Latent fingerprints; G. Blood . . . or other residue constituting evidence of bleeding injuries or other violent trauma . . . hair, fiber, and bodily fluid evidence; H. Computers, cellular phones, memory devices, as well as written instruments . . . which could be evidence of the identity of the persons in possession . . . of the storage unit; I. Any weapons, bludgeons, ammunition, or any other objects that could be used to inflict injuries and/or death; J. Bed sheets, trash bags, electrical cords; (and) K. Any evidence used to commit . . . homicide."

By signing his name on the affidavit for the search warrant, Deputy Jahnke was essentially swearing under oath that the facts he included provided "probable cause to believe that a homicide was committed at 1833 West Buttermilk Road . . . and that Nancy and/or William Styler may have moved evidence of that homicide to the storage units."

In the attached "Statement of Facts," used as a basis to obtain the search warrant, Jahnke listed nine such facts, each one outlining numerous details about that particular fact. For instance, in Fact Four, Jahnke referred to a conversation he had had with Kathy Carpenter at about 9:15 p.m. on February 26 at the Pitkin County Courthouse.

After listing more than forty details about that fact, Jahnke next listed these two: "rr. Carpenter told Sheriff Joe DiSalvo that she saw the Stylers at 1833 W. Buttermilk Road of February 26, 2014; (and) ss. Carpenter told Investigator Gibson that she *did not* see the Stylers at the residence on February 26, 2014."

The very next fact listed, Fact Five, basically repeated what Kathy said to Gibson—except this time she told Deputy Ryan Turner, the officer who responded to Kathy after she found Pfister's body in the closet and called 911 for help—that she *did* see the Stylers at Pfister's residence on February 26.

In three separate accounts, given to three different authorities—including Sheriff DiSalvo—Kathy Carpenter contradicted herself three times. Although that should have been obvious to the judge, the affidavit that Jahnke requested had omitted a few vital facts. Among them was the most blatant failure to disclose information pertinent to the case: after finding her close friend's body, Kathy was so traumatized her words were nearly incoherent during her 911 call. By the time Deputy Turner arrived at her side, Kathy was barely able to stand, nauseous, and still hysterical. After officers took her statement, they took her to the Aspen Valley Hospital emergency department, where she was given two Ativan injections and remained in a state of shock.

Kathy's extremely poor physical and emotional condition continued throughout the next day. Witnesses reported this and voice mail messages confirmed it. In spite of that, police still took Kathy in for more questioning. They did this not long after she had received medical treatment. Kathy was then still under the influence of a very strong, mind-altering drug. According to the manufacturer, Ativan slows brain activity to help a patient relax. Common side effects include drowsiness and dizziness. No wonder, then, that her statements about seeing the Stylers at Pfister's home earlier that day were contradictory. Similar to what happened with Patrick Carney, who was under the influence of strong painkillers during times vital to the investigation, police proceeded as if Kathy's claims were completely sound.

This raises two questions: why did not even one of the law enforcement officers who dealt with Kathy consider her mental state before basing the request for a search warrant on her statements the night of February 26?

***

Brad Gibson's "Application and Affidavit for Arrest Warrant" for Nancy Styler reveals similar problems throughout. For example, Gibson cites as his evidence his February 28 conversation with DA investigator Lisa Miller. He then lists numerous "facts" he got from Miller and other investigators, which led Judge Nichols to sign the affidavit.

Gibson said Miller told him that Merlin went to the Aspenalt Lodge where the Stylers were staying earlier that same evening. There, according to the affidavit, Nancy Styler told Merlin she "did not like Pfister at all," and said "I really did hate (her)." Merlin reportedly told Miller he became uncomfortable with Nancy's statements about Pfister and left their motel room.

What Miller either failed to tell Gibson, or what Gibson failed to include in the affidavit, is this: Merlin was very clear in his interview with investigators. Twice he told them he did not believe the Stylers were involved in Pfister's murder. Fourteen minutes into his interview with Pitkin County Deputy Tiffani Delaney," Merlin says, "I don't believe at all the renters were involved." A minute later, he repeats that sentiment: "I don't feel they're involved."

At other times during the interview, Merlin says the Stylers were "very, very nice, decent people" who were having a hard time moving due to their age. He also told Delaney that the Stylers offered to pay him for his help with their move, but he refused.

Even more important, Merlin said on Monday, February 24, he was avoiding Pfister—just as Nancy Styler was—and for the same reason. He said he didn't want to get in the middle and hear her badmouth her tenants. This is similar to what Nancy Styler told Merlin herself, when he showed up Monday. Merlin shared this with Delaney, when he said Nancy told him she was avoiding Pfister's bedroom, because if Pfister were home, she did not want to see her. The fact that Pfister wasn't up and about, he told Delaney, wasn't odd to him or the Stylers, because Pfister "always slept until 12 or 1 so you never knew if she was there."

In spite of Merlin's statements to the contrary, Miller and Gibson chose to only focus on any statements that would lead a judge to think the Stylers were complicit in Pfister's murder.

Yet anything that could have exonerated them never found its way into a single affidavit. For instance, the fact that Nancy personally notified police on at least three occasions about a civil standby— drawing attention to her and Trey, rather than trying to avoid police attention—was never mentioned. Or the fact that from the first time Nancy smelled an odd odor in Pfister's house, she told several other people about it.

"If Nancy Styler was involved in the murder, she would not have mentioned the bad smell," retired police captain K.C. Bohrer said, "because she would have wanted to distance herself from knowing there was a dead body."

CHAPTER TWENTY-EIGHT

WRONG TIME OF DEATH

The official statements from witnesses who were under the
influence or emotionally unsound, as were Patrick Carney and
Kathy Carpenter, wasn't the only reason the affidavits were
problematic.

Other equally serious errors also crept in. For instance, the time
of Pfister's death as listed on the autopsy report was incorrect. But no
one figured that out in 2014 when the investigation was ongoing. In
fact, more than one year after Pfister was murdered, some of those
who had worked the case still believed Pfister was alive late in the day
on February 24. Defense investigator David Olmsted, Pitkin County
Deputy Coroner Eric Hansen, and even forensic pathologist Robert
Kurtzman, were among this group. And it was all because of one little
note, scribbled in a police investigator's handwriting. Police gave it to
Hansen, who passed it along to Kurtzman, who performed Pfister's
forensic exam Thursday afternoon, February 27, 2014.

Hansen's work on the murder investigation began when he was
paged at 6:40 p.m. on Wednesday, February 26. He arrived at 1833
West Buttermilk Road fifteen minutes later. But he couldn't do much,
because police were waiting for CBI investigators to arrive and process
the crime scene. Instead, Hansen examined the body the next morning, and then took it to the hospital morgue. From there, it went to
Kurtzman's office in Grand Junction.

When asked about how he arrived at Pfister's time of death, Hansen
said it came from another officer. "I have a note here that says there was

an email from her to somebody on [Monday] February 24," Hansen said during an April 2015 interview with investigative reporter Daleen Berry. Since "we know she died in her sleep" that email means she probably died during the evening or early morning hours. "Late that night, the 24th, or early on the 25th, because rigor mortis had passed," Hansen said. "It wasn't likely she died the morning of February 26 or late the night of February 26."

This helped explain why, early in the case, Sheriff DiSalvo told the media that Pfister was still alive Monday afternoon or evening. Zamora's handwritten notes said Braudis heard from Pfister on Monday, when she supposedly sent a text message to him at 3:30, inviting him to a party. Zamora's notes didn't say whether it was 3:30 a.m. or p.m. However, in the audio recording of that same interview, Braudis was heard telling Zamora that he had received an email from Pfister—not a text message. If an email or a text message had been verified, no one from the prosecution said so, and the defense didn't see it.

One can only assume it was an error—which then found its way into Kurtzman's official autopsy report. It listed Pfister's time of death as having occurred during a thirty-six- to forty-eight-hour window prior to the autopsy being conducted. This meant the earliest Pfister was killed would have been around noon on Tuesday, February 25, and the latest, in the wee hours of Wednesday, February 26.

This explains why the time of death listed on the autopsy is unrealistic. "It's too tight a time interval," Dr. Judy Melinek, a professor at the University of California-San Francisco Medical Center, said.

Melinek did not work on the Pfister case, but as a Harvard- and University of California San Francisco–trained forensic pathologist, she has testified as an expert witness in court. "Most textbooks and experts will tell you that time-of-death estimation is fraught with errors because there are so many variables at play," she said. Those variables include "ambient temperature, temperature of deceased when killed, exposure, [and] location."

Pfister's autopsy did provide a thorough investigation of all those variables, but the exact time of death was simply unavailable because the science is too complex and unreadable. A thorough investigation of the scene and Pfister's body should have led to the truth for her family, those wrongly accused of killing her, and the Aspen community.

Unfortunately, thanks to bias and inaccurate information, the truth was doomed from the beginning.

And that one tiny detail—saying that Pfister died later than she did—severely impacted the entire investigation.

That was one reason why Dr. James "Jack" Frost never liked pinpointing a time of death in murder cases. Frost was chief of the West Virginia State Medical Examiner's Office, where he worked as a pathologist from 1977 until he retired in 2003. His peers consider Frost a legend, and his opinions are widely cited in law enforcement and pathology communities.

Kurtzman knew the value of Frost's work, and agreed with him. "In the real world . . . unless you have some sort of a significant indicator, it's very, very difficult [to tell when the victim died]," Kurtzman said, "so you really have to have a range." Since changes in a dead person's body are affected by "so many different factors," Kurtzman said, agreeing with Melinek's statement, "you have to be very careful when giving the time of death . . . [it's] more honest if [pathologists citing time of death give] a broader range than more narrow."

Kurtzman's autopsy wasn't just based on a proper examination of Pfister's body. He also used "a variety of information" that Hansen gave him. The time she died was based "on what the coroner investigator provided to me," Kurtzman said, adding that Hansen gave him "quite a bit." But Kurtzman said it was "obviously [Hansen's job] to validate or dispute that information" before passing it along to him.

That apparently didn't happen, because Hansen had no concrete evidence of an email (or text message) from Pfister the afternoon or evening of February 25.

When asked about the note that Kurtzman received from Hansen's own work, Hansen said he "got that in hearsay from another deputy." And he didn't "validate or dispute" it, as Kurtzman said was his job. Hansen said, "[We don't talk] to police about all those details. We just knew she died earlier that week, because her body wasn't deteriorating that badly."

The most important factor for pathologists to consider is when a victim "was last seen alive and when they were found dead," Melinek said. "It's likely they died sometime between those two points unless [of course] there is an unreliable eyewitness, and you know they are unreliable because the body is completely decomposed and he said he saw him yesterday, for instance."

In Pfister's case, the last known person to see her alive was Kathy Carpenter. She left Pfister's home Monday morning after spending the weekend there—and Pfister was still alive then.

Melinek said the second factor to look at is body temperature. People with "normal" body temperature will lose "about one and a half to two degrees an hour." But that's difficult because what's normal (98.6 degrees Fahrenheit) for one person isn't for another. "Normal range can be between 96 and 101, and if they are on meth or cocaine they could be higher," she said.

Rigor is what pathologists look at next. Melinek said rigor "can set in the jaw muscles in as little as forty minutes but usually within six hours [and in] large muscle groups like the arms and legs, in twelve to twenty-four hours." Most important in Pfister's case, was this: rigor passes in forty-eight hours. This was why Melinek, who independently reviewed the autopsy report, said the window given for Pfister's death was too small. "This body is past rigor mortis and is starting to decompose," Melinek said. "To say that she died thirty-six to forty-eight hours prior to being autopsied is absurd."

Based on a variety of factors that were possible, given the time of year and temperature inside and outside the home, as well as whether the closet had a window that allowed light in, Melinek said Pfister "could have been in that closet a week if it was cold enough in the house."

Furthermore, she said she wouldn't look at the number of hours that had passed from the time the body was discovered until the autopsy was done two days later. "I would ask you, 'When was she last seen alive?'"

If pressed for a more specific answer "about when she died, I'd say, 'She died closer to when she was last seen alive than to when she was found dead.'"

CHAPTER TWENTY-NINE
COURTROOM DRAMA

During her time as an inmate, Nancy never accepted the fact that she could end up there permanently. She continued to believe that the people in charge of the prosecution would finally realize their mistake and let her out—her and Trey.

From the time she was first picked up for questioning until the day she was finally released months later, she believed the DNA evidence would set her free. "I kept writing letters to Beth, saying, 'You and science can get to the truth,'" Nancy said.

Meanwhile, her attorneys felt like they didn't have enough science to do that. Little happened like Nancy thought it would. Once someone has been arrested and charged with a crime, the court system takes over. Nancy would only get out of jail via a judge's ruling—even if that only meant she was free to go on bond. But that couldn't happen until the preliminary hearing.

"What she wanted was for somebody to swoop in and be fair, be reasonable, and look at the facts and the evidence and see that she was not guilty and release her, and there isn't a process for that," Garth McCarty said.

Nancy had to wait for the preliminary hearing, which Garth described as "an archaic-type hearing that just requires the prosecution to show . . . there's enough evidence to establish probable cause." He and Beth didn't feel like they had enough information to counter the prosecution's claims to ask for an immediate preliminary hearing. Unfortunately, the prosecution seemed to have "enough evidence for the judge to entertain the belief that maybe the person charged has committed the offense."

Unlike a jury trial, Garth said, where "all doubts are resolved in favor of the defense," at a preliminary hearing, all the evidence "is required to be viewed in the light most favorable to the prosecution."

Nancy thought that would be her chance to let the judge see that she was innocent, but her attorneys disagreed. "The reality is that if the judge already signed off on the arrest warrant," Garth said, "chances are [s]he's also going to sign off at the preliminary hearing and bound her over for trial." For that reason, the defense wanted to "be ready to destroy the prosecution's allegations . . . [which required] time, work, preparation, and investigation," Garth explained.

It also required evidence—or at least access to what the prosecution had that would benefit Nancy and Trey. But the prosecution wasn't turning things over very quickly. "They were probably in custody for a month before we got any discovery," Beth said. "We wanted to know what evidence they had. We were demanding to be able to see the evidence, and they were saying, 'We don't have to give you anything until the preliminary hearing is set.'" So a lot of time was spent "quibbling about how quickly we were going to get the evidence."

There was one other small window of opportunity the defense team could use to free Nancy. Since she was charged with a capital offense, and therefore being held without bond, Nancy was entitled to a "Proof-Evident Presumption Great Hearing" within ninety-six hours of arrest. It would allow the defense to ask the judge to set bond. Beth and Garth thought the hearing was too risky, though, and perhaps useless.

"We were demanding a bond be set," Beth said. "They [the prosecution] were saying, 'You're not entitled to a bond—it's first-degree murder—until after the preliminary hearing.'"

She continued, "We were going to do the proof-evident presumption great hearing at the same time as the preliminary hearing because we . . . wanted to make a strong case to the judge that there was [insufficient] evidence in Nancy's case." The defense was afraid that even if Judge Nichols agreed to set bond, if she set it at $2 million, Garth said, "that's the same as having no bond for somebody like Nancy Styler."

* * *

While Nancy impatiently waited for someone to tell her she was free to go home, her and Trey's attorneys filed one motion after another. One of the very first motions filed addressed not just Nancy's desire to be set free, but also what the prosecution did that led to her arrest. It also verified that what Joe DiSalvo told Juliana Pfister was correct: Judge Nichols did refuse to give the prosecution the first warrant. In fact, the motion indicated that Nichols refused to sign off on more than one warrant, stating, "Law enforcement has presented this Court with at least three prior versions of the affidavit in support of the arrest warrant, which this Court found lacking in probable cause."

In the "Motion for Specific Immediate Discovery: All Prior Versions of Affidavit in Support of Arrest Warrant," the defense asked the court to order "the immediate disclosure of all prior drafts/versions of the affidavit in support of a warrant to arrest Nancy Styler which was presented to the court and found to be lacking in probable cause."

When asking for the previous affidavits, Nancy's defense team said it was "immediately and easily available to the government and required for the defense investigation to proceed effectively; in its absence, the defense investigation will be unjustly and irreparably impeded."

They also said the denied requests were "of crucial" importance, since "neither Ms. Styler nor her counsel were allowed to see the arrest warrant for seventy-two hours." Once the defense did get a copy of the affidavit, "it became immediately apparent that time-sensitive avenues of investigation were not being pursued by law enforcement and thus risking the loss of potentially material exculpatory evidence."

To prevent losing information that could prove vital to their client, the defense said it asked the DA for permission to "view certain discrete pieces of evidence." However, the DA refused—repeatedly. The defense believed those refusals cost them the chance "to determine identities of two potential alternate suspects."

Finally, the motion summarized what had happened with Nancy's case: "Ms. Styler has been held without bond for two weeks, having been given access to no evidence, with the only source of information coming from an affidavit, of which three prior versions exist that were rejected for lack of probable cause. Precious time and potentially exculpatory evidence may have been lost as a result."

***

Judge Nichols heard this and several other concerns from both defense teams—Nancy's and Trey's—at two hearings, held on March 17 and 18. Nancy and Trey were both present, and heard their lawyers argue that the prosecution was interfering with the rights of both defendants. Chief Public Defender Tina Fang seemed to take the lead, as if speaking for all the defense attorneys there, when she cited problems within the jail.

"In the eight or so years that I've been coming to this courthouse and visiting clients at the jail, the Pitkin County Jail, to my knowledge, they have never kept a jail log for visitors," Fang said in open court, "and they certainly have never requested me as an attorney to sign in."

Yet that was what happened the first time she visited Trey in jail. "I was told that they have a new policy where I have to check in. I was asked to present my bar card and driver's license, again for the first time in eight years. So it's curious to me why it is the jail is suddenly changing jail policy related to the Stylers," Fang said. She also said she believed Nancy's attorneys had the same experience, and she thought someone higher than jail officials had changed the policy.

Fang cited another problem for her client: "At one jail visit with Mr. Styler I became aware that I was in a room in which all the deputies had to do to listen in on conversation with him was push a button." Fang said she didn't learn about this until after the visit concluded. "We need to make sure that both [defendants] have access to their attorneys, that these visits are confidential in nature."

Fang offered to talk to Sheriff DiSalvo about those problems, if the judge preferred not to have a hearing about them. Judge Nichols disagreed with Fang's comment about the jail logs. She did, however, offer to schedule a hearing to discuss one of Beth's concerns about Nancy's case.

Beth told the court that "the evidence in this case as to my client is razor thin." However, since the prosecution was still waiting for forensic results, the defense hadn't gotten a chance to see what evidence they had against Nancy. Because of that, Beth asked for a hearing to discuss the question of bond. "There are specific circumstances that the court could find is justification for setting bond," Beth said.

Judge Nichols said a hearing was required to discuss the question of bond. "I am offering you the hearing. If you choose not to take me up on it, then that's your choice," she said, "but you may have the hearing."

In the meantime, the judge said the defense had "no right to discovery, not unless the time schedule kicks in . . . so you do not get any discovery before the preliminary hearing." Nichols then told both defense teams that she was giving them two weeks, "but then I'm probably going to go ahead and set it [and] we can address bond at the same time."

When Nancy learned the preliminary hearing would be held so soon, she was ecstatic. She told everyone she spoke to on the phone, and all her new friends inside jail. *I will be out in just two more weeks! Trey and I can see each other again!* Unfortunately, like everything else in this case, that was not how it played out.

CHAPTER THIRTY
SHOW ME THE SCIENCE

Since she began practicing law in 1987, Beth Krulewitch had learned a lot of hard lessons about innocence and guilt. That's why she believed "the truth is pretty fricking elusive, because people's own versions of the truth can sometimes be shaded by what they want to believe." And she knew just how elusive, because "innocent people get convicted all the time."

Beth said her "first love" was doing criminal defense work. Before meeting Nancy Styler, she had helped free three other people who were wrongly imprisoned. If she succeeded in the Pfister case, Nancy would become her fourth—and the first woman Beth had helped free.

Two of the three other cases also came from working as a public defender; she was hired to represent the third person she helped. Beth now has a private practice but, like Garth, the public defender's office appointed her to represent Nancy. Her work in freeing innocent people included random cases with "people who were accused of a crime, [and others who were] convicted of a crime they didn't commit, [which she] was able to get . . . undone." Because of those accomplishments, Beth received the Champion of Justice award from the National Association of Criminal Defense Lawyers.

She didn't feel like she had any special expertise in representing innocent people; she believed there were simply many innocent people in jails and prisons throughout the country. "That's one lawyer in one state that's had four people," Beth said, "so I just think it's important for people to understand that our system makes mistakes."

***

Beth hadn't been in Aspen long when she was assigned the case. Originally from Denver, she recently married another attorney who was a longtime Aspen resident. Beth knew what it felt like to be an outsider, like Nancy and Trey were. And before taking Nancy's case, Beth herself wasn't really well known in the small town. Most of her caseload was three hours away in Denver.

But when people found out she was representing Nancy Styler, her status changed. "All of a sudden I became one of the most interesting people in Aspen, because people wanted to talk to me," she said.

As a result, Beth soon realized it was entirely likely that the Stylers were innocent. "When I took Nancy's case, I didn't know if she was innocent or not," Beth said. For her, "the driving force [is to] make sure that the process is fair."

But she kept hearing from different people who didn't know each other, and they told Beth stories that helped her better understand the case. "People would talk to me about Nancy Pfister, [people] who knew her," Beth said, "and there were three different people that said to me, 'I wasn't surprised that she ended up murdered.' Three different people!"

Although the chatty Aspenites didn't have any idea who murdered Pfister, they told Beth things that led her to understand that Pfister "lived such a risky life, and she put herself in dangerous situations."

When Beth sat down to talk to her new client the first time, the advisement hearing was behind them, so the two women had briefly met. But nothing prepared Beth for meeting Nancy Styler, a woman who not only had been accused of murder, but who was older that Beth herself.

Criminal defense attorneys are trained to focus strictly on the evidence. "That's easy in theory," Beth said. "But when you have a client who is looking at you and wanting to believe that she's innocent," that's more difficult. "I mean that's usually a place you don't have to go to as a criminal defense lawyer."

But Nancy was insistent: she had to know that Beth not only would represent her, but that Beth knew *she was* innocent—that she had nothing whatsoever to do with Pfister's death.

Suddenly, Beth was in a quandary. "I do my job whether I believe that person is innocent or guilty, and my job is to look at the evidence, to analyze potential defenses based on the evidence, and to investigate witnesses for their credibility," she said, "so that I can cross-examine at trial, so that the truth or the best you can get will come out."

But Nancy wasn't just your average client. And Beth found herself telling Nancy what she needed to hear—not to appease her or put her mind at ease, but because Nancy convinced Beth she was innocent. Not just innocent of being involved, but innocent of knowing anything about the murder.

That's because Beth's visit was the first time Nancy learned that Pfister had been murdered—that her death wasn't a suicide, but instead, someone had bludgeoned her former landlady.

***

Defense attorneys should be humane, Beth said, but "your main job is not to comfort your client. You main job is to defend your client." While Beth longed to comfort Nancy, she knew she couldn't. And shouldn't. There was an invisible boundary there, and Beth wouldn't cross it. "I was constantly going back and forth between wanting to do what I'm trained to do," she said, "which is just focus on the evidence and evaluate it and apply the right strategies and develop the case from a defense perspective, to wanting to put my arms around her and say 'It's going to be okay, honey, I know you're innocent.'" To do her job well in Nancy's case, Beth had to get to "all the evidence and [wait] for all the DNA to trickle in."

That took a while, so in the beginning, she, Nancy, and Garth were all at a disadvantage—none of them had access to the evidence the prosecution had. But because Olmsted had overheard the chatty two women on the airplane talking about the case, they did realize a brutal murder had taken place. When Beth, and later Garth, after he returned from New Orleans, received copies of the arrest warrant affidavit, they learned even more about Pfister's murder.

The first time Beth sat down and talked to Nancy inside the Pitkin County Jail, she not only had to tell her client what had happened to Pfister, but she also had to tell her what kind of evidence the police had—and why prosecutors suspected Nancy and Trey of murdering their landlady and the woman they once considered their friend.

"I think when the autopsy results come back," Nancy began, "they'll find she killed herself. She wasn't a happy person. And she drank and took a lot of pills. And I thought [things] didn't work out in Australia like she thought [they would], because she had gone to Australia because she was interested in a guy there. Apparently that didn't work out, or she was running out of money, and that's why I thought she was coming back. It certainly wasn't to deal with us, because she would have Kathy deal with that. She had Kathy deal with all her renters, any other time there were rental problems. And if Pfister was a happy camper there, there's no way she would have come home," Nancy explained, as the story poured out in one long stream. "And once police get the toxicology report, they'll know we're innocent. They'll open the door and we'll be free to go."

Beth was flabbergasted that Nancy was so unaware of any of the specifics of Pfister's murder, or how it had happened. She was amazed that her client was convinced it would only be a matter of time before she and Trey would be released.

"I'm innocent, and so is Trey," Nancy insisted.

Beth smiled, feeling like she was trying to pacify a stubborn child. "Well, good, then. But Nancy, this was not a suicide. Pfister did not kill herself. She was murdered; someone bludgeoned her to death." Beth explained how someone had hit Pfister in the head while she was sleeping, then dragged her across the carpet, tied her up, and locked her inside her own closet.

Nancy's eyes opened wide, and her mouth dropped open. For a second, she was speechless. Finally, she said, near tears, "No matter what she did, she didn't deserve that. No one does."

Beth searched her client's face for any sign of insincerity, but she saw none. "[Nancy] was so horrified," Beth said, that she knew then and there her client was innocent.

"I didn't know you didn't know any of this," Beth said.

"How could I? The only way we even knew someone was dead was because the morning they busted into our room, and I asked Trey if I was dreaming, one of the officers said, 'No, there's a dead body.'" The look of horror was still on Nancy's face.

"I kept trying to get someone that day to tell us what happened," Nancy said, "but no one would."

"Well, now I understand," Beth said. "There's something else I need to tell you, though. On the Friday morning before you and Trey were arrested, police received a call from a Basalt city employee named Robert Larson," she began, watching Nancy carefully as she spoke. "He was on his regular trash route when he found a bag with a bloody hammer, some papers belonging to you and Trey, and some personal items of Pfister's."

Beth paused to let those details sink in. "Nancy, they found the trash bag right behind your motel room, in front of Alpine Bank."

"What? A bloody hammer? In a trash can behind our room? What kind of papers?" Nancy asked, rapidly firing questions at her attorney. "What personal items? What does this mean? We didn't have anything to do with her death. I don't understand."

Patiently, Beth explained it all. She told Nancy how the small town of Basalt had a policy against private individuals dumping their personal trash into the city's cans, because it leads bears to try to get into the trash. When Larson found a big trash bag while doing his morning trash route, and noticed it looked like it contained personal items, he opened it. The first items he noticed were prescription pill bottles; they were written out to "Nancy Pfister." Then he saw an iPhone, and some paperwork that bore the name "Styler." There were also utility and credit card bills in Pfister's name.

But Larson's last find was his biggest: the object had fallen to the bottom of the bag because it was heavier than all the other objects combined. It was a bloody hammer. Larson had heard the news about the deceased Aspen woman, so when he recognized her name on some of the belongings, he immediately alerted police. The bag and its contents were sent to the CBI laboratory to be tested, but initially police felt they had enough evidence to link the Stylers to Pfister's death.

Beth told Nancy she didn't know everything the bag contained. The bigger problem was the bag was identical to the ones Nancy had used to pack up her and Trey's clothing when they moved out of Pfister's house. But Nancy wasn't the only one with questions; Beth had questions of her own.

Nancy was ashamed and mortified. *Everyone in town believes Trey and I did this horrible thing, committed this grisly crime.*

"Look, I wish I didn't have to, but I'm afraid I have more bad news," Beth said. "It isn't just the bag of trash with what could be the murder weapon inside that we have to worry about. It's the owner's closet key." She stopped, again watching Nancy's face for any trace of self-betrayal.

"Kathy always kept the key," Nancy began.

"There were two keys," Beth said.

"Right, but Kathy kept them both. I had to call her whenever we needed to store things in there for Pfister, and have her bring the key over."

Beth jotted something on the notepad lying on the table. "Okay, that's good to know. But what worries me is where this second key was found."

Nancy looked directly into Beth's eyes, and Beth saw the confusion in her client's face. "It was found just outside your motel room, about twenty-five feet from your door, the morning you were arrested."

The look on Nancy's face couldn't have been more telling: she was shocked.

"How did that happen? Who found it?" she asked. "I mean, it couldn't have come from me or Trey; the police searched every inch of our motel room that day, the first day they came and took us in for questioning."

Beth explained to Nancy how Aspenalt owner Christopher Szcelina was walking through the property around noon when he saw a key on the ground. It had a round white label attached by a tiny wire ring that read "owner's closet." The words were handwritten. At first, Szcelina picked it up. Then he put it back down. Szcelina then went to tell one of the two officers who were sitting inside the police cruiser, watching the Stylers' room. CBI officer Bruce Benjamin took photos, then gave it to a deputy. The key was eventually sent to the CBI lab for processing.

When Beth finished telling Nancy the story, Nancy said something that made even more sense. "Our room has been guarded the entire time by two officers, and no one saw someone drop that key outside our room? How is that even possible?"

Beth made more notes on the notepad. "I don't know, but is it possible someone is trying to frame you?"

Nancy looked at Beth in disbelief. "Why would anyone want to do that? Who would do that? I don't know anyone I've met here who would!"

Beth was silent. "Kathy Carpenter, maybe?"

Nancy stared at her. "Kathy would never do that. She's not that kind of person. We were friends, and Trey saved her life." Nancy thought back to the day before Pfister returned home, when she texted Kathy asking if they could exchange cars for the move. Kathy said yes, "we can do that." Then she asked if Merlin was helping with the move. Nancy said he was.

In fact, phone records would later confirm Nancy's recollection was correct. On February 21 at 8:31 a.m., Nancy sent Kathy the following text, "Merlin is helping tomorrow and will remove the heater. Call me when you are on your way and bring the closet key so we can put more stuff out they did the roof this pm."

Nancy told Beth about that, and about the day Kathy couldn't breathe, and how Trey had driven over and given her an emergency inhaler, and took her to the hospital.

Beth didn't know what to think. She went back to her other theory. "Okay, then, what about your husband? Do you think there's any way that Trey could have done this?" Beth was relentless, trying to get Nancy to look deeply into Trey's psyche.

"No way! I've known this man for thirty-two years, and he is the most gentle man in the world," Nancy said, launching into the same story she told Gibson—how she had watched Trey with his patients, and how kind and loving he was with them.

Nancy and Beth talked about how Trey was far too brilliant to take the murder weapon, Pfister's personal items, and the Stylers' legal papers, then toss them all into a public trash can. "He's the smartest man I know. He wouldn't be that stupid," Nancy insisted.

Sitting there watching Nancy, listening to her, Beth could tell that "Nancy knew him as a loving, kind, warm man."

That person was the polar opposite of whoever killed Pfister. That's why, Beth later said, Nancy simply could not envision that Trey could have murdered Pfister: "I mean, she just did not think it was possible," Beth said. "And I really believed that."

Nor was she worried about Nancy having been any part of a conspiracy to murder Pfister. Even though Nancy repeatedly told police they were "always together," Beth didn't take that literally.

"I was never terribly troubled by that, although I knew if we ended up being in a trial situation that was certainly something that would come back to haunt her," Beth said. "For most of the time that I defended Nancy, I believed that they were both being framed."

During that first visit and the ones to come, each time Beth confronted Nancy with the available evidence, "Nancy was consistent throughout." Plus, she had reasonable answers that simply made sense. Beth said none of Nancy's responses indicated that she had murdered Pfister—or helped someone else murder her.

"Nancy's emotional responses were absolutely appropriate," Beth said. "She didn't believe her husband had anything to do with it because she presumed him innocent."

Trey never so much as intimated to Nancy for a single second that he had even seen Pfister since her return, much less had an argument or anything else that would have led him to kill Pfister, Beth said. "She believed him."

Beth sighed. There was only one more question to ask. "Okay, then. I need you to direct me. Should we pull the bank video of the trash can?"

"Absolutely. You won't find me on there," Nancy said, continuing to insist that science would free her—and Trey.

"Show me the science," she told Beth, a defiant look in her eye.

***

But if neither she nor Trey killed Pfister, that seemed to only leave Kathy Carpenter. Beth explained again why she believed Kathy was framing Nancy and Trey. She pointed out that Nancy herself had told Beth about Kathy and Pfister's love-hate relationship, which was based on booze as much as the way Pfister treated Kathy like her personal servant. Beth reminded Nancy that Kathy had been sober until Pfister returned from Australia, when Kathy apparently fell off the wagon. But what Beth didn't realize was that this information had not come from Nancy. It had come from the evening deputies went with Kathy to the hospital—where even they couldn't agree whether she had been drinking.

Nonetheless, based on what the prosecution seemed to believe, Beth posited another scenario: what if Kathy had grown so enraged at Pfister during a drunken bout that she had killed her, passed out, then, when she woke up and realized what she'd done, knew she had to hide the evidence—so she made it look like the Stylers killed Pfister?

"I don't think Kathy is mean enough to do that," Nancy said. "She wouldn't lie about us, either."

"But what about the bag of items tossed into the trash?" Beth asked. None of Kathy's belongings were inside—only Trey's, Nancy's, and Pfister's. Finally, there was the key that only Kathy had access to, found outside Room 122, the room where the Stylers had stayed.

"That key didn't have your DNA on it. It didn't have Trey's DNA on it," Beth said. "It had Kathy's, though."

Nancy finally admitted that perhaps Kathy did set them up. But in the back of her mind, she still harbored doubts. Not because Kathy couldn't get angry or drunk enough to do that, but because of how well she and Kathy got along. Nancy thought about all the pep talks she gave Kathy while Pfister was gone, encouraging her to keep up the great work in her AA program and not to let Pfister suck her back into being her drinking buddy. Nancy knew that by the time Pfister returned, those pep talks, coupled with all the hair and beauty treatments she gave Kathy, had helped reinforce Kathy's own desire to reach her true potential. Kathy had done most of her own work, using AA's 12-step program, but Nancy knew she had helped. A part of her didn't want to believe Kathy could ever betray her like that, by killing Pfister and then setting her and Trey up to take the fall for her.

But given all the evidence Beth put before her that day, Nancy felt like it was the only theory that made even a little sense. So part of her accepted Beth's rationale, because Nancy felt like she had no other choice.

CHAPTER THIRTY-ONE

AND THREE MAKES MURDER

Listen to the audio recordings of police interrogating Kathy Carpenter, and don't be surprised if only one word comes to mind: badgering.

There is no other way to describe what happened to the former Alpine Bank teller, especially when CBI Agent John Zamora and DA chief investigator Lisa Miller interviewed her. So it's no surprise that after being grilled in that fashion for more than twenty hours in several separate interviews, the sheriff's office stationed round-the-clock guards at her home on March 2. On March 14, a Tuesday evening, Kathy Carpenter was arrested. Her arrest came eleven days after Nancy and Trey's, her charges identical to theirs: first-degree murder and conspiracy to commit murder, both felonies that made her ineligible for bond.

Somehow, in the eyes of law enforcement, Kathy went from being viewed as a traumatized victim who found Pfister's body stuffed inside a bedroom closet to being a suspect who planned and then helped the Stylers carry out the grisly murder.

But Kathy's troubles began long before she ever agreed to help the police, when she willingly went in for questioning—all because she wanted justice for her dead friend. During her lengthy 911 call that spurred the whole investigation, Kathy said she saw blood on the "headboard," which a dispatcher mistakenly heard as "forehead."

That one-word error created a series of mistakes that snowballed out of control.

The first mistake occurred when Zamora sent a copy of the 911 call to his CBI buddy Agent Kirby Lewis in Denver. Lewis listened and sent back a transcript, along with an attached note for Zamora.

"After me listening to this 911 call," Lewis wrote, "Kathy Carpenter is guilty."

In his official report, however, Lewis stated, "The call revealed thirty-nine indicators of guilt knowledge and no indicators of innocence."

"Well, I flunked the 911 call," Kathy said, looking rueful. Greg Greer, Kathy's publicly appointed defense attorney, said that's what Kathy told him the first time they met.

Before long, everyone involved in the prosecution agreed with Lewis' report, not knowing their opinions were based on that one wrongly transcribed word. Nor did they realize that Lewis incorrectly analyzed Kathy's 911 call throughout—beginning with who the real victim was.

In his report, Lewis said Kathy's "very first statement is to request help for herself, saying, 'Help me.' Innocent callers are focused on getting help for the victim, not requesting help for themselves. In this case, the request for help for the caller is an indicator of guilt."

Lewis, who performed his analysis from his desk in Denver, used only the 911 call as the basis for his findings. He had no clue that for three days, Kathy (and Nancy) were worried that Pfister may have met with foul play. He didn't know they considered her missing, that they were trying to find her. Nor could he know that when Kathy saw the blood on the headboard, and then opened the closet door, the smell alone would have told her that her missing friend was already dead.

Pitkin County coroner Eric Hansen, who arrived at the crime scene later the same evening, said as much. "We could smell her body downstairs, even before [going upstairs] in the bedroom." It was the odor one associates with a dead animal or human, the "off-gassing" that occurs when decay takes place, Hansen said.

So Kathy obviously knew it was too late to help her friend—which is why she cried, "Help *me*," when she called 911. She was terrified that the killer was still in Pfister's house, and she could be next.

Clearly, without knowing the context of Kathy's situation, Lewis' ability to analyze the 911 call was limited, which explains why he confused Kathy's call for help as being for Pfister, rather than what it really was: a cry for help for her.

***

That was only the beginning of Kathy's problems. But she was in no shape to realize it. After police found her hysterical and in a state of shock following her 911 call, paramedics transported Kathy to the emergency department of Aspen Valley Hospital.

There, they audio recorded what occurred during the next hour. The recording captured one of the three male officers at the hospital asking a doctor if Kathy could take a Breathalyzer test. The doctor said yes, one of the officers obtained her permission, and police administered the test. Two of the officers discussed Kathy's condition, as she is heard crying and moaning in the background. The two men can't agree if she'd been drinking.

The first officer, the one in charge, said he was just being "cautious . . . in case we need it down the road. I think it's an important piece," he said. "I don't know; the whole thing's bizarre to me."

The second officer asked Kathy if she had had anything to drink, then returned to tell the first officer what he learned. "She says zip, zero, nada, she hasn't had a drink in such and such a time. It's probably the guy I was picking up earlier."

"You don't smell booze on her?" the first officer asked.

"I don't. I've been smelling booze since the first call I was at."

The first one, who later admitted he had a cold that night, said, "I may be out of my mind, but I've got a pretty good nose and I've been smelling booze."

"Go for it," the second officer said.

***

They did—probably because Kathy was in shock and by then heavily medicated from having received two shots of Ativan, a tranquilizer.

Two men are heard helping Kathy in and out of bed so she wouldn't fall, and then into a chair, where she breathed into the Breathalyzer.

The audio recording shows how shaken and drugged Kathy was. "Little bit at a time. We're not in a hurry," one of the men said.

"Go ahead and stand up. You can do this, Kathy," the other one said. "One step at a time. Slow that breathing down. You're doing good."

The first man spoke again. "All you have to do is turn toward him, have a seat."

"Help us, come on," the second one is heard urging Kathy on as she apparently tried to blow into the machine, but she ended up coughing instead. The men told her to breathe in and out as intermittent moaning sounds continued.

The medical staff realized Kathy was in no shape to answer their questions, so they asked police for her ID. Another male voice (probably a doctor or nurse) and the lead officer discussed getting Kathy to give them a urine sample, which the deputy said he'd like to have. "I just want it handy, in case we get there," he told the hospital staffer.

Not long after, the same deputy introduced himself to ADA Bryan. "Hi Andrea, thanks for coming out," he said.

Undersheriff Ron Ryan called next, and the same deputy said that after the nurse finished with Kathy, he planned to bag her clothes and put them into an evidence bag. "Then I'm not leaving her side," he told Ryan.

After hanging up, he told two other deputies, Jeff Fain and Chip Seamans, who were also at the hospital, what Ryan told him. "They said, 'We don't know what's going on yet so keep an eye on those clothes.'"

When the nurse came out of Kathy's room, she said something too low for the recording device to catch. "I know we have a deceased person at the scene and she found the body," the same deputy said. "We don't know if she has anything to do with it." The nurse is then heard saying that Kathy "is scared; she thinks they may come after her, too."

He later asked a male nurse if the staff was "doing a blood draw on her." The nurse told the officer to ask the doctor in charge.

The deputy spoke to Kathy next. He asked if she was feeling better. "I called a counselor so if you feel like talking to someone. Okay?"

It sounds like Kathy said "no," as she continued to moan and softly cry.

A female nurse led Kathy into a restroom, told her they were taking her clothes because of the doctor's orders, and asked her to pee in a cup, "and then we'll put you in a room."

When the deputy received another call, he is heard saying, "Her health's the most important thing. She's quite a bit better than she was."

The deputy and his caller discussed the drugs Kathy was given, and the question of alcohol came up.

"No, but I'm confident I smelled it on her breath," the deputy with Kathy replied from the hallway near her room. "I do have a cold. She's in AA and she doesn't drink. Not calling her a liar."

Then he said that Kathy "naturally is a person of interest. Not saying she's involved, but until we get more information, she is."

***

Police records show that local law enforcement was well aware of Kathy's past problems with alcohol, and her problems with Pfister, when they were drinking together. That may be why police immediately treated her as a suspect. But when they left the hospital later that night, taking Kathy to talk to officers at the courthouse, they also knew how traumatized, and how heavily sedated, she was. So why did they believe her accusations about the Stylers were valid?

Kathy's comments to the sheriff and other officers that night weren't recorded. But later interviews were. In them, Kathy is seen gesturing with her hands toward her own hair. While doing that, she is heard saying she saw Pfister with blood throughout her hair. DA investigator Lisa Miller said that wasn't possible, because Pfister was wrapped up in such a way that no one could have seen her hair.

But that isn't necessarily true. The very first crime scene photo of Pfister shows a small section of plastic sticking out from beneath the blanket. Upon closer examination, it is revealed to be the plastic covering Pfister's head. Given that Kathy did see blood on the headboard, she could have either made the mental leap that her friend's hair was bloody, or she saw enough in that little bit of plastic to understand the plastic contained hair covered with blood.

Or it's possible that Kathy lied to police, when she said she didn't touch or attempt to unwrap Pfister. That lie would be similar to Coroner Eric Hansen's own statements when he spoke about not touching Pfister's wrappings. He said this twice. But when asked how he knew what police found in the closet was "a dead human, and not an animal," Hansen admitted he wasn't fully forthcoming. "Okay, I did pull down a little corner and looked."

Then there is the question of Kathy's statement to her mother. Chris Carpenter told CBI Agent Zamora that Kathy said Pfister was wrapped in sheets. Yet Kathy didn't tell police this. Perhaps that's because Kathy's mind made the connection between the missing sheets and the body in the closet. If so, she then told her mother that she saw Pfister wrapped in sheets—but she said this at the hospital, the night she was traumatized after finding the body.

By the time Zamora and Miller interviewed her, Kathy's mind was clearer and it's possible she never even remembered what she told her mother the night of February 26.

Either way, those subsequent interviews show that police conducted a wild variety of tactics, many of which defense attorney Garth McCarty took issue with. "They did such a bad job of articulating," Garth said. "They talked over each other, they were having these 'gotcha' moments, where she really wasn't agreeing with them, but they were saying 'Aha! So then you agree!'" when Kathy really wasn't agreeing at all. And, Garth said, they lied to Kathy, like the investigators did who also interviewed the Stylers.

Retired police captain K.C. Bohrer says police should be judicious when lying to suspects. "Lying while doing interviews is very dangerous and must be very heavily considered and weighed as to the potential gain," he said. "Credibility and also issues of coercion can come in to play."

Bohrer has been a police officer for thirty-seven years, working major crimes and cold cases in Berkeley County, West Virginia, and Frederick, Maryland. He also has training as an FBI crises negotiator, and is known for his honest and compassionate concern for suspects. When he conducts his first interview, his goal is to "gain all the info I can, true or untrue. Then investigate and confirm or discount [the] information." That interview becomes the baseline for any subsequent interviews, and helps him determine which information might "be implausible or false . . . I never generally become confrontational of lies on the first interview or even second, because it is detrimental to the rapport process."

Bohrer says rapport is usually established by the third interview. That's when a police investigator can make suggestions such as, "'help me understand why this happened, why you felt you had to do what you did.' It's a process wherein you become a bit like a priest in being the one who can help, and in fact you do help the person who has done something wrong [to] confess and move beyond the issue."

Listening to one suspect interview after another, that is not how the Pitkin County or CBI investigators interacted with the three suspects.

* * *

It's also possible Zamora and Miller denied Kathy her right to an attorney, because at one point in a later interview, she says she's done talking— yet they ignore her statement and continue to push her for answers.

Although he defended Nancy, and had nothing to do with Kathy's legal representation, Garth was outraged at the way police treated her. "They lied to Kathy Carpenter many times during her interrogations, and put words in her mouth, and then dishonestly reported her reactions to those situations," Garth said.

Like the Stylers, Kathy later received two public defenders to help fight her charges. Greg Greer and Kathleen Lord were both in private practice, but the Alternate Defense Counsel appointed them to Kathy's case. Greer and Lord were also vocal about Kathy's mistreatment.

When a reporter asked Greer what the prosecution did wrong, he said he'd never seen such "egregious" errors. "I've never had a case like this in thirty-two years."

His partner, Kathleen Lord, said the prosecution got off track in a serious way that resulted in innocent people losing their freedom. "I'm very, very disappointed in the criminal justice system."

The entire ordeal ruined Kathy's life. The police took her car. Her reputation was ruined. She lost her job and had to move in with her mother. She lost friends—Pfister, Sarah, the Stylers, her colleagues at the bank, and many others who thought she was involved in the crime. Aspen residents turned on her, even though police arrested her without a shred of evidence.

Greer said Kathy was unemployed and homeless, all "because she called 911."

***

Listening to police interviews, it seemed like police were browbeating the suspects. But Kathy experienced police badgering on a different level. It's possible that happened when, a day after finding Pfister dead, Kathy went to Alpine Bank and took $6,000 from what police continued to call Pfister's safety deposit box.

It also seems probable that Kathy, who didn't have much income and likely had no savings to her name, felt forced to do this because the police left her stranded and without any access to her own money—just like they did the Stylers on February 27. They did this the evening Kathy called 911, as confirmed by a call she made to her AA sponsor, Sarah, the next day.

During the one-minute voice mail message, the anguish was evident in Kathy's voice. At times it was impossible to tell which was affecting her worse: her own distress or the tranquilizers, as Kathy seemed to find it difficult to compose her thoughts well enough to speak. "Hey, Sarah," Kathy said, before pausing as she sniffled.

"Sarah, it's Kathy," she said, moaning and crying for a second, before composing herself, "and I wanted to talk to youuuuu."

Kathy's voice broke and she is heard crying. "Something bad's really happened and I just wanted to talk to you."

There was a pause, then Kathy cried throughout the next few sentences. "I don't have my phone. The police department has all of my stuff. Could you please call me on my mom's number?"

Kathy gave Sarah her mom's number, then tried to end the call on an upbeat note as she told her AA sponsor goodbye. "I hope you're having a good day. Bye."

***

Kathy also removed a ring from the safety deposit box that Pfister planned to give her daughter, Juliana. When confronted by police, Kathy told them she didn't know why she took the money. But she took the ring because she knew how much Pfister distrusted her trust-fund attorney, Andy Hecht. Knowing that, Kathy was afraid Hecht might take the ring and Juliana wouldn't get it. It's entirely possible she took the money for the same reason: she was afraid Hecht would end up with it. Or it could be that Kathy, who didn't receive a salary or payment for her services from Pfister, for all the errands and chores Kathy did on her behalf, felt like she was entitled to the money. Kathy didn't tell police why she took it; she simply agreed it was wrong for her to do so.

The more likely reason Kathy took money from the safety deposit box, however, was that she shared it with Pfister and felt there was nothing wrong with taking it. Both women's names were on the legal paperwork as signers for it. Bank officials knew that. (So did Patti Stranahan, because she told police this in her interview.) At different times during their friendship, possibly due to an argument between the two women, Pfister did get another safety deposit box entirely her own. But the one containing the money and ring belonged to Pfister and Kathy—so she had some legal right to its contents.

Kathy never told Miller or Zamora that. At no time did she try to defend herself, by saying, "Why shouldn't I have taken the money and the ring? It's my safety box, too!" Why not? Attorneys who worked for the defense, as well as for Nancy and Trey Styler, said it was because Pfister treated Kathy like a doormat for so long, she eventually felt like one. Also, they said, Kathy felt eternally guilty, all the time. They believed she suffered feelings of guilt for some past wrong, real or imagined, she committed.

In spite of that guilt, the audio recording of Kathy's interviews showed that her AA meetings had held her in good stead. Because for all the pressure Zamora and Miller exerted on her, repeatedly accusing Kathy of lying, and saying she was a bad person who was going to hell for her actions, Kathy never caved. Even though her voice was at times shaky, her self-confidence never wavered. "I am a good person," Kathy insisted.

***

Several times during that early interview, when Miller and Zamora couldn't get her to say something they wanted to hear, or when Kathy gave them the same answers she had during a previous interrogation, they cut her off. Or, they insisted she was lying. They did this even though there was not one item in the more than 25,000 pages of evidence to support the accusations they leveled at Kathy. Kathy stood firm, throughout more than twenty hours of interviews, and Garth was impressed. She remained insistent: Nancy Styler was upset with Pfister, but she never intended to kill her; she and the Stylers never conspired to murder Pfister, and she certainly didn't kill her friend, either.

In her earliest police statements, Kathy insisted Nancy Styler didn't kill Pfister. It wasn't until police told Kathy the Stylers were arrested and charged with murder, and twisted Kathy's words in an attempt to use them against her, that Kathy even began to believe the Stylers might have murdered Pfister.

Those first few interviews supported her 911 call, when she didn't outright name them, either. While talking to the 911 operators, she said something about problems Pfister was having with her tenants, but never once did Kathy say they killed Pfister.

Garth said it was easy to see there was no way Kathy was involved in the murder, because she stood by her story and gave the police the very same answers—every single time.

Both police officers and defense attorneys know this is not normally what guilty people do; their stories usually change from one interview to the next. Kathy's stories, her telling of situations and people as she knew them, remained consistent, never changing. Not even when Zamora and Miller browbeat and threatened her.

CHAPTER THIRTY-TWO

OUTGUNNED AND OVERWHELMED

Winning or losing a legal battle often comes down to a single reality: whoever has the biggest guns wins.

Taken figuratively, "biggest guns" includes possession of the most resources, such as money, manpower, and time, to help the prosecution and defense fight their battle.

However, taken literally, "biggest guns" refers to whoever is in charge of a given situation. No one from the defense team knew exactly who steered the prosecution. After Tina Fang, who led Trey's defense, publicly called the sheriff out for being too biased, DiSalvo told the media he wouldn't release any more details about the case.

Denver's KDVR station reported this during a Monday, March 17, hearing, where the Stylers were finally—and formally—charged with first-degree murder. Fang spoke of the sheriff's close friendship with Pfister and accused him "of failing to run an objective investigation into Pfister's murder."

***

By October 2014, four months after the case was technically over, the defense still didn't know who was responsible for the arrest of innocent people. "I would love to know who was calling the shots," Garth told investigative reporter Daleen Berry.

They desperately wanted to know because of their long list of questionable police actions: the use of male police officers to photograph nude female suspects; interviews conducted on traumatized or medicated witnesses whose judgment and memories were arguably compromised; and the forty-page affidavit filled with statements taken out of context, half-truths, and incorrect facts, which were then touted as evidence and used to arrest the wrong person. It all smacked of misconduct.

Some members of Nancy's defense believe the majority of the prosecution's mistakes stemmed from lack of experience because none of the key players had ever investigated a murder prior to Pfister's case, but Garth wasn't one of them. Like Fang, Garth believes Sheriff DiSalvo's close ties to the Pfister family skewed the investigation.

Prior to Pfister's murder case, if anyone had asked him which county had the most honest law enforcement, Garth said, "I would have said Pitkin. They are the most cerebral, thorough, and fairest I've ever dealt with." Specifically, the sheriff's office was "more accommodating of people's civil rights."

But something dramatically changed with this case. "If [Pfister's] relationship with the sheriff was strong enough to ask Joe to evict [the Stylers] when he had no authority to evict them," Garth later said, "that suggests an old and friendly relationship."

In addition, he found the speed with which the Stylers were arrested unusual. "It was surprising to me that they made these arrests before completing their investigation," he added.

Throughout the case, the defense fought to get copies of the emails Pfister had sent DiSalvo while she was overseas, asking him to evict the couple, but those motions were denied. The defense did receive copies of a February 18 email Pfister sent to Deputy Jesse Steindler (and former sheriff Bob Braudis), asking him to "please evict these losers ASAP."

When it came to the sheriff's behavior during the investigation, Beth and Olmsted disagree with Garth. Beth doesn't think DiSalvo intentionally did anything wrong. "I know Joe DiSalvo knew her, and considered her a friend, but how close that friendship was, I don't know," Beth said.

She believes he showed more bravado than necessary when talking to the media about the case and how he was going to make sure Pfister's killers were caught, because "[the police] were always operating under the premise that it took two people to commit the crime." And he "said some things in the news conferences that were unprofessional," including becoming choked up about Pfister's death. "But he's a human being," Beth added.

Olmsted, who has lived in Aspen longer than Beth, believes the sheriff is good for Aspen. "I think Joe DiSalvo is very good at what he does [based on] what this community needs," he said.

Aspen doesn't have much serious crime, so "when these kinds of things happen, especially with a high-profile case like this, they're out of their element," Olmsted said. "This case was unusual, and not what DiSalvo was used to dealing with."

Other people who worked the case are equally critical of DA Sherry Caloia, who was no stranger to hot water. The DA's office earned some bad press after Caloia made what at least one staffer felt was an anti-Semitic comment, and her tendency to micromanage her team led some staffers to resign. That wasn't Caloia's only problem; she became DA in 2012 and simultaneously, her private practice firm represented the tiny town of Marble in Gunnison County. The town sued Caloia after her firm's bookkeeper embezzled more than $329,000. Caloia denied any knowledge of the bookkeeper's alleged theft. The bookkeeper committed suicide while the investigation was pending. The suit was later dropped.

**

As it turned out, the answer to Garth's burning question was in the prosecution's own paperwork. That very topic was discussed during Juliana Pfister's revealing taped interview with CBI Agent John Zamora and DA chief investigator Lisa Miller. In addition to telling the two investigators that DiSalvo promised her he was going to "get the Stylers," Juliana talked about how much help her family had received.

Before she agreed to the interview, though, Juliana told the investigators she didn't want to say anything that would lead to trouble for DiSalvo. Miller reassured her, saying Juliana wouldn't hurt them, because she and Zamora were close to the top people in the investigation.

"We're sitting in the high-level meetings with the chief [Ron Ryan] and the sheriff—," Miller began.

"—two, three, four times a day," Zamora finished.

After openly saying that DiSalvo and Ryan were, in Garth's words, "calling the shots," Juliana spoke up. "I know that there is a lot of close connections between the Aspen Police Department and my mom, and a lot of people in here [the sheriff's office]."

She thanked Zamora and Miller for their part in the investigation. "And I'm so happy those fuckers are in custody right now," Juliana added.

Neither investigator denied that local police had close connections to the Pfister family. Instead, Zamora said, "We're working them [the Stylers, apparently] and we're going to continue to work hard."

Juliana finished by revealing another detail that DiSalvo shared with her: the discovery of what police believed was the weapon used to kill Juliana's mother in a trash can in Basalt. "Joe told me," she said, after he warned Juliana not to mention anything he said to another soul.

And she didn't—until she told Miller and Zamora.

***

In a figurative sense, the prosecution certainly had the "biggest guns" in the Pfister murder case. They had more money, manpower, and time for their quest to find and convict Pfister's killers.

Three people in Aspen were charged with Pfister's murder in March 2014. Their charges included first-degree murder and conspiracy to commit murder, which are capital crimes. Those convicted of capital crimes in Colorado may face the death penalty. Therefore, state law stipulates that each defendant accused of a capital offense must have two attorneys apiece. Trey and Nancy Styler and Kathy Carpenter had six defense attorneys combined, as defendants in the Nancy Pfister murder case.

When it came to manpower, Beth Krulewitch and Garth McCarty were the two attorneys appointed to handle Nancy Styler's defense. Assisted by paralegal Jody Visconti Clow and three private investigators, six people comprised Nancy's entire legal team.

On the other hand, the prosecution had a plethora of resources to pick from, in the area of manpower alone. DA Sherry Caloia, ADA Andrea Bryan, investigator Lisa Miller, Sheriff Joe DiSalvo, Undersheriff Ron Ryan, and a slew of at least fifty city, county, and state police officers were at the state's disposal. Nancy's team was about the size of a squad, whereas the prosecution had enough to be called a platoon.

By mid-March, it became clear that the prosecution didn't have a case—yet Nancy and Trey were still in jail. Part of the problem was the slow rate at which the prosecution turned over discovery to the defense. Discovery is the legal term for any facts or findings that both parties to a legal action must disclose prior to going to court. In general, Rule 16 of the Colorado Rules of Criminal Procedure says the deadline for discovery to be revealed to opposing counsel in a criminal case is thirty days before going to trial. This includes tangible items being held as evidence, such as the hammer and closet key believed to be connected to Pfister's murder.

However, prosecutors are supposed to turn over any statements made by defendants as soon as it's practical, but no later than twenty days after filing charges. Charges weren't filed in this case until March 17. Since Nancy's defense team received her statement and Trey's, too, early on, that didn't interfere with their ability to fight for her freedom.

Something else did, though. It was the sheer amount of evidence such a huge prosecution team compiled. With more than 100,000 pages, audio and video files, as well as tangible objects like the hammer, the numbers were staggering, their combined weight massive. Each document equaled evidence—and became one more piece of the puzzle—any one of which could solve the crime.

"There were thousands of documents and hundreds of hours of multimedia to review," Garth said. He was so busy working on Nancy's case that he barely had time to hike, bike, or go to the gym like he normally did. Casework and caring for his daughter became his primary activities for three solid months.

Winning Nancy's case wasn't just a question of the sheer number of documents, videos, and audiotapes of witness and suspect interviews the defense had to read, watch, and listen to. It was *how* the defense team could do that: in the case of most items other than paper documents, which were saved as PDF files, they had to find ways to transfer the information from the prosecution's files to their own. There was so much data in discovery that it required driving to Office Depot and other stores that sold computer products, Jody, the paralegal, said, and buying up every single 1TB hard drive within a fifty-mile radius. Then there were conflicts between computer systems. The prosecution created files using Windows-based programs, but some members of the defense had Apple computers that wouldn't even open the discovery files without a workaround.

Garth said the situation was quite frustrating. "One of our many, many challenges during this case was . . . trying to use files that were sent to us but were not easily viewable."

Jody said they even "had to consult with IT experts to get [the files] to work." More specifically, the prosecution "sent us several recordings that required specific programs, some proprietary to the agency that recorded them, others . . . recorded in unknown formats, but they didn't provide the program players or even give us the necessary information so we could find the players on our own."

Another problem involved corrupt files, "full of malware," from the prosecution. Jody said their IT guy advised the defense attorneys not to open the files, "for fear of downloading unwanted files and possibly system-destroying viruses to our computers."

Those were two of the bigger dilemmas that occurred after receiving discovery. However, obtaining discovery was also a challenge. "There were a few instances when we were not given discovery until we asked for it," Jody said. "The DA provided it to the Public Defender's office," who represented Trey, but not to Garth and Beth, she added.

CHAPTER THIRTY-THREE

WHAT NANCY NEEDED TO HEAR

Unlike the police badgering that Kathy Carpenter tolerated, all without an attorney, for hours at a time, and which Trey Styler tasted briefly during his February 27, 2014, interrogation, Nancy's experience with police while in Pitkin County was radically different.

She has her son, Daniel, to thank for that. Of the three murder suspects, Nancy was the only one who listened to a family member's advice and hired an attorney. Nancy met Beth Krulewitch, one of her two public defenders, on March 4 at her advisement hearing. The two sat down for a two-hour visit not long after, when Beth laid everything out for Nancy: the closet key, the hammer, why the DA was seeking to convict them for first-degree murder. A few days after that, Garth McCarty, Nancy's other attorney, went to visit Nancy. He had just returned from a legal conference in New Orleans. And, like Beth, Garth said he'd never met anyone quite like his new client.

In many ways, she was a mess. Garth discerned that she had been "pretty despondent during [the] last couple of weeks," and extremely stressed. "She was frazzled . . . Nancy's a very proud person, and she takes a lot of pride in being well-kept and looking presentable," Garth said, "and she really just felt like she was being treated like an animal because they wouldn't let her have her medicine or hearing aids, things like that."

While Garth noticed that, he paid more attention to Nancy's atti-tude. He found her "courteous and extremely friendly," but also "very assertive." And she looked Garth directly in the eyes every time she answered a question.

"She was defiant, there was a desperation to her," he said. "She was very sad, she was humiliated, she felt dehumanized, and she seemed des-perate to find someone that she could trust and who would listen to her."

Garth was a part-time single father of a young daughter, which may explain why he was so attuned to Nancy's basic needs. But he was also observant. For instance, he sensed that Nancy "felt quite isolated in the Aspen area to begin with, and to then have lost contact with her husband" just made the situation worse. He could tell there were times when life in jail was almost unbearable for her. In part, that's because the design of the Pitkin jail allows inmates to look through a "window and see the person you're isolated from and still not be able to have contact with him."

In addition to the trauma of being arrested for a serious crime of murder, the "psychological impact of being isolated and alone" was harder on Nancy, because she was "a very social person." Even under the best of conditions, Garth said, the most social contact she could hope for was seeing her attorneys maybe twice a week.

* * *

After initial introductions, Garth asked Nancy to tell him everything she could about herself. She did, starting with her French grand-mother, who was a seamstress back in Boston, and ending with the alterations Nancy did for Monika Olinski, the owner of Faboo, a high-end women's clothing shop in Aspen. Along the way, she touched on the assorted legal and medical problems she and Trey had had since 1999, including the most recent ones with Pfister.

One of the smaller problems that Nancy didn't expect to be so troubling was the way Pfister insisted that her houseguests ingest only organic and natural food and drink. She wouldn't allow them to use ice in their drinks, saying, "It's bad for digestion." And the microwave was off-limits, since it's "bad, bad for you." Also, they could store only organic food in Pfister's fridge.

If Nancy put some of her Fanta orange soda in the fridge, Pfister threw it out, saying she "knew the horrible things that [are] put in soda." While expecting her guests to live by her house rules, Pfister didn't. She brought home lunches that weren't organic, which she kept so long they spoiled. But when Nancy tried to toss the ruined food out, Pfister got upset.

At first, it was just little things. Then, over time, Nancy said it became apparent that Pfister's hypocrisy extended into other areas of her life. Like her sexual relationships with a different man every week, or bringing home married men she met on some trip or another. Then there was the drinking. Pfister's alcoholism was on a level all its own. Nancy told Garth that Pfister drank all the time, and usually swallowed a handful of pills with her Champagne.

Finally, Nancy reached the part of the story where Pfister went missing and Kathy later found her body. She went through every detail she did with Detective Gibson on February 27, explaining how they moved out before Pfister returned from the airport; how they couldn't get all their things out in time, so they planned to return for the rest later; how Pfister was trying to milk them for more money; and how she called the police and asked for an officer to join them when they went back to Pfister's, in case she grew angry and nasty. Nancy told Garth how Trey repeatedly called Pfister, but she never answered, so all he could do was leave her messages, asking her to call them back.

In the meantime, they had moved into the Aspenalt until they could find another rental home; Nancy was chasing down leads for aesthetics work at various hotels in the area, and they were trying to move on with their life. Since Pfister never returned Trey's calls, they drove back to her home so they could get the U-Haul truck off of the road above her driveway, and the rest of their things out of her house. When Pfister didn't answer the door, Nancy went inside and found Gabe all alone. She noticed an odd odor, but chocked it up to Gabe defecating all over the place. At the same time, she told Kathy she was worried because Pfister wasn't home. By Wednesday afternoon, no one had heard from Pfister, so Nancy and Kathy decided Gabe should go home with Kathy after she left work that day. It was the last time Nancy talked to Kathy, because the next thing she knew, friends were calling, telling her police vehicles were going up West Buttermilk

Road. A few hours later, police banged on Nancy and Trey's motel door and hauled them in for questioning.

Next, Garth brought out the forty-page affidavit, which claimed to represent "why she was sitting in a jail cell." He went through all of the concerns he had that could potentially prove to poke a hole in their defense argument.

"Okay, look at this one," Garth said, pointing to a sentence saying the prosecution found blood in the Stylers' Jaguar.

"That's Trey's blood," Nancy said. "With his disease, he bleeds all over the place."

For every single point in the affidavit that worried Garth, Nancy had a logical explanation.

Then there were the "bad facts," as he called them, like having the murder weapon and the closet key turn up near your motel room. Finding the murder weapon, left like a calling card, right by the motel, was what worried Garth the most. Nancy didn't have an answer for that, but insisted there was a good one. "The police just haven't found it yet."

Later, when the defense finally received copies of evidence the prosecution had, Garth and Beth learned that Kathy Carpenter saw a therapist just across the street from the motel. The defense team thought the prosecution believed Kathy might have planted it to frame the Stylers.

"We were drinking the Kool-Aid," Garth said afterward.

Continuing with the "bad facts" in evidence, Garth asked Nancy, "What about the hammer they found, which we've been told has Trey's blood on it?"

At his mention of the hammer, Nancy didn't even look worried. "We lived in the house, so our DNA was everywhere. He probably used the hammer for repairs around the house, because he did plenty. Or even to hang pictures on the wall. Before Pfister returned, he hung her pictures back up, so everything would be like it was when she left."

At the time, that explanation made sense to Garth, as did all of Nancy's responses. The prosecution and defense both later learned she was right: DNA testing, for items like the blood in their car, which police cited as a reason to arrest her and Trey, proved Nancy right.

"Sure enough, it was Trey's," Garth said. "Every drop!"

After hours spent talking together, Nancy handed Garth a stack of papers. "This is my account of what happened, from the first day we arrived in Aspen."

Garth glanced through the handwritten pages. "This is really good, and it's going to be very helpful. Thank you." Then he paused. "I hate to say this, but it's not safe to write down anything in here."

"But I'm in solitary confinement," Nancy said.

Garth gave her a serious look. "You never know whose eyes might see it. There are always snitches in jail, on the lookout for things just like this."

* * *

Listening to Nancy's accounts of her life with Trey was the easy part. Hearing how terrible their relationship with Pfister had become wasn't difficult, either. And he thought Nancy's details about Pfister's disappearance seemed straightforward enough. But then, Garth said, "it became clear that she wanted to trust that she was in good hands with her attorneys, but she was not believing, necessarily, that she was." Even more striking than Nancy's need to trust her attorneys was her need, her desperation, even, "for somebody to see that she was innocent."

Garth didn't trust lawyers who got personally invested in their clients. "I think that is a dangerous way to practice law, generally," he said. Part of that may be because during his years spent as a defense attorney, "ninety percent of the clients I represent are involved or at least know something" about the crime.

Nancy was different.

"You don't run into Nancy Stylers very often," Garth said. "You don't run into cases like this very often. Where they're as tragic and as emotional as this, and where somebody's life is just really on the line."

Like Nancy's was. "And it was pretty clear she knew it," Garth said.

* * *

Just as she had with Beth, Nancy asked Garth directly: "Do you believe I'm innocent?"

"It's not my job to believe you, because I'm not your judge and jury," Nancy recalled Garth's words. "I'm here to make sure you get a fair shake."

Looking back now, Garth laughs. But he didn't that day. Tall and trim, with a shaved head and warm brown eyes, Garth said he was worried—first about his ethical obligation to do the best job he could regardless of Nancy's innocence or guilt and, second, about having a client who didn't trust him. "It's just a very uncomfortable question to be asked by your client because it's no secret that not everybody that we represent is innocent," Garth said. "They're innocent in the eyes of the law, until proven guilty, and I like to think that I'm a professional enough attorney that I advocate equally for all my clients, regardless of my opinion." For that reason, Garth made it a habit "not to even form an opinion."

But Nancy "wouldn't let me evade the question. She cornered me and demanded to know whether I believed what she was telling me, that she was innocent, and I believed the facts that she had told me," Garth said.

It was a sticky wicket for sure, one the thirty-eight-year-old defense attorney wasn't used to. Or prepared to answer, because he'd just read the affidavit from ADA Bryan, which contained enough "suspicious stuff in there, for instance, [the] proximity of the murder weapon to her hotel room," to make Garth worry.

That day, Garth had no idea how strong a case the DA had, and he'd only just met Nancy. But none of that mattered to his client, who refused to "let me sidestep that question."

Still, he was torn. "In this business we're supposed to be cynical. We run into people who have done bad things." And while he tried to "take people at their word," in his line of work, that was not easy. During their four-hour meeting, Garth tried repeatedly not to give Nancy an answer. "I tried to sort of thread that needle, saying, 'Well, first of all, it's none of my business to make that judgment, and I want you to know that you're going to get the best representation that you can find out of me, regardless of my personal opinion. That has nothing to do with my job, and I want you to understand that.'"

He took the intellectual approach, "which of course we're taught as lawyers, but which is not satisfying to the person who's sitting in jail wanting to have someone believe that she's innocent."

It didn't work. "I need you to believe I'm innocent," Nancy said, giving him that direct look again.

Finally, Garth caved and told Nancy what she wanted to hear. "She's the first client I think I've ever had who actually persisted," he said, "until I said, 'You know what, I do believe you. I do.'"

When he left the Pitkin County Jail not long after, Garth felt like he'd compromised his own principles. Until later that night, after he'd tucked his daughter into bed. *It wasn't just a courtesy. She really did need to hear someone say it*, he realized.

"She needed to go to bed that night knowing that there was somebody out there, other than her husband, who believed that she was a good person, because she is a good person," Garth said, "and that she was not guilty of this crime. And that's what it came down to—it was a necessity."

CHAPTER THIRTY-FOUR
BECOMING NANCY

O
n Friday, March 21, 2014, Jason and Sara, two guards from Pitkin County Jail, escorted Nancy to her new home at the Eagle County Detention Facility. The time had finally come for her to be completely separated from Trey. Sheriff DiSalvo didn't want two codefendants in the same jail; since her March 14 arrest, Kathy Carpenter had been lodged in the Garfield County Jail.

However, because of his medical condition, the prosecution agreed Trey should stay at Pitkin. So Nancy was transferred to the ECDF, ninety minutes from Aspen. And from Beth.

And Trey.

***

When she first arrived at Eagle, Nancy was devastated: for the second time in her life, through no fault of her own, she was forced to strip naked in front of complete strangers. The first time was in Room 122 of the Aspenalt Lodge, after the team of male police officers serving the search warrant made her disrobe for photographs. The second time happened when Nancy arrived at Eagle.

The process is humiliating and degrading, and requires the removal of one piece of clothing at a time. Nancy handed each item over to Teresa, a female guard who scrutinized the process. Even her hearing aids ("I'm almost deaf without them") had to come out.

Next, Nancy was told to "squat, cough, and spread your cheeks." It's the term inmates have given the procedure implemented in prisons all over the country. Basically, it works like this: Nancy placed her hands above her head and spread her legs. After the guard patted her down "down there," Nancy had to take her hands and pull her butt cheeks open. Next, the guard told Nancy to squat and cough, in case "you're hiding any contraband *up there*," she said. Finally, the guard looked in Nancy's mouth and ears, and instructed her to shake out her hair, which had to be free of any elastic, braids, or barrettes.

While her March 17 strip search was Nancy's first at Eagle, it certainly wasn't her last, because every time she reentered the jail—for instance, when she was transported to and from Pitkin for a hearing—Nancy was strip-searched again. That was seven times total, not including the February 27 search inside the Aspenalt Lodge.

Another indignity she eventually experienced while at Eagle involved being handcuffed and shackled for almost nine hours at a time. That would occur during transports to and from Pitkin County for court hearings, and it would result in bruises that Nancy showed the nurse and asked her to photograph.

Nancy wasn't allowed to wear her underwire bra in Eagle, either—female inmates are only permitted to wear sports bras. That's because hooks, eyes, and underwires can be used to fashion a weapon or tool. She decided a man established the prison system, since they obviously didn't consider such necessities as comfortably supported breasts.

Some things, like the bra policy, were the same. Other things were different. In Pitkin, the lights went out at night and inmates slept in the dark, punctuated by thirty-minute flashlight breaks, when guards came around to check on them. But in Eagle the lights stayed on all the time, even at night.

Even if the lights were off at night, Nancy probably wouldn't have slept any better. Eagle was different, and not in a good way. Other inmates shared their horror stories with Nancy, who also came to have stories of her own during her stay at Eagle.

A holding cell across from the front desk became Nancy's dining room for her first night's fare inside Eagle. The accommodations included a thin mattress on a concrete slab and a metal sink-toilet combo. A guard gave her a blanket, a meager dinner, and a cup of warm Kool-Aid to take into the cell, while she waited for the shift change to end. Nancy asked for ice, one of the few luxuries provided at Pitkin. She got nothing but a roll of the eyes. "You're in jail, Styler."

After lockdown, a guard escorted Nancy to her cell. There she would share a two-cell, four-bed pod with two other inmates. The two other women, her pod-mates, were both "frequent fliers," back in the jail for probation violations. They were only weeks from release. They knew the guards, the guards knew them, and even a routine cell check ended in a hearty round of exchanging profanities with the guards.

Nancy looked around, feeling lost in the cold, unwelcoming environment: the somber room's only furnishings were a combo sink-toilet, a closet, and a concrete post to help climb up on the top bunks. The plastic-encased mattress looked an inch thick, the pillow—if you could call it that—about the same. Nancy lay down on the narrow bunk, feeling the metal frame cutting into her back. She closed her eyes and tried to nap, but sleep wouldn't come. *How did I ever come to be in this awful place?*

***

Since she couldn't sleep for the first several nights, Nancy began writing: about her move to Eagle, how the guards treated her, the terrible food, and even the view from her top bunk, which had a small window. She wrote about anything and everything. But mostly, she wrote about all the women she met in jail, starting with the ones in Pitkin.

There was Barbara, in for a series of DUIs. She had violated probation. She was also a victim of domestic violence—a frustratingly common theme in the lives of the women she met. And, like most of the other female inmates, Barbara was trying to get her life back on track.

Nancy met Barbara during her few visits to the dayroom, which came near the end of her Pitkin stay when the guards had become more lax because Nancy would soon be shipped to Eagle. Like all female inmates there, Barbara wore an orange and white striped shirt on top of her orange jail uniform. The striped shirt was the designated uniform for female inmates. Nancy wore one, too.

Everyone knew why Nancy was there. "I was the old lady murderer," she said, but she didn't know Barbara's story. Not when she first sat down. But by the time they parted, Nancy felt like they were old friends. She learned Barbara's entire life story, as she would with each and every woman she later met at Eagle.

Then there was Janelle, a native Spanish speaker Nancy also met inside Pitkin. Like Barbara, she was also young; Janelle was only nineteen and already the mother of one child. Nancy said she wore her long, curly hair in a topknot, and she had a full beard. "I didn't know her name was Janelle. I thought it was Jannie," Nancy said, "because Janelle had a full beard." She, too, wore an orange and white overshirt.

At the time, Nancy didn't understand the significance of the overshirts. A few minutes after Janelle left the room, Nancy turned to a male guard sitting nearby. "Why do I have to wear this orange and white striped top? Is it according to your crime?"

"No, it's because you're a woman," the male guard said.

"Well, what about the person I was just talking to out there?" she asked. "Why do they have a striped top on?"

"That's Janelle, and she has a hormone problem. She doesn't shave in jail."

It wasn't until later, after Nancy was taken to Eagle, that she learned Janelle was "on the inside" because she had allegedly cashed stolen checks. That didn't matter to Nancy, who said, "Janelle was one of the nicest people I've ever met." And much later, Trey would tell Nancy how kind and helpful Janelle had been to him when she handed out the laundry inside the Pitkin Jail. He said Janelle also helped him when he was having problems getting his medicine.

Nancy found she and Janelle had a common love, as Janelle was also an avid reader. "She was reading three or four Danielle Steele novels at a time, and she read both English and Spanish," Nancy said. Janelle kept Nancy (and the guards) busy asking for pronunciation help with her English.

**

Because Nancy was in solitary at Pitkin, she only met a handful of inmates. It was very different at the Eagle County facility. Women came and went all the time. Nancy's attorneys warned her: never believe anything another inmate tells you.

She learned they were right; it was a big problem on the inside, because you never knew who was telling the truth and who was lying. When Lynn, who knew her way around Pitkin, was transferred to Eagle County, too, she and Nancy ended up living in the same pod, but not the same cell.

"I know your husband, back in Aspen," Lynn said. "I'm going back for trial next week. Do you want me to fly a kite to him?"

In jail, "flying a kite" means sending a message to someone, and Nancy often had to put a kite in for the nurse, to get her medicine, or if she fell ill. But she never took any of the other inmates up on their offer to get a message to Trey for her.

"I didn't want to violate any of the rules," Nancy said, "and I didn't want [the guards] to say, 'These two were communicating.'" She was afraid someone could take a perfectly innocent situation and make it sound like she and Trey were conspiring, or planning to do something wrong.

Besides, for all Nancy knew, Lynn might be a snitch who hoped to get Nancy into trouble with the authorities. Garth warned her about people like that, and even if she didn't already naturally follow the rules, she wasn't going to take any chances while inside.

***

Nancy met many women during her stay in Eagle County whose lives, she said, were far worse than hers. In fact, hearing about their situations made her realize how great her own life was. Take Thee, a woman in her sixties who had been arrested for having underage boys stay overnight in her home. Her charge? Thee told Nancy she was charged with contributing to the delinquency of a minor.

When Thee first came to her cell, Nancy was naturally curious.

"Oh, you're a cougar!" Nancy said.

"No," Thee said, "I'm a turkey vulture."

Nancy looked puzzled. "Why do you call yourself that?"

Thee laughed. "I still like the chase but I'm too old to take down the prey."

Nancy and Thee chatted and before long, Nancy did with Thee what she did with everyone—she had them telling her their entire life's story, even the darker parts they normally wouldn't share with strangers.

One of Thee's ex-boyfriends deliberately ran over her with his truck. Her injuries were so bad she was unable to work as a nurse any longer and eventually became addicted to the painkillers. Nancy thought about how Thee had first become a victim but afterward, she was in and out of jail repeatedly for DUIs and contributing to the delinquency of a minor. Both acts were a form of self-victimization, leading to further incarceration.

When Nancy met Thee, her boyfriend was an older fellow who lived nearby. Thee told her that relationship "wasn't anything that she felt really good about," helping Nancy realize that even though he was her boyfriend, he wasn't someone Thee could count on. That might be a problem if she didn't know when she was getting out, but Thee had a finite sentence; she was only in jail for eight days—yet she didn't even know if her significant other would be there for her, to pick her up when she was released.

The day of Thee's release, she didn't have any money in commissary, so Nancy helped her out. She called Thee's boyfriend who, as it turned out, did come and get Thee from jail. But one week later, Thee called Nancy with more bad news: after leaving jail, Thee found an eviction notice on her front door. She had three weeks to find a new place and move out. It was an eerie feeling, taking Nancy back to the horrible experience she and Trey had had with Pfister.

***

Thee's situation made Nancy think about how many women on the inside weren't self-reliant. Who, instead of helping themselves, depended on unreliable men. "It was a pattern that I saw in a lot of the women," Nancy said, "that when they were getting out they weren't sure who was going to be there for them. If anyone at all would be there. They felt very insecure."

Seeing that situation time and again broke Nancy's heart. "To see all of these women, and most of them had that same [problem]." They were never sure if their man was going to be there for them, and while "they were thrilled when it did happen," most of the time it didn't and they just accepted it as though their disappointment in those around them was normal.

Their experiences felt foreign to Nancy, because she "just knew that I was getting out. That my family would be there." If Trey was released before she was, which Nancy didn't think would happen, since she expected them to be released together, "Trey would have been there in a minute."

Nancy said that was never a situation she faced in her marriage. "I never had to think about, would he be there or wouldn't he be there? If he could be there, he'd be there."

And because she didn't think Trey would be there, given the fact that they were in separate jails, then if Daniel "could be there, when I got out, I knew he would." Someone who loved her would see to it that Nancy wasn't left standing alone, on the curb, with no way home.

Seeing and hearing about the lives of her fellow inmates helped Nancy realize how different her life was from theirs. "I never felt unloved by Trey, or that I had to question his love," she said. "I never, ever felt that."

By the time she had been in Eagle County for two months, Nancy had seen enough to know that most of her fellow inmates had no support from anyone on the outside. She believed most of their problems, or at least that most of the reason they landed in jail, had to do with lack of self-esteem. Nancy could tell that most of the women had never had anyone tell them how wonderful they were—as children or adults. There was also a high incidence of attention deficit hyperactivity disorder (ADHD) among her cellmates, who self-medicated with alcohol and illegal as well as legal drugs.

"I learned a little about AA from Kathy," Nancy later said, "but I got a complete education in jail by attending some meetings and reading their books."

In comparison to her cellmates, Nancy felt like her own life had been charmed, because it had been filled with people who believed in her from the time she was born, people like her mother, Tess, who told Nancy she could be anything, do anything, she wanted. And even though she and Trey had lost almost everything they owned, including their once-fabulous lifestyle, and had been reduced to living in a small mountain motel, Nancy knew for certain that the life she'd had was priceless.

CHAPTER THIRTY-FIVE

FALLEN ANGEL

On March 28, 2014, Nancy met Emily McClung, her new cellmate, or "cellie," and the young woman who would help Nancy endure a kind of loneliness and isolation she had never known. Emily had just spent a week detoxing in a holding cell before jail officials moved her into the general population.

The first time Nancy saw Emily, when a guard led her to Nancy's cell, she was shocked. The young girl's face was covered by her long, blonde hair. When she turned her head, Nancy saw how beautiful Emily was, even with a fading, ugly bruise that covered her right eye and reddened her bright blue iris. Later that night while Emily was undressing, Nancy saw the full-size angel wing tattoo on her new cellmate's back. "All I could think was 'fallen angel,'" she later said.

"What are you in for?" Emily asked Nancy.

"First-degree murder—that I didn't do!" Nancy said.

"I'm just in for a violation of probation," Emily said. "For a drug charge." Then she told Nancy that she had "done it all: heroin, crack, and more."

"What happened to your eye?" Nancy asked. "That looks painful."

Emily grimaced. "My boyfriend beat me up for using up all of his cocaine."

Later that night, Nancy helped Emily make up her bed and gave her some toiletries. Then they settled down for what turned into a very long night: Emily yelled and screamed and cried in her sleep. The next morning, Nancy asked the nurse to get Emily the medication she needed, "so we can both get some sleep tonight."

Fortunately, the nurse did.

The following day, facing almost ten hours of lockdown and with nothing better to do, Emily shared her story with Nancy. She was thirty-two, just two years older than Nancy's son, Daniel. After a childhood riddled with abuse, Emily "turned to the needle" and was soon addicted to heroin.

Despite the trials Emily faced, she was a natural storyteller and had Nancy laughing in no time. She told Nancy about the first day she arrived at Eagle. "The deputy behind the desk said, 'Emily, you're drunk!' and I replied, 'And you're fat!'" She later apologized when he brought her room supplies. But every time Nancy and Emily saw him they shared a good laugh.

Emily had been in and out of jail several times over the years. She was arrested and charged with the same repeat offense: possession. Her last stint in jail came about not long after Nancy arrived at Eagle.

"I called the cops on myself," Emily said, adding that she was on probation at the time. "I was bored with the lifestyle, I was bored with drinking, I was bored with doing drugs." Emily wanted to start over.

Like many of the women Nancy met in jail, Emily was abused as a child, and a victim of human trafficking, which led to bad choices as an adult. Which led to more abuse—at the hands of boyfriends who battered her—and at her own hands.

Nancy thought about how dramatically different their experiences were that brought her and Emily together. She could tell that—unlike Daniel—Emily had graduated from "the school of hard knocks." Nancy also saw how little self-esteem Emily had. Because Emily told Nancy her story in such a candid, childlike way, Nancy was drawn to her.

***

Emily could tell right away that Nancy was different from everyone else. "She was so shocked to be in jail, and the whole experience. She'd never been through anything like it, and she was in shock. It was like, 'Wow, I'm in jail!'"

Whenever a new inmate arrives, it's common for the "old-timers" to ask what the inmate did that landed her in jail. But when Nancy told Emily why she was there, Emily "could tell from the beginning that [she wasn't a murderer]." In fact, she was shocked that Nancy was even accused of murder.

"I never had any notion that she had anything to do with [Pfister's death]; she just doesn't have that in her," Emily said. "Nancy just didn't strike me as a person that would be in jail for any reason." Incarceration can have an upside, after all: Emily said it sharpened her skills, making her a good judge of character. Nancy's character didn't cry out "murderer!" Just the opposite, in fact: Nancy was "kind and quiet," Emily said, but she was also "a funny lady, who's got a good sense of humor."

Then there were the rules: Nancy refused to break them. Not even the little ones.

"You know, I would hide food all over the place. Fruit, I loved the fruit," Emily said. So at mealtimes, she would "keep some fruit . . . take it, just hide it somewhere in the room so that they wouldn't find it and then I could eat it later." Storing leftover food was something "everybody does," but Emily said Nancy never did.

It wasn't just Nancy's personality that led Emily to believe Nancy was innocent. It was the way people on the outside saw her, and tried to help boost her spirits while she was inside. "Her family loves her, you know; people are writing letters to her that she doesn't even know," Emily said, "from other parts of the country and stuff, you know, people who'd been touched by her somehow."

The mail situation inside Eagle County was frustrating for Nancy. All incoming mail had to be scanned and it "never showed up on time. It was like at least thirty days later," Emily recounted, "and [Nancy] swears that the people there were doing it on purpose, because she would get lots of mail." So, instead of getting a letter from her mom, Tess, every day, they all came at once. "It was frustrating for Nancy," Emily said.

Even though she was stressed out or worried about Trey or wondering why her mail wasn't arriving like it should, Nancy focused more on Emily than on her own problems.

And Emily needed it. When she arrived at Eagle County, she "was at a burned-out stage . . . I had a possession charge—I have aspirations and dreams and I couldn't go anywhere with them."

That's why she turned herself in, so she could clean up her act. "I'm going to jail for ninety days because I'm ready to get off probation," Emily said.

Once she was back in jail, though, Emily was all alone: she had no money and no boyfriend. Her romantic relationship ended and she refused to call and ask him for anything. But Emily found support and comfort in Nancy, and thus more positive experiences than she did during her past incarcerations.

***

Inmates don't often share their food and personal possessions with each other, because they don't usually have that much to share. Well, that and they're . . . criminals. Many of the inmates Nancy encountered committed a crime that involved theft or worse. Being generous with others isn't their strong suit—especially not on "the inside."

"Nancy was a giving person. She always had lots of snacks. She would share her snacks with me," Emily said. "And in jail when you don't have a lot, a snack is like a huge thing."

Take a cupcake, or a pack of Jolly Ranchers, which Nancy always had a ready supply of. Emily described why something as small as a cupcake in jail "is like a huge deal. Because everything changes in there. Like you're scraped down to hardly anything, and it's a gesture when somebody shares with you. Because a lot of people don't, they don't even care."

Nancy was different. "I mean, Nancy shared with whoever didn't have anything."

Because of all the support from her family and friends, Nancy always had money on account for the commissary. "She just always helped people out that needed help."

Most of them appreciated Nancy's help. "It just touches people when they're incarcerated and somebody reaches out like that," Emily said.

Many women are in jail because they defended themselves against abuse, or because they got caught up in something by mistake. But then there are the women who have actually committed terrible crimes, which means they will be incarcerated for a long time. To them, gestures like Nancy's have the capacity to be life changing.

One woman, Traci, who was awaiting trial for murder, was so different, with serious mental problems, that many inmates wouldn't have anything to do with her. "She probably will never see the light of day again, let's just put it that way," Emily said. "And Nancy was even nice to *her.*"

For this woman, who "seriously didn't have anybody for probably the rest of her life . . . a bag of Jolly Ranchers was a big deal," Emily said. "And this girl, you know, was really touched by that."

When Traci wanted to talk, "Nancy would just sit there and listen. [But] everybody else, we could not handle her talking, because she would just drive us nuts," Emily recounted. But not Nancy. "She totally was able to do that," even if it meant listening to Traci talk for hours at a time. "Nancy has a giant heart," Emily said.

At times, however, Nancy's generosity led other inmates to take advantage of her. "I was like, 'Nancy, you gotta chill out on that because this person is simply just using you.'" Once Emily "gave her the low-down on what was going on," Nancy tried to see what Emily meant. But it was difficult, not only because Nancy enjoyed helping other people and sharing with them, but "because she's so sweet, so nice. And nice people get walked all over, you know, generally," Emily said.

Over the time they were in jail together, Nancy began to discern who genuinely needed help versus the ones who were merely using her. Emily explained it another way. "Nancy started growing a pair eventually," Emily said, laughing. "You know? She did."

* * *

Emily had been a cheerleader and an ice skater, so the two women shared similar personality traits, being very upbeat most of the time. Nancy asked Emily to design a program for her and be her personal trainer. Emily showed her how to use Gatorade bottles for training weights. But the empty bottles couldn't be refilled with any other liquid, since inmates were known to try to make "jailhouse hooch," so when Nancy began working out, she faced the same dilemma as Emily: whether to drink the Gatorade or save it to exercise with.

"She wanted to get rid of her bingo wings, you know? That's what she called it, like the arm part right here?" Emily pointed to her triceps.

While Emily, who was "eating like a crazy person at night," found losing weight difficult, Nancy, at just 115 pounds, "didn't get fat at all. She's got that skinny body."

Emily didn't exercise just to lose weight—she did it to keep her sanity. "I needed to, being enclosed like that." And when Nancy saw Emily working out, she wanted to join her. Emily used the T25 program, a strenuous workout for the fittest person, but because of her mastectomy surgery and her age, Nancy didn't have that option. So Emily took some of the exercises from the program and modified them for her new friend and cellie. Then she and Nancy worked out twice a day. "Once in the morning and once in the evening, like maybe thirty minutes each time, so it got us moving," she said.

Emily said it was just the two of them. "Nobody else really joined, from our little pod. Like they just looked at us like we were crazy."

Being stuck in a tiny cell together for three hours after dinner, the workouts helped the two women break up their evening, because there wasn't much to do otherwise. By the end of Emily's ninety-day stay, they had a great exercise schedule and compared themselves to Jack Spratt and his wife when eating their meals. Nancy wouldn't eat any "mystery meat"; Emily didn't want to eat carbs. Emily, a constant blur of movement, was always moving—even in her sleep. That made her the perfect person to motivate Nancy to exercise. Emily nicknamed Nancy "white chocolate," a name that Nancy's family laughed at and immediately adopted.

***

Jail life is the opposite of real life, and in some ways, what most people dream of: it gives you all the free time in the world. There's only one problem: there isn't enough to do on the inside to fill your days, unless you get really creative. That's what Nancy did, and that's how she stayed sane.

Because of her past trips to jail, Emily was familiar with many workarounds, which required an inventive mind. For example, she taught Nancy, a trained aesthetician, how to make eye shadow, lipstick, and face cream. Nancy was more than willing to experiment. "She was just so funny," Emily said. "It's funny how you do things in here."

Deodorant formed a base for the shadow, and colorful magazine advertisements provided the color. They took a bit of deodorant and rubbed it into an area on the ad with the color they wanted, "and then you rub it on your face."

There is a drawback, though. "It's pretty, but not good for you because you break out like a crazy person," Emily said, "because you're putting deodorant on your face."

Chapstick became a type of wrinkle cream for the face. "I don't know if it worked, but it had cocoa butter in it, so I thought it was better than nothing." A $1 jar of cheap Vaseline cost $4 on the inside, so they used it "very sparingly." Emily said, "We'd be like, 'Okay, well, that's good enough.'"

Then there were Jolly Ranchers: when dissolved in hot water, they could be used in place of hairspray to slick their hair back. Jail toothpaste, which was clear and colorless, doubled as hair gel and paper glue.

Nancy, ever the beauty expert, even curled Emily's hair. She took toilet paper rolls and twisted strands of Emily's hair up with it. "And it worked! Really well," Emily said. There was only one problem: the paper rollers were considered contraband. So the guards woke them up at 3 a.m., telling Emily she had to "get rid of all my rollers because it was contraband," Emily said. "I had curly hair just for that day."

Nancy's own hair looked quite different by then. Anyone who knew her knew that Nancy was naturally a dark blonde with salon highlights. Long before Nancy ended up as a jailbird, Tess had asked her daughter what her untouched natural color was, and Nancy laughed. She told her mother she didn't ever plan to find out.

"But after three months in jail, I did," she said.

Since Nancy's hair wasn't long enough for an elastic band, Emily French-braided it. The other inmates loved having her plait their hair, and she was very fast. Emily told Nancy she had to be, because she used to braid the entire cheerleading squad's hair on the bus en route to competitions.

Nancy was delighted when Trey, who was sitting behind her in court during their first hearing, whispered, "I love your French braid." After that, whenever Nancy knew she would be seeing Trey at a hearing, she would ask Emily to braid it for her just for him.

***

Some days, Emily and Nancy just stayed in their narrow bunk beds and read books. Emily preferred fiction, but Nancy always read non-fiction, usually biographies. Nancy read 196 books during her incarceration. She admittedly relished not having "to deal with my phone or email or make any decisions. It reminded me of the old adage 'Be careful what you wish for, you just might get it.'" When they weren't reading, working out, or creating their own designer line of jail cosmetics, Emily and Nancy went to "the beach."

The beach was a rooftop cage next to the recreation room. Nancy told the guards they needed their vitamin D, and asked if she and Emily could "go to the beach" when it was sunny. "We even got them to bring our lunch out there a couple of times," Nancy later said.

"We'd lay out [and pretend it was] the seashore," Emily said, laughing. They even tried to get a tan.

But when other inmates interrupted because they needed to talk, Nancy would let them. "So much for the day at the beach," Nancy told Emily, in a tone of voice that cracked Emily up.

"I'd just start laughing," she said.

Laughter on the inside is usually rare, and when it happens, it's like a delicious, forbidden treat. But there was no shortage of laughter in Nancy and Emily's cell. "We laughed a whole lot more than we cried," Nancy said.

In fact, some young teens came by the jail with a program called "Scared Straight." The guards opened the window to the cells so the teens could see the inmates in their native habitat. Nancy and Emily were playing cards and were laughing so hard they were crying.

Still, most inmates, Emily and Nancy included, needed an antidepressant just to deal with being locked up in such a small, confined space. And sometimes the jail ran out of medication. "The jail nurse would say, 'Oh, well, we don't have any but we'll get you some in a couple days,'" Emily recounted. When that happened, "Girl, you better watch out. There was intense neurochemistry going off the chain. Antidepressants kept us all sane. Prozac helps you, helps you stay centered in the midst of chaos, and not think everything's gloomy."

***

Emily said she's "met interesting people" in jail, but no one like Nancy who was wrongly accused of a crime as serious as murder. "That's stressful, and she was just like, flabbergasted, I guess you could say." She met other women who were innocent of other, less serious crimes, but "I've never met anybody like that because the people I've met generally all did whatever they were in there for."

Nancy stood out as different, and because of that, Emily said there wasn't one person who didn't like her, because Nancy was the woman who planned special parties for the other inmates, who took the lead in making greeting cards to celebrate when someone was getting out, and who shared her food with everyone else, passing out Jolly Ranchers or chocolates as if she didn't have a care in the world.

"Everybody liked her in jail. Nobody gave her any problems," Emily said. "Because she didn't ever create any problems."

***

Nancy's demeanor, her take-charge attitude, and her confidence were what made women on the inside like Emily pay attention to what she said. "I always was talking about how I was going to get fake boobs when I got out," Emily said, adding that she was going to have a boyfriend pay for them. "Nancy was like, 'No you're not.' She said, 'You're going to pay for them,'" Emily said. "I'd always relied on men or always relied on other people to take care of me and give me what I wanted."

Nancy stressed the importance of being self-sufficient, instead of relying on someone who may or may not come through. She told Emily that when she got out, she should apply for scholarships so she could pursue her dream of studying IT and becoming a web developer. Emily recognized she lacked self-confidence. "I was lacking at that point, you know, in my whole self," she said.

Mostly, Emily said she didn't feel good about herself because she "was just screwing up, [not] putting the right foot forward," and letting her past, which involved human trafficking, get in her way. But then Nancy helped Emily see that she could do better. "She just motivated me to do more, you know—get more independent and believe in myself and do well."

Nancy told Emily she should go back to school. "You're going to make it," Nancy told her. "You're gonna be able to take on the world." Nancy was "so sweet about it," Emily said, "and it was nice to hear that from somebody."

Emily learned about Nancy's son, Daniel, who was finishing up his doctorate degree, and his girlfriend, who was working on her degree and already had a good job. Nancy told her that if she worked hard, she could pay her own way. "And I wouldn't have to have somebody buy me boobs one day," Emily said, smiling.

***

The love went both ways. Nancy was so happy Emily landed at Eagle, "because she truly became an angel to me. Her positive attitude, energy, and sense of humor helped me get through my time in Eagle. Because of her, I laughed more than I cried while I was there."

Being with Emily, who was young enough to be her daughter, made Nancy think even more about Daniel. She agonized at the tremendous burden that had been placed on him, knowing that his sheltered, suburban upbringing could not ever have prepared him for dealing with two parents facing first-degree murder charges. Nancy hoped Daniel would find his footing with the tools she and Trey had given him, and later she was rewarded to learn that he did.

"As it turns out, Daniel not only found his footing, he stayed on his path," Nancy said. "My family told me over and over how well he was dealing with everything. He kept them informed, managed finances, and dealt with the media, all while working on his dissertation."

In the year since they were together at Eagle County, Emily said Nancy is never far from her thoughts. "I've thought about Nancy a lot since I've been out," she said, "and my life's completely turned around since then. I mean completely. Like it's not even the same thing."

She believes meeting Nancy made a world of difference. "It was in the back of my head the whole time, because she was right—because now my whole life's opened up."

Emily, who had been clean for six months in April 2015, is now in college, studying IT, in pursuit of her dream. Nowadays, instead of using toxic chemical substances, Emily is addicted to her gym workouts and running. "Everything's going good. I've been sober," she said. "No alcohol, no pot, no nothing." Fortunately, Emily broke the cycle that so many women don't, whether in prison or out. She gives Nancy all the credit for that.

CHAPTER THIRTY-SIX

NEVER SEEN THIS DEAD WOMAN BEFORE

Armed with the details Nancy gave him from their first meeting, Garth began combing through the arrest warrant affidavit and other documents the prosecution gave Nancy's defense team. He was puzzled about several things, including why male police officers had photographed his female client in the nude. And why not wait until police took the Stylers in for questioning on February 27, instead of snapping photos right there in the couple's motel room?

"We want to see if there's any marks or abrasions or bruises, anything that could have happened during a struggle," Detective Brad Gibson told investigative reporter Daleen Berry. "Especially when you have a search warrant, you don't want to wait," adding that during the twenty-mile transport, the seatbelts could leave bruises on a suspect, or the handcuffs might scratch them. "We want to take pictures of them as we found them."

When police served the search warrants for the Stylers' bodies, "both Stylers were photographed with no clothes on." But Gibson said, "Nancy Styler was given more privacy. We didn't, you know, make her disrobe in front of us. She was taken to a walk-in closet or a bathroom inside the motel room."

Nancy disagreed. "That's bullshit! That room didn't have a closet, and the bathroom wasn't big enough to have any focal distance to take photos. There was only enough room for a tub and toilet and very little else."

Gibson said the Stylers "were both photographed with no clothes, per the search warrant, and that's normal."

However, in the motion Judge Nichols ruled on for that search, only Trey Styler was mentioned as having had nude photos taken by police. When Berry told Gibson this, he said he didn't know why the photos of Nancy weren't mentioned. "I don't have anything to do with the motions; that's all the DA and defense." And when told that Nancy said a man photographed her in front of all the other men, until someone spoke up and said they should bring a woman in to do it, Gibson said he didn't "recall it that way." The team who served the search warrant "wouldn't want to impose ourselves *that* way," Gibson said, before offering a caveat. "If we had to [let a male officer take the photos], we would. If there was a woman available, we would have used her." Ultimately, though, it had nothing to do with the officers themselves. "We had a search warrant saying we could, by a judge."

Nancy said that was exactly what happened. Even after someone stopped the male officer after he began taking photos, "they still waited a while after the remark until Heather came to snap the rest of the pictures and let me pee." When Heather took the rest of the photos, "I was in the bedroom, with a bunch of men watching," Nancy said.

The entire defense team was vehement in their disagreement with Gibson's rationale for having photographed Nancy Styler naked and the manner in which it happened. They also questioned why police ever thought Pfister's killers would have defense wounds. "It seems a little silly because she died in her sleep," Garth said. "There's no rationale to think there would be injuries on either Nancy or Trey."

Nancy's defense team also wanted to pin down the source of a rumor floating around town, at least in law enforcement circles: namely, that Pfister emailed Sheriff Joe DiSalvo in early February, asking him to evict the Stylers. If true, it would indicate the two had a very close friendship, which, while troubling, would not be surprising.

DiSalvo's relationship with Pfister could explain the authorities' urgency to arrest the Stylers more quickly than they normally did with suspects in criminal cases. "They were under a lot of pressure to make an arrest quickly," Garth said, "but why?"

While true that Pitkin County rarely had a murder to contend with, Garth still found it perplexing. He wondered if political pressure was behind the swiftness with which police had the two suspects in their sights. District Attorney Sherry Caloia lost the 2012 election in Rio Blanco County, tied in Garfield County, but won in Pitkin County. That meant that Pitkin voters elected her to the Ninth District. What if, when later faced with the facts about Nancy's innocence, Caloia was afraid to back down? What if she feared the people of Pitkin County would disapprove of how she had handled the case—and tell her so when they return to the ballot box in 2016?

***

It didn't take long for the defense to find evidence that their client was telling the truth: Pfister was renting the chalet, which was owned by her family's trust fund, for cash under the table. They discovered that Nancy was also correct when she said Pfister had a long and colorful history of having problems with her tenants.

"Rita Bellino and her son used to live at Nancy's, but then something went wrong," Nancy told Garth. "I can't say why, or what exactly happened, just that Pfister told me they nearly came to blows over her first Labradoodle, which she also named Gabe." Pfister and Rita hadn't talked for several years, as a result.

Then there was Gayle Golding. "That was a real fiasco," Nancy said. Sure enough, court and police records validated Nancy's story: Gayle and her son rented Pfister's house once and got her approval to grow marijuana on her property, since Gayle had a medical marijuana license, making the operation legal. But when Pfister returned early from an overseas trip, she called the sheriff's office to report finding marijuana being grown on her property. Deputies responded, and, not long after, Gayle arrived and denied Pfister's claims that the marijuana was illegal. She showed police her license, but Pfister was so unreasonable that Gayle moved out anyway. Later, she filed a suit against Pfister for emotional and monetary damages. The two women eventually settled out of court.

Bellino's own words confirm what Nancy told Gibson. Pfister "liked to rent her house out, but she really never liked people being there. She would always come home before she originally planned," Bellino wrote in a journal she gave to police.

Eventually, the defense also discovered that Pfister had, indeed, asked the sheriff to help evict the Stylers. Pfister emailed Deputy Jesse Steindler on January 20, 2014, saying she wanted the couple evicted. Then she told Steindler to "get Joey after them," a clear reference to the sheriff.

Pfister also copied former sheriff Bob Braudis on that email, as she did many others that contained information about the rental dispute. That meant that within minutes of Kathy's 911 call, Braudis and DiSalvo, who were together when they heard the call come over DiSalvo's police radio, had time for an unofficial chat about Pfister's alleged problems with the Stylers.

A few hours after Pfister's body was found, Braudis began forwarding those emails to the sheriff. They later became part of the discovery prosecutors turned over to the defense. Later, Braudis told CBI Agent Zamora during an interview that Pfister copied him "on scores of emails ... [with her] bitching about [the Styler's supposed] nonpayment of rent, utilities, leaving her car in the snow, as opposed to putting it in the garage."

Braudis also believed Pfister's lies, that the Stylers were deadbeat tenants, as shown when he said that during her absence, Pfister's attorney had been dealing with "the legal shit, trying to get them to either pay up or get out." The sheriff was aware of all this prior to Pfister's death, too. "Joey has all of those ... I can print those out," Braudis told Zamora.

"I'm sure the sheriff got some of those as well," Zamora said.

"He got some of the more entertaining ones," Braudis replied.

Later, when the defense filed a motion to obtain copies of those emails, the judge denied its request.

Before long, Chief Public Defender Tina Fang, Trey's defense attorney, publicly called out DiSalvo for refusing to release evidence and other documents. In open court, she told Judge Nichols that DiSalvo was too close to the victim to be objective, as shown by the fact that Pfister's Labradoodle was staying at DiSalvo's home.

Continuing to dig, Garth learned that several of the statements in the affidavit used to charge Nancy and Trey were "erroneous and

deceptive." The entire defense team soon believed that someone—
whoever was behind the plan to arrest the Stylers—came up with a
theory about their guilt, and then tried to find facts to support that
idea. Nothing else makes any sense.

Granted, the DNA from the hammer may have linked Trey to
the murder, but not Nancy. Besides, even if Trey were involved, which
seemed highly unlikely, given Trey's condition, that didn't mean Nancy
was.

"There is no law that I'm aware of where if a husband is arrested,
his wife is, too," Garth later said.

***

On April 16, Garth had an important task before him, but he wasn't
looking forward to it. He gathered up his iPad, put it in his case, and
followed the curvy, mountain road leading from Glenwood Springs to
Eagle County Jail. It was a gorgeous spring day but Garth barely noticed,
so focused as he was on the unpleasant task ahead. He told Nancy he
believed her, and he did. But he still needed to make sure—the defense
had to find out if their client knew anything about the murder.

When he arrived at the jail, Garth checked in and then went
through security. A guard led the defense attorney to the library, where
he and Nancy would meet. A few minutes later, Nancy was led into the
room. She sat down and after Garth briefed her on what they'd found,
she shared funny stories from the past couple of weeks from her "life
on the inside." As usual, she was chatty and talkative. But not for long.

Garth pulled his iPad from his case. "Nancy, I brought the crime
scene photos with me. Do you want to see them?"

Nancy didn't hesitate. "Yes, I want to know what I'm accused of
doing."

The first couple of photos didn't show much. It was even difficult to
tell that the mound of blankets someone had piled inside on the closet
floor hid a body. If not for a tiny place where a bit of plastic peaked
through one end of the blanket, showing what looked like it might be
hair covered in red, it would be more difficult to tell that it was a body.

But the next couple of photos showed a bulky form of what Nancy
could tell was a body, and she could see it had been wrapped up like a

burrito. However, the photos taken after the coroner removed Pfister from the closet, but prior to the autopsy, were particularly disturbing. The first few showed nothing more than a body wrapped up in sheets and towels, and then covered with plastic bags. But Nancy recognized the linens: they were the same ones she washed and stored away while Pfister was gone, that had been part of Betty Pfister's bridal trousseau.

In the photos that followed, though, Pfister was shown from several angles, her legs and arms hog-tied with a yellow extension cord, so that her body was doubled in half. The photos of the head, wrapped in her mother's white towels, monogrammed in forest green with the initials EHP for Elizabeth Haas Pfister, were the worst. They were almost impossible to look at—and all that remained of Pfister.

Nancy, who typically talked nonstop, went silent as she looked at every photo. For thirty minutes she remained that way, not so much as a single syllable escaping her lips. Garth, experienced in reading the reaction on his clients' faces, watched Nancy's face intently. All he saw was sadness, and a complete absence of the socially learned behavior a guilty person would exhibit.

"At that moment, I thought, 'This lady has never seen this dead woman before,'" Garth later said.

CHAPTER THIRTY-SEVEN

FREEING NANCY

The past three and a half months, starting on February 27, 2014, with police pounding on the door of the motel room, seemed a nightmare from which Nancy still didn't feel entirely awake.

Yet she knew that's what Beth told her: they're letting you go.

She and Trey were free! Any minute now, he would walk through the door and they would walk out together, hand in hand. Nancy wanted to pinch herself, just to make sure she wasn't still asleep.

"Nancy, did you hear me?" a voice asked.

Nancy turned her gaze back to Beth, remembering when Beth first entered the room a few seconds ago. "Good news, you're leaving," Beth said, hugging Nancy.

"I thought I'd lost you there for a minute," Beth said, smiling with Nancy. She had just given her client the good news, and Nancy was "obviously elated."

Nancy shook her head, as if to banish the daydream bunnies bouncing around in there. "Did I hear you right? Did you really say we're getting out? Trey and me?" The words came out in a rush, one long sentence, and ended on a high note that sounded so excited and hopeful that Beth was torn between Nancy's happiness and a sense of worry over what she had to do next.

"Yes, you're getting out, but—," Beth stopped, not sure how to finish, and instead brushed her hair from her eyes, not looking at Nancy. "But, you know, before you get, too excited." Beth stopped again, unable to find the right words.

Then she sat up straight, forcing herself to look Nancy directly in the eye. "I need you to understand that, that Trey is pleading guilty. He's taking responsibility and you need to read this letter. It's from Trey. He gave it to Tina, and she gave it to me for you."

"What are you talking about?" Nancy took the envelope from Beth's hand, pulled out a three-page letter, and began reading. By the time the door opened and Garth joined them, Nancy was sobbing. As Garth took a seat, Nancy continued reading.

Garth wished Beth had waited for him, so they could have broken the news together. He knew it was going to be their only victory and he wanted to share in that moment, to see the smile on her face when Nancy heard the news that she was free. That moment was long gone, with only tears in its place.

The room had "a much more sullen atmosphere than I was expecting," Garth said later. Beth was watching Nancy, too, and said she went from a feeling of jubilation to being panic-stricken.

"I never, never entertained any serious belief that she was involved at all, but when I told her first off that she was getting out, she was obviously very, very happy," Beth said later, "and then I told her hold on a second, you know, there's something else you need to know . . . that was the clincher to me."

Beth felt terrible that she had to deliver the news to Nancy that the person she loved and had lived with for thirty-two years was pleading guilty. The letter was ambiguous, telling Nancy that he knew she was innocent and she "should believe the same of him," but he was pleading guilty anyway.

"What does this mean?" Nancy asked. "Did he do it and you're just not telling me?"

"We think you were driving around with [Pfister's] phone and the murder weapon," Beth said, trying to help her understand Trey's letter, "but we're not sure."

"We don't really know," Garth said. "Tina and Trey are afraid you will try to fight this decision, but please don't." He said Trey would be sentenced in three days. In return for his plea, he would receive a twenty-year sentence. "You should thank Tina every day of your life for such a good deal."

Looking at Nancy's face, both attorneys suspected what she was thinking, just before Nancy said as much. "Oh, my God, Trey's falling on his sword, just to get me out of jail!" Neither Beth nor Garth knew what to say.

Nancy was suddenly hysterical at the thought of never being with Trey again, and of him confessing just to get her out.

But then, Garth saw another emotion, too—one that worried him.

"It was the moment that she trusted us least. She went back and forth, trusting us. I think there were moments where she trusted us and moments when she didn't," Garth said, "but I felt like that moment was the moment she had the least amount of faith and trust in us."

Beth saw it, too. "She was distraught. In her cell crying, because she could not believe that her husband actually did this."

It was easier for Nancy to believe her attorneys had "pulled some legal trick and threw Trey under the bus and . . . her innocent husband is now going to prison because of some trick that her lawyers pulled," Garth said. "That certainly is not what happened," he added.

Just before he headed back to Pitkin County, Garth asked jail officials to monitor Nancy until her release. He feared Nancy might do something to sabotage Trey's confession, and he hoped she wouldn't try to give a false confession just to save Trey. He knew it was a crazy idea, but he also saw Nancy's distrust. Garth wished he could have stayed longer, but he had to appear at Nancy's hearing, where the charges would be dismissed.

Beth stayed with Nancy for a while, but as she left, she thought that if she had had any doubts before about her client's guilt, Nancy's reaction to Trey's letter had chased them away. Beth was convinced that Nancy was totally innocent.

***

Nancy was alone back in her cell. Emily had been released the day before, so she wasn't there to comfort Nancy. Another inmate who was charged with murder held Nancy and tried to comfort her, as she sobbed most of the day. Inside her mind, Nancy's thoughts wavered, going back and forth between thinking Trey confessed to save her, to wondering if he confessed because he actually did kill Pfister.

By the time the guards came to tell Nancy she was being released, hours later, she still hadn't completely grasped what had happened. She could not believe the gentle, kind man she loved would ever be capable of murder. Especially not a murder like Pfister's.

Nancy took the bag with her belongings and went outside, leaving the bars and heavy steel doors behind her. Jill, the same guard who had given her such a hard time over the bleach incident, transported Nancy to a meeting spot where Patrice was waiting for her, and when Nancy saw her, she fell, sobbing, into her arms.

* * *

Patrice took Nancy back to her house, where Nancy would spend the next few days. When they pulled into Patrice's driveway, Nancy looked up and for the first time during their time in the car, saw something that caught her attention: hummingbirds. Nancy suddenly realized she was free; she was finally free.

All evening, Patrice treated her with so much tenderness and love, waiting on her, running her a bath, encouraging her to relax, that Nancy felt like a princess. Later that night after they'd eaten, Patrice led Nancy upstairs to the spare bedroom, where a featherbed was piled high with all kinds of pillows.

"Since you told me you didn't have a [good] pillow in jail," Patrice said, "I wanted to make sure you had enough here."

Nancy hugged Patrice tight and felt tears well up again. By the time she was tucked in, Nancy felt some of the tension ebb away. Lying under the covers, she felt like the fairytale princess who sleeps on a tall bed piled high with mattresses.

The bed even had its own pea, as Nancy's first night of sleep outside prison walls was disrupted by nightmares of Trey's letter.

CHAPTER THIRTY-EIGHT

CALLING BOSTON

Daniel was in Boston at his aunt Cindy's house on June 16, preparing to fly home to Denver the next day. When Beth Krulewitch called him, he couldn't have been more surprised.

"Where are you?" she asked.

"I'm in Boston for a family wedding," Daniel said.

"Will you be available tomorrow?" Beth asked. "Because something big is happening, but I can't say anymore."

"Yes, I will. My flight leaves here tomorrow afternoon."

After hanging up, he turned to Cindy. "Well, I wonder what's happening now."

***

Daniel got another call from Colorado a few hours later. This time it was his father. He and Cindy looked at each other: either the news was really good, or really bad. But it wasn't just bad—it was terrible.

Cindy couldn't hear Trey's words, but whatever he was saying wasn't good. When the phone rang, Daniel had been holding a nail in his hand, and as he listened to his father, he dug it into the workbench where he and Cindy were working. Cindy grew so nervous that she took the nail from Daniel.

"Why? Why are you doing this?" Daniel asked his father.

Cindy watched as Daniel fell apart and began sobbing. "I love you, Dad," Daniel said just before he hung up. Cindy had never seen Daniel so upset. Daniel didn't get upset. He was stoic and wore a protective shell to keep from being hurt. He just didn't show pained emotions.

Until this time, when he got off the phone. "Dad said he's pleading guilty. He says he's very sick and is probably going to die soon," Daniel said. "He said, 'I want your mom to go free.'" Daniel was so upset he could barely stand. Cindy held him and hugged him, trying to console her nephew as best as she could.

"It's going to be all right, Daniel," she kept saying.

"No, it isn't!" he said. "I'm going to be forever known as Daniel Styler, the son of the man who murdered Nancy Pfister." With that, Daniel began crying again.

Cindy looked at him squarely in the eye. "No, you're not. You're going to be Daniel Styler, the man who does great things with his life!"

***

When he was calm enough, Daniel called Tina Fang, his father's attorney. He had questions. "Is my father really dying? Is he doing this to save my mother or did he really do it? Did he kill Nancy Pfister?"

Tina had no answers. She reminded Daniel of the attorney-client privilege and said she was only allowed to share what Trey gave her permission to. She wished she could tell him more, but ultimately, his father needed to answer those questions. Tina did tell Daniel that if he spoke to his mother before she got the news from her attorneys, to plead ignorance. Besides, there was always a chance she might not get out the next day. It might take a day or two. "Let her attorneys handle it," Tina told Daniel.

He had barely enough time to tell Cindy what Tina said when his mom called. It wasn't expected, because they normally coordinated time for her calls from jail. Daniel didn't breathe a word of what Tina or Beth had told him. Basically, he told his mother he was "coming home tomorrow. Give me a call in the evening and I'll let you know I'm back safe."

After Daniel hung up with his mom, his third call that day from Colorado, he and Cindy had a long heart-to-heart. They began with the RV trip the Stylers took in 2013. It was just before they moved to Aspen.

"He was so hell-bent on that RV, he felt like that was going to be his salvation," Nancy later said. Trey had always dreamed of getting an RV, taking Nancy, and "just going where the winds took us."

At the time, she thought it a good idea. "I looked at that as giving him the mobility that he didn't have on his feet. That the RV were his wings, basically."

Unfortunately, the vehicle was a lemon that resulted in one problem after another throughout the trip. Plus, driving down California's Highway 1 wasn't any fun for Nancy or Daniel, who had been persuaded to join his parents for "one last family vacation."

"It was too big and too imposing, and it wasn't as enjoyable a ride as that would have been in a car," Nancy said.

Trey and Daniel shared the driving while Nancy lounged in the back, reading. Trey was at the wheel when suddenly she smelled burning brakes. Daniel was yelling at his dad to pull over. But Trey was so set on getting down the mountain that he wouldn't stop—until together, Daniel and Nancy convinced him.

When they went outside, the brakes were on fire. By then Nancy was vomiting inside the RV, and Daniel was sick outside. So Nancy didn't hear Daniel tell his father he was cutting the trip short and flying home.

Daniel never forgot his father's reply: "I might as well kill myself, and you don't know who I might take with me."

Daniel stayed, viewing the comment as a warning of sorts.

***

As he and Cindy talked about the "RV trip from hell," the entire situation with defense attorneys and plea deals and murders felt so surreal that Cindy couldn't help asking: "Daniel, do you think it's possible that he did it?"

"I don't know," Daniel said, still distraught.

Cindy couldn't help herself. She did think it possible. She remembered the late-night call from Nancy, after Garth showed her photos of the murder. Nancy was so disturbed by what she'd seen she had to talk to someone close, someone she loved.

"I can tell you this, whoever did this was angry," Nancy said.

And at that precise moment, a small seed took root in Cindy's mind. She'd seen Trey's temper, so the angry part of the murder—that would fit Trey. She tried to work out different scenarios in her mind: What if this? What if that?

As Nancy rattled on, Cindy pictured herself flipping her mother's mattress, because Tess was too short to do it herself. Cindy knew it wasn't difficult for her, even though she wasn't very strong. That's when it hit her: *This is about height and leverage. Not about strength.*

Cindy began asking Nancy questions: How far was the closet from the bed? You said there was an extension cord involved, that you plugged into the machine to clear off the flat roof? Where did you keep it?

"In the bathroom sink cabinet," Nancy said.

Cindy knew then that whoever killed Pfister was familiar with the house, which left Trey and Nancy. *I know it's not my sister.*

Her next thoughts were equally stark. *Oh, my God, he didn't kill Nancy Pfister so much as he did John Powell and everything else.*

***

Then, suddenly, Cindy had an epiphany: *The white whale won*. Taken from Melville's classic book, *Moby-Dick*, the white whale symbolized unfinished business. Captain Ahab was on a lifetime quest to capture the white whale. If Trey did commit the murder, it wasn't Nancy Pfister he was killing—it was Powell, who was his unfinished business, the one thing he couldn't let go. Pfister was an innocent victim, who merely served as the conduit for all the years of anger Trey had harbored at Powell.

After Nancy hung up, Cindy texted Daniel, "OMG, the white whale won." Daniel replied, but Cindy could tell he didn't understand what she meant. So she never breathed a word to him or his mom about what she believed really happened.

And on June 16, after Daniel told her Trey was confessing, Cindy knew she was right. Trey did kill Pfister. *He isn't pleading guilty to save my sister. He's trying to make himself look like a freakin' hero.*

Deep down, she suspected Daniel believed that, too, even if his belief was yet one step removed from the reality of it all. Cindy also knew it was much easier for Daniel to believe his father was being noble, and saving his mother.

* * *

Being released from jail was the easy part for Nancy. Trying to return to some semblance of a normal life on "the outside" was a far more daunting task. Nancy spent one night hibernating at Patrice's mountain cabin. She tried to remember she didn't have to rise for breakfast at a certain time, or open her mouth and stick out her tongue to show a nurse she really had swallowed her medicine, or hear the loud click of metal against metal whenever a steel door closed behind her. And when she went into Patrice's bathroom, Nancy felt like crying. It was the first time she had used the toilet in complete privacy in months.

Nancy sipped on a Diet Pepsi with ice, telling Patrice and Purl all about her prison life. Nancy read Trey's letter again and again, trying to decipher some hidden message just for her. She had to know if he was trying to tell her he killed Pfister without really saying it.

Nancy refused to believe it. She had thirty-two years full of memories of life with a kind, loving man who would never dream of killing another human. No, Trey couldn't kill someone, especially in such a violent, gruesome way. She was sure of it.

"He fell on his sword," she told Patrice and Purl and anyone else who would listen. "That's how much he loves me. He did this to save me. I know it."

Following her June 17 release, Nancy needed time to regain her bearings. Time was one thing she didn't have, though. Not when she had to find a good defense attorney to take his case, to appeal the sentence and get him out. It was the least she could do, after what he had done for her. Nancy was determined: she would fight the rest of her life if she had to, until Trey was free.

After one night of complete tranquility at Patrice's cabin, Nancy had to pick up the threads of her frayed life—and try to go forward. It would be the most excruciating project she'd ever taken on. The scariest part was, Nancy didn't know if she could even do it.

At sixty-three, she was homeless, penniless, and widowed. That's how she felt—like a widow, who wasn't allowed to grieve for her still-living, convict husband. She was also without a mode of transportation, since the Jaguar, considered evidence in the murder case, was still impounded. Staying with Daniel wasn't an option; considering the continued media interest in the case, they both knew Colorado wasn't a good place for her. That only left Boston.

The decision was made easier when Nancy or anyone in the McDaniel family read the headlines: every time one came up with Pfister's name, or Trey's, hers was right there, too. Except, instead of saying she was free because she really was innocent, the authorities helped cast a cloud of suspicion over her head. Sheriff DiSalvo, ADA Andrea Bryan, and DA investigator Lisa Miller repeatedly told the media they had to let Nancy go, but they weren't happy about it.

The defense team was still angry about the authorities' actions. "The prosecution has absolutely nothing to offer, in terms of inconsistencies or evidence against Nancy Styler," Garth said. "And ultimately, we didn't force them to dismiss Nancy's case. We never forced that issue . . . it's not like we stormed into Sherry Caloia's office and demand[ed] that she dismiss Nancy's case. They did that on their own, because they accepted Trey Styler's confession."

Garth believed the prosecution wanted to have it both ways: "To say, 'Shoot, we arrested the wrong person, and we kept her in jail for three months. So now we've got to let her go, but, wouldn't it be nice to also save face in the community by suggesting that, there's more to the story than that.'"

The DA's office chose to dismiss the case, with prejudice, agreeing that they would never charge Nancy again. By telling the public she was still guilty, Garth explained, they were basically saying, "Well, of our own volition, we released a murderer."

Is that something they would even do?

Garth was skeptical. "I doubt that."

***

The day after Nancy's release, Daniel met his mother at the infamous storage units in Basalt. During the drive, the past twenty-four hours ran through his mind like a looped recording.

His mom had called after her attorneys had delivered the news. "I'm getting out," she said, sobbing. "Your dad told them he did it to save me."

Within seconds, Daniel was crying into his cell phone as he stood next to a Sbarro pizzeria inside Boston Logan airport. By the time he landed in Denver hours later, he had a text from Beth saying his mom was out, and six voice mails from different Denver media outlets begging him for a comment. He didn't return their calls.

Daniel drove four hours up the mountain and when he saw his mom at the storage unit, they hugged for the first time in months, and didn't want to let go.

Beth met them there with the keys, and when they opened the doors, Nancy found a huge mess. During their search for anything that might connect the Stylers to the murder, police had basically ransacked their belongings. If she had had any tears left, she might have cried. Instead, she just tried to find the things she needed most, to move on with her life.

Nancy had to transport some of the contents, including her aesthetician's equipment, back East. Without them, she couldn't support herself. But without a car, she wasn't sure how to even do that. After talking to Cindy, it was agreed: for the time being, Nancy would leave behind what she couldn't fit in a suitcase. Then she would fly back to Boston, and her family would help her figure it all out. Realizing she couldn't even afford to rent a car, much less a place of her own, Nancy knew her only option: she had to move in with her eighty-three-year-old mother.

"Just come home, Nance," Cindy told her over the telephone. "We can't wait to see you."

"You stay strong," Tess told her eldest daughter. "Everything's going to be okay."

Later, Cindy said their "mother was amazing throughout," despite being a mess knowing what Nancy was dealing with. "My mother was a rock star. She might have broken down with me. But with my sister on the phone, she was strong."

In the coming days, it was a trait that Nancy would appreciate having inherited from her mother.

***

Cindy had to lie to Tess, telling her Nancy's flight was due to arrive two days later than it really did. She didn't want her mom to try to make the drive to the airport, a dicey one for the best of drivers—which Tess was not.

When Nancy came through the arrivals gate at Boston Logan International Airport, Cindy turned to her friend, Donna. "How is she even upright?" If she had been in Nancy's shoes, Cindy knew she would have been in a wheelchair or comatose, from the wear and tear of the last year.

As soon as Nancy was close enough, the two sisters hugged. "I prayed on this moment," Cindy said.

"Me, too," Nancy said.

There were no tears, only laugher. The drive to Tess' took a while, and it was 8 p.m. when they arrived. Inside, Nancy held back as Cindy called out for Tess. "Mom, are you there?"

Tess replied. "What is it?"

"I'm out here," Cindy said. "Will you come here?"

When Tess, dressed in her nightgown and robe for the evening, saw Nancy, she stopped. Then both women started sobbing as they held onto each other as only a mother and daughter can.

***

When Cindy's phone rang a week or so later, she, Donna, and Nancy were chatting in her kitchen. It was July 3 and Daniel was calling from Denver. His voice sounded weird, and Cindy could tell he was upset.

"Hi, are you going to be with my mom for the next hour?" Daniel asked.

Cindy told him Nancy was already there. "Why?"

"Tina's going to be calling," Daniel said, "and I just want to make sure somebody's with her."

***

Nancy's cell rang less than an hour later. She looked at it, her eyes opened wide. "It's Tina Fang," she told Cindy and Donna. Nancy took the phone and went into Cindy's backyard. She was walking around in the garden when Cindy, watching through the kitchen window, saw Nancy's hand fly to her mouth.

The sensation in Cindy's gut was there before her mind could even register her thoughts. "At this point, I know what's coming," Cindy later said. "Trey had already confessed. Nancy was released. What more can it be? I read my share of Nancy Drew books."

As Nancy's hand touched her lips, Donna told Cindy, "Get out there."

Cindy quickly crossed the room and was out the door, standing beside Nancy before she knew it. Nancy was sobbing and trying to speak at the same time. "But how? How? When? This doesn't make sense. Are you sure?" she asked Tina.

Cindy tried to hug Nancy, but when she felt, rather than saw, that Nancy's knees were growing weak, the hug became a tight grip as she held Nancy up to keep her from falling. It didn't work. As they got to the doorway, Nancy's legs buckled and she fell to the ground, sobbing like a child.

Cindy had never seen Nancy break down like that for anything or anyone. It was scarier, even, than watching Daniel go through the same anguish a few weeks earlier.

"Seeing her like that," Cindy said, "if anybody had any doubts . . . there's not an actress on this planet that could have pulled that off, that could have feigned [not knowing]."

That day in Cindy's garden, when she learned the real truth from Tina Fang, Nancy was "truly shocked and devastated and brought to her knees. Literally." Cindy said her sister was "just sobbing and sobbing. Like I've never seen her sob in her life."

It took many long and painful minutes before Nancy could talk. When she did, she simply said, "I slept next to that man for three nights and I had no idea that he killed somebody."

***

Cindy drove Nancy home later that day, and throughout the evening, Daniel must have called a dozen times. "How is she?" he asked Cindy. He was so worried about his mom, after the gravity of everything hit her.

"She's good," Cindy said, knowing how worried Daniel was.

Cindy and Tess put an exhausted Nancy to bed. "Promise me you're not going to do anything stupid," Cindy told her sister as they said goodbye.

Nancy promised.

Next, Cindy turned to Tess. "Mom, you keep close tabs on her."

"I will," Tess promised.

And she did. She was like a nurse doing her rounds. Every hour she tiptoed into Nancy's room to check on her daughter, not even sleeping herself.

***

The story of how Tina Fang went to see Trey in prison has become almost a legend in some Colorado circles. What is less known is that her visit was spurred by a phone call from Daniel. "Did my dad really kill her?" he asked Tina.

She reminded him that she didn't have his father's permission to discuss it.

"Then tell him, 'If he won't let you tell us what went on, I know what went on,'" Daniel said.

He never learned whether Tina told his father that, but he does know that once there, she sat across from her client and told Trey he was being cruel by not coming clean with his wife and son. By not allowing them to know the truth and by not permitting her to tell them, Tina said Nancy and Daniel would spend the rest of their lives fighting for his freedom.

Trey gave Tina his consent to tell them the truth herself. But he said he couldn't bear to tell them, for fear of how they would view him. Trey knew he'd never see or talk to Nancy or Daniel again, once they learned he really did murder Nancy Pfister.

CHAPTER THIRTY-NINE

HOARDING BY PROXY

A lthough Nancy was free and starting to rebuild her life in Boston, one major problem remained: nearly every possession she'd accumulated in her many years was scattered in storage units throughout Colorado.

Nancy and Trey were always better at accumulating possessions than getting rid of them. Nancy loved to shop, so their 6,000-square-foot house in Greenwood Village had been packed to the gills. Trey's love of tools and technology, and a garage jam-packed with materials for their failed printing business, added that much more for them to store. And after moving four times in three years, each time to a smaller home, most of their material belongings were in storage.

Even after losing two storage units in Castle Rock (for nonpayment shortly after their arrest), the costs were daunting. This was due, in part, to the snow that led to one moving van becoming stuck in Pfister's driveway. That meant the other vans never made it to Pitkin County. So much of the furniture, printers, TVs, clothing, tools, and family heirlooms ended up being locked away in fifteen five-by-eight-foot storage containers with a no-name moving and storage company in Denver.

Then there were the belongings she and Trey packed up when they moved from Pfister's home on February 24. After being released from jail, Nancy realized that everything she needed for everyday life, as well as a full spa and sewing studio, was sitting in two of the largest storage units in Basalt, much of it disheveled or destroyed from many police searches. No one knew where anything was, even precious mementos like scrapbooks and baby pictures. When combined, the storage costs came to nearly $2,500 per month.

Although Daniel had managed to locate most of the storage for his parents in the weeks after their arrest, paying rent on them proved to be a formidable challenge. He raised funds from family and friends, sold what he could, and maxed out his own credit cards to pay the bills. He joked with his aunt Cindy, in times of levity, that his biggest job while Nancy and Trey were in jail was to be a "hoarder by proxy."

The costs didn't stop with Nancy's release and her departure to Boston, though. Also, she needed some semblance of her life back, even if it was nothing more than a few pairs of high heels, a box of family pictures, and a sewing machine.

Then, of course, there was everything seized by Pitkin County authorities, including Nancy's vehicle. They had kindly returned her ID upon release, and Daniel had bought her a new phone the next day. However, she had no car, no wallet, no purse, and, worst of all, no computer, which held all her financial and personal files.

Nancy and Cindy arrived in Colorado in mid-July to get the storage situation sorted out and retrieve everything taken into evidence, including the Jaguar. They drove four hours up to Basalt in a rented car to load what they could into a moving truck. After two tearful days sorting through her life in a sweltering storage unit, Nancy returned the keys to the empty units that she later learned Trey had rented with bloody hands.

Unfortunately, Pitkin County wasn't quite ready to release the evidence they had taken. This felt like another slap in Nancy's face, and in addition, it meant another four-hour drive back to Aspen. So she and Cindy returned to Denver, the car fully loaded down.

The ride back was somewhat cathartic for Nancy. She took pictures of the Eagle jail to show her mom, and she met Emily, her former cellie. They arranged to meet at a rest area along the highway. Nancy met Emily's dog, and they took selfies. She learned how well Emily was doing and felt so happy because this time, Emily really was on the right path.

***

Back in Denver, Cindy, Daniel, and Nancy went through the opened wooden storage containers at the storage warehouse, sorting the important and the "nice-to-have" from the trash. Each time they opened another box, new memories flooded back. Family photos from Disneyland, when Daniel was only nine or ten, or a ragged fake fur coat that had been passed down in the family as a gag gift.

It was physically and emotionally exhausting for everyone, especially Nancy. Knowing that Trey would likely never be a free man again, she knew she had to let go of his clothing—and everything else that belonged to the man she'd loved for so long. Letting go of his physical presence was yet another painful reminder of the lost soul who sat incarcerated just a few minutes away in prison.

With Trey's guilt hanging upon them like a leaden mantle, every crutch, every pair of glasses, every watch, and most of all, every hammer left in a toolbox, reminded them of the loss of the man they had loved, and then, of the man he'd become.

As if that weren't enough to weigh her down, Nancy soon realized that despite paying nearly $5,000 since their November 2013 move to Aspen, to keep their possessions safe, it hadn't worked. Many of the most expensive items, like TVs or printers, were in storage boxes that the moving company claimed it couldn't find, or had no record of. Jewelry and designer clothing was missing too, but since the company's workers had unloaded the trucks for Nancy and Trey, who were already in Aspen, there was no reliable manifest to check.

***

On Friday, two days before Cindy and Nancy were due to fly back to Boston, the clock was ticking. Nancy needed her things back from Pitkin. She and Cindy originally planned to drive a rental car up to Aspen that morning, to haul away what remained. They would also get the Jag the police had towed away back in February. The sheriff, however, was dragging his feet.

When Beth called Nancy at noon, she said the sheriff's office was finally going to release things, "but they close at five. Have somebody get up here ASAP, because I can't fit everything in my car and they can't release it all to me."

Nancy knew she needed to stay in Denver and finish sorting her stored belongings, so she sent Daniel and Cindy to get everything that was left in Pitkin County, before the office closed for the weekend.

Daniel was *not* amused. "Oh, for fuck's sake," he said, sighing in frustration. "Of all places on earth, you want me to go *there*!?"

The last few months had been hell for him. Between the trauma, the media harassment, his assistance to the legal team, his attempts to manage financial affairs he knew nothing about, and the social horror of his parents' public arrest and prosecution via the evening news, Daniel was already worn down and nearly broken. After the soul-crushing shame of his father's deception and eventual tearful confession, Daniel just wanted to lock himself away, someplace where no one would bother him and where no one knew his family's shame.

Yet, there he was, Cindy in the passenger seat, racing toward the very last place he wanted to be: the Pitkin County Courthouse, in Aspen.

It was a tense ride. He and Cindy had always been close, even more so as his parents' lives fell apart. She was one of the few people who saw their fragile emotional state and was as scared as he was. Daniel vented some of the anger he hadn't been able to for months. He vented about the media. The arrest. The hundred days of fighting his parents' financial battles, of enabling their ridiculous storage needs. He vented about his mother, who was too busy processing her own pain to notice his, and who had the gall to send him up the mountain to Aspen.

"My parents are the reason I don't want to have kids," Daniel joked. "I already have them."

But he vented most sharply about his father, and the ten years of crazy deeds he had wrought on their family, culminating in a horrifying murder and forever tainting the Styler name. Daniel ranted about the prosecution's ridiculous claim that his father could never have killed Pfister by himself. Daniel had no such doubts. He knew that his father could and did carry out the act alone, that he was more than capable.

Daniel told Cindy how he'd seen his father throwing luggage into the RV the summer before the murder, and moving boxes just months before. "He just paid for it later," Daniel said, thinking of those times, and how Trey would then have no energy left for a day or two.

"That singular truth is key to understanding how [Trey] could seem so weak and still," Daniel told Cindy, "without any doubt, flip a mattress."

Cindy listened with a reassuring ear, commiserating where she could and using humor to ease Daniel out of that dark place. "I know, Danny. We can set up a kiosk in Aspen and sell 'Justice for Nancy' T-shirts," she said.

It would give Nancy some seed money to start her new life, and Cindy figured the locals would assume the shirts meant Nancy Pfister—and gobble them up—when really, she meant justice for her sister, Nancy McDaniel Styler.

"Really, Cin?" Daniel asked dryly.

Gradually, as they reached the Roaring Fork Valley and turned toward Aspen, his anger gave way to fear and sadness. Despite growing up in Colorado, and his parents' brief residency there, Daniel had never been to Aspen. After the murder, he decided he never would. For him, the entire drama had played out remotely, by phone, by email, and by reading newspapers.

Aspen was a faraway land where terrible things happened. It was the "belly of the beast" as Melville wrote, and he didn't want any part of it—not the jail, not the courthouse, and least of all the road to the crime scene—to become real. Moreover, if he felt ashamed walking around in Denver, where only the occasional store clerk recognized the "Styler" name from the TV news and started asking questions, Daniel couldn't imagine walking around a tiny town where everybody would know nothing of him—except his father's horrible act. He held Cindy's hand, for strength, as they pulled into the Pitkin County Courthouse parking lot.

Beth was waiting for them when they arrived. They were ushered into the courthouse and escorted into a conference room full of more boxes. These, though, were covered in evidence tape and paper. Cindy and Daniel went through what they could, leaving behind the cleaning supplies and trash bags collected as evidence, and saving the computers, hard drives, and personal effects.

At one point, someone dropped a box. Out fell a copy of *Fifty Shades of Grey*. "What a shitty book," Daniel said. "Well, *now* I'm ashamed."

Cindy agreed. "Of all the things my sister was accused of, having this book is definitely the worst."

Even the deputy cracked a smile.

They took what they could to a trash bin across from the Pitkin County Jail, where Daniel's parents had recently resided. The young woman who was helping them stopped Daniel. "Not that it's any of my business, but do you still talk to them? I can't even imagine."

He looked at her, worn out. "My mom didn't do anything. Not so much him."

* * *

They walked back into the building, through the same door in the same brick hallway where the reporters had waited to get fresh pictures of the "murderers," and Cindy paused as Daniel wrestled a handcart around the corner. "Wait, Danny, stay there." He looked to the side, at the wrought-iron seal built into the wall, featured in so many pictures, then looked over at Cindy, holding her camera phone. "Smile!" And somehow, he did. His aunt did always do her best to make the most of a bad situation.

After Daniel's car was loaded up with their personal effects and computers, they followed Beth to a public works lot, where the Jaguar was waiting among snowplow blades and piles of sand. The small, blue car was covered in dirt, salt, mud, and what seemed like miles of EVIDENCE seal tape. Daniel looked over at Cindy. "You know there's no way in hell I'm driving that car like that, right?" She grabbed his hand and squeezed. "Well, I am. We didn't do anything wrong. I'll hold my head up high."

Cindy and Daniel cut open the seal on a door, and miraculously, after most of a winter and spring, the car started, but just barely. Since the car had been torn apart during searches and then neglected for months, every warning light lit up, and the three-and-a-half-hour drive home was full of unexplained noises and warnings, as well as a gas station stop to refill the "Evidence Mobile." Eventually, almost four hours later in the summer traffic, they arrived back at the hotel.

Outside, as they unloaded the boxes of evidence-taped computer and photography gear from the luggage cart, Daniel stopped his mom and aunt. Concerned about what other hotel guests would think of their crime scene cart, Daniel and Cindy agreed: "if anyone asks, we're in town for a forensic science convention."

Cindy, Nancy, and Daniel knew they had accomplished what they needed to. The storage was consolidated and almost ready to load into a truck the next day and head to Boston. Daniel would sort out the computers, transfer his mom's files onto a working machine, and consolidate his own. They had a car, her iPad, and, thanks to Beth, they finally had all of Nancy's personal effects that police confiscated.

That left only one thing to do. At midnight, Cindy and Nancy drove the Jaguar to a car wash in a quiet Denver suburb. There, the two sisters talked about the last year of Nancy's life. Cindy reminded Nancy of the August 2013 wedding she and Trey returned to Boston for, and the heartbreaking talk Cindy had with Nancy that weekend. That's when she told Nancy she was "worried about Trey unraveling and you being consumed by this."

Nancy told Cindy she was exhausted from years of taking care of Trey. Cindy said she wondered "how on earth Trey could go out and kill someone and come back and Nancy not notice?" She said the "old" Nancy would never have missed that.

"If my sister was at the top of her game," Cindy later said, "there was no way she wouldn't have noticed that her husband had killed someone."

After they finished talking, they blasted off the evidence stickers. As she swept the power-wash gun against the tape lining the car hood, Cindy chuckled and looked over at her exhausted sister. Nancy's makeup was patchy from a day full of crying.

"Oh, Nancy, you bring me on the best vacations."

CHAPTER FORTY

THE SADDEST DAY

Even though Nancy returned to Colorado at the end of July, she hadn't spoken to Trey since her release. She tried to visit, but both times jail officials turned her away. Her driver's license didn't have her correct address, plus she still showed up as a felon in the prison's computer system. In addition, it took a while for her new cell phone number to be added to his phone list of approved callers.

So Nancy was back in Boston before she talked to Trey for the first time since her June 17 release.

"Did you do it?" she asked.

"No," Trey said, "I didn't."

Nancy knew they were on a recorded line and thought perhaps Trey didn't want to admit to it because of that. But even so, she still had believed him right up until July 3, when Tina called and told her the truth.

***

Having to hear her husband confess to being a murderer over the telephone would have been bad enough. But hearing that truth in person from the man she loved and thought she knew was far more painful. That happened on August 15. Nancy waited patiently in the same room where all family members who visit do, seated at a little table. The first thing she noticed—other than the wheelchair—was how old he looked.

Nancy hugged Trey before she could stop herself, and the hug felt like a millisecond. But to prison officials, it was too long, so the guard reminded them nothing longer than a short hug was allowed. They held hands across the table as they talked, and Nancy kept thinking that part of Trey was still there. Another part of him was gone.

He said all the things she thought he would: "I love you, I miss you, it's so good to see you, it's so good to hold you." But when he asked how her life was going, he was surprised at how difficult things had become for her. He didn't know about all the people who still didn't believe Nancy was innocent; he found it strange that she had trouble getting car insurance or passing background checks. It was as if he had never considered what life would be like for her, once she was released from jail.

Trey also thought, like many people do, that appearing on national TV shows like *Dateline* and *20/20* would have helped her financially. He was shocked to learn they didn't pay for interviews.

"No, I'm pretty much broke," Nancy told him.

Nor did Trey understand why no one would give Nancy a job.

"Because until the court seals my record, I'm still a felon, so when they do a background check, no one wants to hire me," she said.

Seated across from Trey, Nancy knew that she still loved him—no matter what. But it felt so surreal to see him sitting there in an olive green jail uniform. She also noticed that he had lost a lot of weight, and his hair was growing long.

"He was like a shadow of himself, almost," Nancy later said. "I could see glimpses of him in there, but I didn't really know the man that was in front of me."

When they finally crossed the invisible boundary between them, and discussed the murder, Nancy felt sick all over again, just like on July 3, when Tina Fang's phone call shattered her world. Nancy needed to hear the words from Trey's own lips, but it was all she could do to listen as he explained how had he killed Pfister, hidden her body, and then snatched up some of her personal items, including her pearls. Nancy couldn't even imagine it, much less visualize Trey committing the act. Nor did she want to. The one phrase that stood out to Nancy, after she left the jail that day, was Trey's claim that it wasn't really him.

"The man who did that is not me," Trey said. "Someone else took over my body."

Nancy realized he was right, in a way. "Obviously, he's not all there. And it's hard for me to get too angry with a sick person."

Many other people, including her own family, "have all this anger and want to slap him," Nancy said. But not her. "I'm not feeling anger. I'm feeling more sadness. Just sadness for what could have been. I thought, 'Boy, what a waste of so many lives.'"

***

Nancy once told Trey that she would rather "live with you in a cabin by a creek without any money" than live without him. She told him that after he warned her of his suicide plan.

In the year and a half since they were first arrested and taken to jail, Nancy found out how it really felt to live without Trey. At first she was heartbroken and sad. But anger wasn't an emotion she encountered. The shame and numbness and shock had to wear off for that feeling to break through.

But first, she would suffer several more indignities before that happened: feeling like she had no choice but to file for divorce, so her name wouldn't forever be attached to a murderer; filing for bankruptcy; and finding out that while she and Trey were in jail, she had become a victim of tax fraud when someone stole her identity, filed her tax return, and took what little bit of a refund she hoped to receive.

Nancy has rented a space and opened up her own "spa" of sorts, a little place where she does waxing, facials, and eyebrow extensions, every Monday through Saturday. It certainly isn't enough to pay rent, so she still lives with her mom, but it's a modest start. An honest day's work, for a woman whose name was once known by scientists and researchers around the world—both for her love affair with the Victoria lily and for her groundbreaking work in the field of malignant hyperthermia.

On June 19, a year after she was released, Nancy spoke to Trey for the first time in a long time; she hasn't had money to put on his prison account so he can call her collect. "This is the saddest day of my life," Trey said.

"Why?" Nancy asked.

"I had to sign the divorce papers today," he replied.

When they hung up, Nancy began thinking about the last few years of her life. That's when she began feeling it. The anger that had been buried under a mountain of compassion, empathy, and understanding for a man who was slowly going crazy finally reared its head.

"My life is in shambles because of him," Nancy said. "I'm pissed off right now." She said she's just begun to realize how sick he was, and how well he hid it from her.

Nancy couldn't see it at the time, but now when she looks back, she sees that Trey was still highly intelligent, but his mental capacity was already diminished by the time he got involved with the corrupt attorney who stole their money. "Or he never would have let John Powell do that to us," Nancy said. "Brilliance is an asset and also a liability."

When it comes to their future—hers and Trey's—Nancy is blunt. "There is none," she says.

CHAPTER FORTY-ONE

SNAPPED

On April 9, 2015, during an eight-hour prison interview, Dr. William "Trey" Styler revealed for the first time to investigative reporter Daleen Berry exactly what happened that led him to kill Nancy Merle Pfister. It was the only interview request he honored, and he only did so to help clear his wife's name. Trey revealed many details during that interview, including how he went from being a mild-mannered doctor to a murderer.

Anesthesiologists walk a fine line between life and death all the time. Their goal, Trey said, "is to keep you alive, while you are in a deathlike state." His specialty was working with people who had bad experiences while under anesthesia.

"There's a certain very small percentage of people who claim at least to have awakened during surgery, from inadequate levels of anesthetics," Trey said. "People don't die [from] anesthesia in surgery except in extreme cases."

If people who have had problems with anesthesia need more surgery, Trey said they often become full of fear. He saw this firsthand during his medical residency at the University of Colorado, when he was assigned to the upcoming surgery of a recovery room nurse who wanted to have children but couldn't.

"She was utterly panic stricken," he said. "It's a little-known fact, but if you're seeing a patient before surgery, and the patient says to you, 'I think I'm going to die during this operation,' they might."

That panic and fear induces physiological changes that can actually scare them to death. That's what happened to the young nurse Trey was in charge of. "This woman was scared to death," he said.

So he spent three hours with her the night before surgery, telling her exactly how he would ensure she didn't have another bad experience. "I will be there with you. I will listen to every beat of your heart. I will listen to every breath you take. I will be watching you so closely that it cannot happen when you're under my care," Trey said. "I will not allow it."

The woman came through the operation "just fine. No problems whatsoever." She later had to have three more surgeries, and Trey said "she wouldn't let anybody else take care of her. She would only trust me."

That young recovery room nurse was one of many such terrified patients. He kept them alive and safe. "I would not let anybody hurt them," Trey said. "I would not let those kinds of things happen. And I was able to convince them that they were safe with me. They trusted me. It meant a lot."

By then, Trey was tearing up as he spoke of the patients he loved, and the lifesaving work he did. "I haven't cried this much in months," he said.

After finishing his residency training, the University of Colorado hired Trey as a faculty member, where he was in charge of cardiovascular anesthesia. There, two-thirds of their cardiac anesthesia patients were newborns.

"Babies this big," Trey said, holding his hands about eight inches apart. They had congenital heart disease and the medical team "knew damn well that if we didn't do anything, they would be dead in twenty-four hours or less."

These were very sick babies, who were "weak at the outset. And so we had to try." But Trey said it became commonplace for many of the babies to die. "There were a lot of things that we could not fix. And I personally pronounced over 100 babies dead."

Trey's job was to join the surgeon and deliver the sad news to the waiting parents. But first, he would take the babies, who were still on the heart machine, and dress them up in operating gowns, hats, boots, masks, then bring them in to the operating room to say goodbye. The parents came in to say goodbye, and then Trey took the babies out again.

"We would cover them up—all that was visible was their head— we would kiss them and tell them goodbye," Dr. Styler said, sobbing like a baby himself as he related his experiences.

Those were the babies whose hearts were too weak to be taken off the heart machine, because their tiny, broken hearts would not work. And Trey was the doctor who, once a baby was dead, had to "make the official legal declaration that, okay, as of this moment, this patient is dead."

He did it for two years—until he could do it no more.

Dr. Styler was so traumatized by the experiences of those two years that "it was years before I would do any kind of cardiac anesthesia. On adults, even."

Since then, Trey has had to declare a lot of people dead. "I declared more babies dead in those first two years than all the other people I've declared over the thirty years that followed," he said.

The man who tried to save babies never intended to kill Pfister— he simply snapped.

When Trey went to Pfister's house Monday morning on February 24, he was still the same gentle physician who had taken a vow "to first do no harm," the same man Nancy fell in love with. He was still the same conscientious doctor who voluntarily quit his anesthesiology practice when his neurological illness negatively impacted his memory, leading Trey to fear he might endanger his own patients. He simply went there before Pfister began drinking at noon, as was her habit, in the hopes of having a reasonable conversation. He wanted to work out a resolution to everyone's satisfaction. Trey needed to do that so she would release the $150,000 worth of equipment she was holding, in return for the $13,000 in damages she claimed he and Nancy did to her house.

"I intended to challenge her and to demand that she retract her demands for more money," Trey said, "and allow us to take our equipment and try and make a living some other way."

If she didn't, and persisted in holding hostage their equipment, he and Nancy would be destitute. Without it, they couldn't make a living. And if that happened, he would have failed Nancy—his Nancy. Failing as a husband was not something Trey could do; his father had instilled in him that taking care of one's family was a man's first and foremost responsibility. But that day, Trey felt like a failure.

And he almost left Pfister's house that morning, after calling her name and getting no answer. Instead, something caused him go up the stairs and into her bedroom, calling her name out as he went. That's when he realized Pfister was there, but she wouldn't respond. He didn't know she was asleep, her earplugs in and eye mask on. Trey said he thinks it was seeing the legal papers, the insurance and registration from the Jaguar, lying on Pfister's nightstand, that enraged him. That caused him to snap. By then, the good doctor was nowhere in sight.

"In retrospect, I realize she probably was. I think there was a part of me that was thinking that she was playing asleep," Trey said. "That she was just not responding. I think that's what I was still thinking when I did snap . . . she was there, she was sleeping peacefully while my life was going down the tubes, and the next thing, I mean, in a real sense, the next thing I knew, it had been done."

That is the last thing Trey Styler remembers. His next lucid thought occurred after he looked down and saw her lying there. "The next thing I remember with any clarity is trying to figure out, 'Now what? She's dead, now what do I do?'"

On some level, he knew what he had done—after all, the hammer was still in his hand. But Trey couldn't even recall where he got it. "All I know is there she was, and there I was."

Since then, he's had second thoughts, of course: what he would "have done differently that day, starting with not going there at all, proceeding through not killing her. If instead of trying to cover it up, I just walked away and then came back on Tuesday and said, 'Oh, my goodness, look here, I guess we need to call the police!'"

If he had done any of those things, "I might be with Nancy now," Trey said.

Of course, he didn't. It was too late for that.

"I did not intend to kill her. The thought never went through my conscious mind," Trey said. "The first thought I can remember having is, 'I did kill her.' Past tense."

***

When Trey realized that he had struck Pfister on the top of her head, near the crown, and she wasn't responsive, his physician's training made him believe that she went from "sleep straight to unconscious-ness." The very next thought was that it was probably fatal, because the force of the blow would have done enough damage inside Pfister's skull that it was "not a survivable injury unless she had immediate attention, and probably not even that."

However, since he did not strike the base of Pfister's skull, where the brain stem is, he knew "she would probably continue to have a heartbeat and blood pressure for some minutes." That meant Pfister could have had some sense of awareness that she was dying.

What Trey did next does not seem to be the act of a hardened murderer.

"I've done the deed," he said, "let's make sure that she is at least spared any awareness of, the psychological agony of being aware that—that she was dying."

Trey then struck Pfister again, twice, so she wouldn't suffer, hit-ting her once in each frontal lobe, where consciousness occurs. "And so, I wanted to make sure that, that whatever time it took before—before she died—that she would not awaken."

But just after saying that, the man whose mental illness caused him to take Pfister's life in the first place added a chilling statement. "I'd like to say it was because I knew that she was beyond saving," Trey said. "I'm afraid that there was part of me that wouldn't have wanted to." It almost sounds like Trey is saying he didn't want Pfister to live, that he wanted her to die—until his next sentence. That is, that once he realized he had struck her the first time, he didn't think there would be enough of her left to save. In other words, had he not struck Pfister again in the frontal lobes, there was a remote chance she could have survived, living the rest of her life hooked up to machines.

"Suffering has always struck me as being worse than death," Trey said.

***

Next, he rolled Pfister's body onto a sheet that he placed on the floor. "And I rolled her off of the bed onto the floor, and then dragged the sheet, on my knees." Still on his knees, Trey said he would pull it a little bit at a time. Then, still on his knees, he would back up, then pull again. "I mean it was only about ten feet."

He was able to do it that way, he said, because he still had enough upper body strength, even though his "lower body was shot."

Trey wanted to contain the bleeding, so he wrapped her head in towels, "grabbed some big trash bags, put one over her head (and) was going to put the other one on her feet" when he realized that wouldn't work. "So, I used the extension cord to kind of . . . it was just a handy way to fold her up." He wrapped her up in sheets and then put her in the closet. Locked the door, and took the key.

He thought he would return later and move the body, but he couldn't think beyond that. During the forty-five minutes or so Trey was there, he flipped the mattress over to hide the bloodstains. He said it was not difficult at all.

In an attempt to make it look like she had run off somewhere, Trey said he grabbed a few items he knew Pfister would take with her, like "her phone. A string of pearls that she wore all of the time." He stuffed everything into a trash bag and left the house. He said he didn't get a drop of blood on him.

But Trey then made the mistake that would lead to his downfall: he put the bag into the trunk of the Jaguar and forgot about it. He drove back to the Aspenalt, where he found Nancy awake and wondering what had taken him so long. Trey told her getting the storage units had been a hassle, and she didn't think twice about it.

It wasn't until two days later, when Nancy told him about Susan Waskow's phone call, saying police and emergency vehicles were seen heading toward West Buttermilk Road, that Trey remembered—the bag with Pfister's things was in the trunk. He suspected the police had found Pfister's body, which was what triggered his memory. So when he and Nancy returned from Glenwood Springs, after taking back the U-Haul, he parked the Jag while she went across the street to tell Merlin Broughton they were too tired to join him at Heather's. Trey grabbed the bag from the trunk and quickly dumped it into a Basalt trash can.

* * *

Trey didn't want to suffer, either. He knew if he confessed, he would lose Nancy, and he didn't think society would be in any danger if he were free, instead of behind bars. But mostly, he didn't want to suffer by losing his Nancy. She was the woman who, on April 9, 1980, he had decided to marry.

During the interview, when Trey realized it was April 9, he began crying. "So I told my mother that night that I was going to marry Nancy. And I did. She gave me all the best years of my life."

In fact, until the John Powell situation, they had never really argued. Nancy was the reason Trey had such a good life. "Because she's one of the wonderful people of the world," he said. "She's beautiful and sexy. She's brilliant. I mean, she's smart as a whip . . . She's—she's so nice she doesn't even dislike her ex-husband."

Nancy was the reason Trey went to see Pfister in the first place, because she—like him—had grown so depressed, she was also talking about suicide. Trey just wanted to save Nancy. He thought by trying to talk sense into Pfister, he could do that.

"God, I wish it'd never happened. I do," Trey said, sobbing some more.

***

Trey had that same wish when Tina Fang came to see him after he and Nancy were arrested. By then, they had been in jail for three months. She told Trey the prosecution had a jailhouse "snitch" who planned to testify against them. The snitch, Cody Chiarelli, would tell the court that Trey told him Nancy was involved in Pfister's murder. Trey told Tina he had never said any such thing to anyone— because it wasn't true.

There was another problem, Tina said. The DA had Pfister's cell phone and it was possible the GPS had saved locations on it. If they could link that to either Trey or Nancy, it would make the defense's job even harder. In fact, Chiarelli's testimony alone was enough to get Nancy's bond denied at the upcoming preliminary hearing. That meant she would be sitting in jail for another six months, Fang said, if not longer.

Hearing that—even though Trey insisted Chiarelli was a liar whom he had not given the time of day to—he knew it didn't look good. "They were going to prosecute us as though Nancy was my coconspirator and accomplice and accessory," Trey said.

If they did that, and if the jury found Trey guilty, Fang believed the jury would undoubtedly convict Nancy, too.

But if Trey pled guilty and told the prosecution what he knew, ADA Bryan had told Fang, then they would let Nancy go. He didn't have to think about the offer for long, and twelve hours later he gave Fang his answer. "I'll do it," Trey said, believing he had no other choice.

"I knew that Nancy had nothing to do with it. I knew that she was totally and completely innocent," Trey said. "I also knew that if I had told her anything about it, she would not be able to keep the secret."

It wasn't just her propensity to talk that led him to that belief. It was Nancy's character. "My wife is so honest, she's a terrible liar, and if she knew what I had done, she would not have been able to conceal it," Trey said. "She might not even have wanted to conceal it, I'm not sure."

CHAPTER FORTY-TWO

THE EVIDENCE FINALLY VINDICATES NANCY

Throughout the past eighteen months, Nancy Styler has been called a murderer and an accomplice to murder. Her attorneys said she was arrested simply for her marriage to the man whom police believed did murder Nancy Merle Pfister. But since police also believed Trey was physically incapable of moving Pfister's body from her bed to the closet, they mistakenly believed that Nancy Styler had helped her husband commit the murder.

Or, at the very least, knew about it.

In fact, Sheriff Joe DiSalvo said as much in the July 22, 2014, edition of the *Aspen Times*, one month after Nancy's release. "I do believe she knew after the fact." The basis for his opinion? "When you're sitting in a 200-square-foot hotel room and you've had everything removed, I find it hard to believe, I find it impossible, that [Nancy Styler] didn't know," he was quoted as saying.

Even the defense had mistaken beliefs. "We believed Kathy set up the Stylers, because that is more believable than what actually did happen," Beth Krulewitch said.

There were other problems with the defense. The one tangible item it lacked, based on how the police interviews occurred, was someone else with a motive to kill Pfister. That's because police didn't ask Suzanne Pfister Kelso about the February 28 land sales, or the granting of her the right-of-way that same day, the one that her sister Nancy

Pfister had repeatedly refused to grant. The one that would increase Kelso's property value.

In fact, during their interview with her, police asked Kelso very little. They didn't even ask her why Pfister told numerous people that if anything ever happened to her, police should start their investigation at Suzanne's door.

Nor did police ask Andrew Hecht, the trust attorney Pfister hated, about the February 28 land sales. Private investigator Pete Fowler, who worked with Nancy's defense team, found details about changes leading up to the sales—but not the sales themselves—when a city clerk called police to report that a real estate transfer tax exemption would transfer ownership of 511 Lazy Chair Ranch Road "from the Estate of Arthur O. Pfister to the Estate of Elizabeth Pfister." Fowler's notes say the city employee found the timing "extremely coincidental."

Apparently neither the defense nor the prosecution followed up on this—or they would have found what Berry did in April 2015. David Olmsted referenced the two land sales, and a quick trip to the county clerk's office produced three deeds involving the two sales. The first deed was for the sale of 511 Lazy Chair Ranch Road. Hecht sold the property to Lazy Chair Lot 2 LLC for $2.5 million.

The second deed sold a property listed only as "TBD Lazy Chair Ranch Road." It was sold to Lazy Chair Lot 3 LLC for $2 million. Of that amount, ten-percent went to Elizabeth Pfister's estate; another thirty-one-percent went to trust funds for Betty Pfister's grandchildren, Juliana Pfister, Daniel Patrick Kelso, Arthur James Douglas Kelso, Chasen Arthur Smith, and Tyler Reed Smith. But the majority of that $2 million, forty-three percent, went to "The 1990 Sep Trust." Hecht handled the sales for the Pfister family, and signed for everyone except Juliana. Her godfather, George Stranahan, signed for her.

As trustee, Hecht is authorized to do this. And a clerk in the Pitkin County Assessor's Office said Hecht has "always looked after Betty and everybody (in the Pfister family)."

What is more interesting, however, is this: these two pieces of Aspen land, which is valued at the highest in the country, sold for less than they were worth. When Berry called the assessor's office, the clerk told her that the sales were considered unfair because the seller had received the parcels for less than anyone else would have.

"Somebody got an exceptionally good deal that you and me would not have gotten," she said.

That somebody is Mark Friedland, manager of the two Lazy Chair LLC's that attorney Millard Zimet formed on February 14, 2014. Friedland, an entrepreneur and real estate mogul who buys and "flips" houses throughout the Aspen area, and whose company, Aspen Starwood, is listed as the grantee (buyer) of the two Pfister properties, got the land for a greatly reduced price.

In 2014, the first property was appraised at $3.615 million; the second, for $2.925 million. Which means that Friedland got them for $2 million less than their appraised value. Some people say that if Pfister was still alive, the land would have been sold for closer to the appraised value. Or that the sales would never would have happened.

Defense attorney Garth McCarty isn't one of them. What he does say, though, is that it makes for compelling "reasonable doubt." And something the defense would have used, had Nancy Styler gone to trial.

The sad part—no matter which camp held them—is that the majority of the "mistaken beliefs" came about largely because of an inept police investigation that smacked of tunnel vision from the time DiSalvo learned Pfister, a personal friend, was dead.

After living more than one year with the title of "murderer" hanging over her head, Nancy is angry.

She is also tired. "I want vindication. I want my reputation back," Nancy said. "This is insane that someone, because of a theory that they have and they continue to stick to, has damned an innocent person to a life where people are going to wonder, all of my life."

All she really wants is an apology. It's possible that Nancy might receive one, too, for buried within the thousands and thousands of pages of evidence is the proof that conclusively exonerates her. It's the May 15, 2014, cell phone analysis report conducted by Michael McGruder and sent to Krulewitch, Nancy's other defense attorney, on May 16. Either the prosecution never saw it or the defense missed it—or by then the wheels were rolling for Trey's pending plea deal, so no one bothered to look too closely at its contents.

Either way, it's highly likely the prosecution also had access to the same conclusive proof in Nancy's favor, since they had forensic experts analyze all three of the Stylers' cell phones. If so, the prosecution may be guilty of withholding exculpatory evidence from the defense—and of knowingly keeping an innocent woman behind bars.

McGruder's report reveals that Trey and Nancy were telling the truth the whole time. It shows four brief calls coming from the Basalt area during the time Trey killed Pfister. Those calls verify that Nancy was, indeed, inside Room 122 at the Aspenalt Lodge—and not with her husband as he carried out the murder.

In fact, Nancy didn't even know where Trey was, since she was asleep when he left. And because Trey took her personal cell phone with him, so it wouldn't wake her, Nancy couldn't find it. She had to dig the business phone out of her purse. She used that phone to try to locate her cell, thinking it was somewhere in the room. Nancy also tried calling her cell from the hotel landline.

Private investigator Pete Fowler first discovered that calls were being made from Basalt, as shown in the defense's timeline of events he created. But it appears the defense team did not realize Nancy was in Room 122 making those calls. The defense attorneys didn't have a time of death until Trey confessed, so Nancy's attorneys said they didn't know she had an alibi.

That wasn't discovered until May 18, 2015, when Nancy and Berry reviewed McGruder's report. "I was checking to see where Trey was. Because he wasn't back yet. At 10:58 a.m. I made a call from the business phone to my cell," Nancy said. "No answer. At 11:26 I called Trey's phone from the business phone. No answer."

One minute later, Nancy tried again. "At 11:27 a.m. I called my phone again. No answer. At 11:29 I called Merlin, but I don't remember talking to him so he probably didn't answer."

The beauty of McGruder's report is that with it, Nancy was able to retrieve memories she'd completely forgotten, due in part to being strip-searched and wrongly arrested, all of which she believes left her with post-traumatic stress disorder. McGruder's analysis provides information from the cell phone towers used by each phone, showing that during Monday morning on February 24, Trey and Nancy's personal cell phones were in the Snowmass area, close to Aspen and where Pfister's house is located, during the time Trey murdered Pfister.

But Nancy's business phone shows up in Basalt for each of the calls she placed Monday morning, giving her a rock solid alibi during the time Pfister's murder occurred.

***

If tunnel vision had not seriously impaired the law enforcement officers who worked this case, they would have waited for the results of the Stylers' phone analysis before rushing to the conclusion that the married couple killed Pfister. Then they would have seen that Nancy was telling the truth, and her arrest would never have happened.

Equally important, if law enforcement had been proactive, Pfister's murder could have been prevented. In fact, Pitkin County police missed three chances to intercept and perhaps help the man who was so despondent that Ed Aro, opposing counsel in Trey's lawsuit against his previous employer, said Trey wanted to commit "suicide by cop." Instead, when the sheriff's office received a call at 9:40 a.m. on Friday, February 21, 2014, alerting them to a suicidal man, sheriff's deputies went to the wrong house. Had they realized their mistake, it is entirely likely Pfister would still be alive today.

When Kelsey Koenig called the authorities Friday morning, she asked them to do a "welfare check" on a man who had threatened suicide at least twice in the last day or so. Koenig, a mental health care worker, was making the call on behalf of someone who wanted to remain anonymous, but who really believed the man might carry out his threats.

That man was Trey Styler.

In the days prior to this, Trey went to two local businesses, hoping to obtain a loan and hawk his wife's $30,000 diamond ring, respectively. The banker turned him down. The jeweler's offer wasn't high enough. Trey was desperate—so much so, that he told both the banker and the jeweler he should just kill himself. That way, his wife would be better off.

Trey knew that without a loan, and without cash from the ring, he and Nancy were at rock bottom. They had no money, and no friends left to borrow from. They were staying in a motel and didn't know how much longer their credit card would pay for their room. Trey was a desperate man—and desperate men who do not receive help take desperate steps. That's how Pfister ended up dead.

The first chance for police to help Trey, who had a long history of depression and suicidal thoughts, had come in late November or early December. His son, Daniel, then called Pitkin County 911 to report that he and his mother hadn't heard from Trey. They were worried, they said, because Nancy was in Denver and neither she nor Daniel could reach him. They spoke of Trey's suicidal tendencies, and asked someone to go check on him at 1833 West Buttermilk Road. No one did or, if they did, that incident report wasn't turned over in discovery.

The second chance to help Trey, who was often medicated to the point that a trained officer should detect it, came on Sunday night, just past midnight, on February 23. He was speeding alone through Basalt when two city cops pulled him over. They gave him a warning ticket but nothing else. No questions were asked—not even when Trey couldn't find his insurance papers or vehicle registration.

The third chance came with Koenig's call to police on Friday morning, the day before Pfister was due back in town. Official records indicate that sheriff's dispatcher Danielle Madril sent two deputies to check on Dr. William "Trey" Styler at 1833 West Buttermilk Road. They never made it, though.

In a May 7, 2014, incident report, Deputy Jason Kasper told his supervisor that he and Patrol Director Michael Buglione went to check on Styler, but at *1801* West Buttermilk. "I knocked on the door several times and no one answered the door. I left the residence with no contact. Case closed," Kasper wrote, apparently seventy-five days after the incident itself.

Why did Kasper wait so long to file his police report? Why did his supervisors, Jeff Lumsden and Alex Burchetta, wait that long to sign off on the report? Is it perhaps because calls about suicide aren't taken as seriously in Pitkin County, so deputies don't file reports about them?

Did Kasper only file his report then because Fowler later filed a request for the sheriff's office to provide Nancy's defense team with records of all law enforcement calls to the Pfister home? (Actually, Fowler asked for a copy of the report showing Nancy's request for a civil standby; the sheriff's office sent the report about the February 21 welfare check by mistake.)

More important, why did neither deputy call the dispatch opera-tor, to see if they had the correct address? (Pfister's address does appear correctly in the initial incident report.)

Nancy said she and Trey were at Pfister's house at 1833 West But-termilk Road all day Friday, packing up their belongings in prepara-tion for their Saturday move. She said if deputies had shown up at the door, she would have made sure Trey got help—because she had no clue just how far his suicidal thinking had progressed. Nancy didn't learn about the comments he made to the banker and the jeweler until months later.

Why did the deputies not make more than one attempt to find Trey, since that was their mission? Why did they not return to the house a second time? And since the last radio log for that call was at 12:31 p.m., does that mean the deputies waited three hours before going to check on Trey? If so, did they interact with anyone between 9:30 and 12:30? What were the next calls that came in after they went to the wrong house? Did they have to respond to another emergency?

These questions might not seem important, but they are—because people with mental illness commit 10 percent of all U.S. murders, and this group commits more and more mass shootings. One new study currently underway has found that out of 160 U.S. workplace and school shootings, the killers had a mental illness in sixty of the cases. Most of the time, they were either not being treated for their illness or not taking their prescribed medications. Trey fits into the latter cate-gory, but perhaps through no fault of his own. He and Nancy ordered their medicine online, including Trey's antidepressant. The drugs were supposed to be shipped directly to them. But the moves from Denver to Aspen, and out of Pfister's house to a motel in Basalt, delayed their mail delivery.

When Trey, already a desperate man, and a man with a mental illness, learned that Pfister was trying to extort more money from him and his wife, he became even more desperate. His desperation, created from years of spiraling downward, resulted in either a blind rage or a psychotic break that left Pfister dead. No one can say for sure which occurred, and Trey insists he has not received a psychiatric evaluation since his arrest, a crucial tool that could shed more light on his deadly actions.

Putting a value on human life is impossible. But in addition to the loss of Nancy Pfister, the cost of Trey's depression has been astronomical. By now, it is probably well into the millions and counting: from lost earnings, the Stylers' family home, their vehicles, prestige and status, and the fact that taxpayers must now pay to house Trey in Arrowhead Correctional Center, near Canon City, Colorado, for the next twenty years.

So in the end, Trey's mental illness didn't destroy just one woman. His state of mind decimated the lives of two women—both named Nancy. Add Kathy to that list, and you have three women with ruined lives.

There is probably no one who wishes Trey had gotten the help he needed in time more than Trey himself. He sits inside his prison cell, where he's already read three hundred books, but does little more than that. He wants to appeal his sentence, but says his public defender, Tina Fang, won't return his phone calls or answer his letters. Nor will any other attorney take his case, either, given that Fang is listed as his attorney of record.

Nancy thinks she knows why. "Tina was a savior in the early days. But later I discovered they had fights," she says. "Probably because Trey thought he could dictate to her, tell her what to do. Or because he lied to her, tried to manipulate her."

After being released from jail, Daniel told his mother that Trey's relationship with Tina was "very tumultuous," that they "butted heads." Nancy said she believes Trey was still trying to call the legal shots, even though he had a court-appointed attorney. "He had enough knowledge to be dangerous."

There is more. With the loss of his medical license and now, being a convicted murderer, Trey isn't allowed to even use his life-saving skills to help other inmates. That is a huge regret for the man who once loved saving lives, and who chaired the anesthesiology department at St. Joseph's Hospital in Denver.

The man who, along with his wife, even believed he could help Pfister. In fact, other people believed and hoped so, too. When Gerry Goldstein, a prominent Aspen attorney, met the Stylers at Pfister's party, he said as much.

"Thank God you're going to be there for her. Thank God you're going to help her," Nancy said Gerry told Trey that night, after learning about the Stylers plans to open a medical spa in Pfister's home.

Trey thought that was an excessive reaction. But not for long. "I came to realize that he realized that Pfister needed help. And he thought we were going to be the ones to help her."

Trey thought the same. "I thought we were going to be the ones to help her too. But that quickly became impossible." After the Stylers realized they couldn't open the spa—much less help Pfister—Trey wrote Gerry a letter.

His lengthy apology outlines how he had hoped they might help Pfister with her alcohol and other problems. In the end, it turned out they couldn't.

"I always thought of myself as a rescuer," Trey said. "It's what I did for probably thirty years. [I'd] take people in dire straits and make them healthy, or keep them as healthy as possible. And I had fantasies I would be able to help Nancy Pfister, before I realized how bad off she was."

There is a bigger regret. It has nothing to do with that Nancy. It has to do with Trey's family, with his Nancy. He knows he will "never hold her again (or) sleep in the same bed with my wife." That he will never see his wife of thirty-three years, or their son, Daniel, again. That reality is the most painful one.

***

Those regrets are why Trey continued to consider suicide an option, especially behind prison bars.

"And if I could think of a way, that I could surely be successful, I think that's what I would do. Because God knows I'm not having any fun, and God knows she's not having any fun," Trey said. "And I don't think she would be any emotionally worse off, and she would certainly be . . . better off, if I were dead."

In spite of still having suicidal thoughts, Trey said the lack of readily available means in prison makes that idea almost impossible.

"Quite frankly I wish somebody would do to me what I did to Nancy Pfister. To die in your sleep is not a bad way to go," Trey said. "I sometimes think that it was the nicest thing anybody ever did for Nancy Pfister . . . "

EPILOGUE

When, after several years, the expectation is finally realized, it can feel like both a lifetime and a split second have passed at the same time. It's surreal, a feeling that can't be described unless those listening have personally lived through the experience.

On Thursday, August 6, 2015, when Nancy's cell phone rang, she was getting ready for work. It was the call she prayed would never come. And yet, the only one she knew that would truly set Trey free.

It was the Fremont County Coroner's office, calling from Colorado to say that Trey passed away earlier that morning. Coroner Randy Keller told Nancy that Trey hanged himself with his bed sheets in his jail cell. He was sixty-seven.

Nancy hadn't heard from Trey in a month. Prison inmates have one luxury, albeit a woefully small one: they can decide if and when to call a loved one. There is no doubt that Trey wanted to call Nancy. They talked often, even though their pending divorce was nearly final.

When they last spoke, Trey had one minute left of his prepaid phone plan. The plan Nancy refilled, whenever she was able. Lately, she hadn't had any extra money to give Trey to call her. But the minute she did, she paid on his account. Then she waited for his call. She waited a month. During that time, she went to work. She tracked down IRS officials, trying to find someone to tell her what was going on with her stolen tax refund. She went to see her bankruptcy lawyer. And she appeared in bankruptcy court.

***

After hearing of her client's death, Tina Fang said Trey's confession came at a high cost to himself. "When presented with an opportunity to mislead authorities for his own benefit in plea negotiations, [he] took the high road and came clean. Instead of coming up with a lie that the district attorney's office wanted to hear—that Kathy Carpenter or Nancy Styler were involved—[he] told the truth resulting in a worse outcome for himself."

Fang said there was one thing to learn from that. "While much has been made of the brutality of this offense, in truth, Trey Styler himself was a man filled with grace."

* * *

When Daniel learned about his father's death, he was as pragmatic as ever. Then again, he'd had more time to mourn the loss of his father than Nancy had to mourn losing her husband.

"We're getting used to heartbreak," he said. "It was more a question of 'when' than 'if.'"

Nancy was less so. Garth called her with his deepest condolences, saying the divorce was still in progress. Nancy knew then it never would be—Trey died while they were still married, making her the widow she felt like she had become after Trey confessed.

Nancy moped around her mother's house in her pajamas for the rest of that day, rereading all of Trey's letters from prison. His December 10, 2014, letter really tugged at her heartstrings.

"Imprisonment itself is bad enough," Trey wrote. "It may seem strange to some for me to speak of the morals and ethics of others but I don't feel different in those respects from the person I have always been. I condemn my own act as strongly as anyone else could. The knowledge of it, always present, is my real punishment. Imprisonment is just society's revenge, as cruel in its own way as what I did."

Reading Trey's words made Nancy cry even more. But then she remembered what he said, when he called prison a "moral and ethical wasteland." So she was relieved that he was no longer suffering, and she was grateful. Still, she continued mourning. She mourned the man whose life was intertwined with hers for thirty-three years, who gave her a son and a lifetime of happiness, before becoming ill. Mostly, she mourned the man she lost before Trey became ill, before his sick body led to a sick mind, which then led them to financial and every other kind of ruin.

Ever the medical expert, Nancy told Keller not to spare her when it came to her husband's autopsy. "I want to know especially what his brain looked like, if there were any lesions (that would signify brain damage)," she said.

Trey wanted to be cremated and Nancy honored his wishes. She hoped the autopsy would provide valuable clues to help other people learn from the mental illness that stole not just Trey, but also Nancy Pfister.

If it does, then Nancy believes the loved ones of sick people like Trey won't have to "scream into the void" like she did, while trying to get help for her suicidal husband, but finding no one who would listen.

ACKNOWLEDGMENTS

First and foremost, I would like to acknowledge the primary writer of this book, Daleen Berry. She painstakingly reviewed thousands of pages of discovery pertaining to my case. The investigative journalist in her interviewed dozens of people, and she was the only reporter to visit my husband in prison and hear his innermost feelings. In addition to our interviews, we spent countless hours on the phone talking about anything and everything, and her role as a writer was almost surpassed by her support as a friend and counselor as this tragedy unfolded. As a first-time book author, it was great to have a bestselling author and friend to guide me through the publishing process. In spite of the many obstacles that we both faced in our lives, she continued her quest for the truth and she found it. Her discovery validated my innocence, which allowed me to move forward and start rebuilding my life. For that I am eternally grateful.

I cannot thank Michael and Leslie Wright enough for their guidance and putting me in touch with Daleen, and for the entire BenBella team who believed in my innocence and agreed to publish my life story.

I also need to thank my family and friends, who helped me feel so loved during my stay in jail. I have to thank my son and his fiancée for their love and support, and for holding down the fort when Trey and I first went to jail. They truly became communications central. My mom kept my spirits up by sending me 103 letters during my 108-day jail stay, and my sister has continued to keep me laughing through some of the darkest moments of my life. I felt the wagons circling as soon as my family learned of our troubles. What an incredible feeling it is to hear what unsolicited people will say in your defense. It was almost like listening to my eulogy, except I didn't have to die for that to happen. There were many "angels" who came into my life just when I needed them most. I will never forget their kindness. I kept a journal of my "angels" throughout my time in jail, and they number in the hundreds and come from all walks of life. Patrice and Purl could not have been more beautiful. They were the only visitors I had during my stay and they continued to shower me with cards and letters. My son's godparents took their role seriously, guiding our adult son through a tragedy that no one should have to experience. Attorneys Beth Krulewitch and Garth McCarty have been with me since the beginning and continue to support me long after their roles as public defenders ended. Defense investigator David Olmsted helped us to understand the system and was one of the staunchest believers of my innocence. Pete Fowler and Mike McGruder, also defense investigators, were an immense help to my attorneys. Motel clerk Lucia and Merlin Broughton were both early angels who brought us food when we were stranded, left with nothing. The Duran family jumped right in and continues to help me get my life back on track. So many people from my horticultural past wrote letters of support, which triggered beautiful memories of gardens past. My list of angels includes most of the Pitkin County deputies who were in charge of my care during my incarceration in Aspen. They were very respectful, non-judgmental individuals. My time in Eagle County gave me a whole new set of angels. Cellmate Emily kept my spirits high while I waited for justice. Guard Dave brought us movies, popcorn, and snow cones, while Guard Theresa really connected with the inmates, making us feel more human. The books, cards, and letters from around the country were deeply appreciated and made me feel like I could handle anything with that much love and support on my side.

Together, Daleen and I wish to thank the many kind people in Cañon City, Denver, and Aspen, who helped Daleen navigate her way around Colorado. We owe deep gratitude to the Aspen area residents who were afraid to speak publicly about this crime and its victim, but who anonymously shared details about Nancy Pfister and her family. We cannot thank the prison officials with the Colorado Department of Corrections and Arrowhead Correctional Center enough, especially Major Terry Hamilton, Adrienne Jacobson, and Patty Viola, for making Daleen's interview with my husband a reality.

We also are deeply indebted to retired police captain K.C. Bohrer and forensic pathologist expert Judy Melinek, M.D., whose keen insight into police and suspect behavior and autopsies, respectively, was an immense help in writing this book.

Many thanks also go to Asra Nomani, cofounder of the nonprofit, Treatment Before Tragedy, for sharing important statistics about crimes committed by people with mental illness; and to defense paralegal Jody Visconti Chow, who guided Daleen through the chaotic maze of legal discovery.

We appreciate deeply the support and assistance from other West Virginia writers, including Diane Tarantini, Alison Bass, Benyamin Cohen, Dana Coester, Karin Fuller, and Ginger Hamilton.

A special thank you and huge hugs go to Lauren Housman, whose transcription skills saved Daleen's sanity; Susan Stringer Dempsey, Becky Rog-Hood, and Diane Tarantini, for extending much help following Daleen's surgery; Sarah Rosier Nora, a discerning beta reader and librarian; fellow author and WVU professor John Temple; and true-crime writer Diane Fanning; for their gracious help and words.

ABOUT THE AUTHORS

 **Nancy Styler** was a clinical and medical researcher who traveled around the world teaching anesthetists about the diagnosis and treatment of malignant hyperthermia; a former anesthesiology instructor at the University of Colorado Health Sciences Center; the founder of Victoria Conservancy, a nonprofit dedicated to educating the public about the Victoria water lily; and host to thousands of visitors to her former Greenwood Village home and gardens as well as HGTV.

She and her family travelled to the Amazon to study the DNA of waterlilies. She has published a number of scientific papers and many water gardening articles and was the garden editor for *Colorado Homes and Lifestyles Magazine* for three years. Styler has also lectured internationally on medical and horticultural research.

 **Daleen Berry** is a *New York Times* bestselling author who has written or co-written five books, including *Sister of Silence* and *Pretty Little Killers*. She has worked as an investigative journalist for twenty-seven years, and began her career in West Virginia, where she worked on a crime beat and published law enforcement journals, while learning from such renowned pathology, legal, and criminal experts as FBI Special Agent Ken Lanning, Cook County Detective Brian Killacky, renowned medical examiner Dr. James "Jack" Frost, and WVU law professor Franklin Cleckley.